COLOMBO'S
All-Time
GREAT CANADIAN QUOTATIONS

COLOMBO'S
All-Time
GREAT CANADIAN QUOTATIONS

John Robert Colombo

First published in 1994 by
Stoddart Publishing Co. Limited
34 Lesmill Road
Toronto, Canada
M3B 2T6

Canadian Cataloguing in Publication Data

Colombo's all-time great Canadian quotations

ISBN 0-7737-5639-6

1. Quotations, Canadian (English).*   2. Canada — Quotations,
maxims, etc.   I. Colombo, John Robert, 1936–   .

PN6081.C65 1994   C818'.02   C94-930035-7

Cover design: Brant Cowie/ArtPlus Limited
Typesetting: Tony Gordon Ltd.

Printed and bound in Canada.

*Stoddart Publishing gratefully acknowledges the support of the Canada
Council, the Ontario Ministry of Culture, Tourism, and Recreation,
Ontario Arts Council, and Ontario Publishing Centre in the development
of writing and publishing in Canada.*

Contents

PREFACE

*C*olombo's All-Time Great Canadian Quotations is, as its title states, the compiler's selection of the great or essential quotations connected with Canada. The selection consists of 600 essential or basic quotations that effectively dramatize the history of Canada and the development of its society and its people. The arrangement of the quotations is chronological, although within any particular year the arrangement may be somewhat modified from time to time. The aim has been to present an overall chronology to illustrate the country's emergence from the land, the dawning of a national awareness, and the characteristics of the Canadian people.

This book is the first dictionary of Canadian quotations to have a chronological arrangement. That is its first distinction. Its second is that there is a commentary for each quotation. The commentaries are necessarily concise, yet each identifies the contributor of the quotation, places the quotation in its context, delivers information on its source, and not infrequently offers an allied remark by an associated contributor. Access to all the contributors is provided by the index, which is arranged by contributor and gives a précis of all the contributions.

The 600 quotations in the collection are augmented by close to 200 additional quotations that are included in passing in the commentaries. To some extent, the selection of the quotations represents the personal opinions of the compiler. Certainly, no two compilers would ever produce identical selections. Yet the majority of the selections would likely appear in any informed person's list. There are probably 200 quotations that are so important, so interesting, so memorable—and, possibly, so familiar—that they should be on everyone's lips if not in the back of everyone's mind. They should be our famous lasting words. It is hoped that this book will contribute to the task of reminding readers and researchers of these classic quotations and drawing attention to their importance and also to their sources.

The selection begins in 1000 B.C. and ends in A.D. 1995. Is this choice of first entry and last entry simply quirky? The compiler considers otherwise. Communications theorists and economists talk about "the global village" and "globalization." Creative writers take broadly human views of issues. It is timely to see the Dominion of Canada from both national and global vantage points. In these pages, our country is placed in the context of all time and all space.

The selection highlights the history of the country, but society, culture, and people are also featured; national concerns rather than regional matters are emphasized; and individual expression has been favoured over corporate communication. After all, people will be reading the poems and aphorisms of F.R. Scott, Irving Layton, and Louis Dudek long after the reports of royal commissions have been relegated to the stacks of all but the largest reference libraries.

This book is unusual in yet another way. It was edited and designed to appear in the format of a trade paperback. The idea is to make it available to everyone, from student to specialist, especially the general reader: the member of Robertson Davies's "clerisy," who values not only Canada but also the written and spoken word. It is quite likely that the readers or users of this book—not to mention its purchasers!—will already have other "quote books" on their bookshelves, possibly even titles edited by the present compiler. If this is so, it might be useful to place this book in the context of dictionaries of quotations.

Canadian quote books, unlike their American and British counter-parts, are perforce national compilations. They strike a balance between history and society, between policy and personal expres-sion. With fewer celebrated or famous people whose *bon mots* clam-mer for inclusion, Canadian books are inclined to be more serious and scholarly—with less levity—than "quote books" from other countries.

This category of books is certainly popular today. If a ruler is taken to the columns listed under "quotations" in catalogues of current, in-print books in Canada, the United Kingdom, and the United States, the ruler measures 150 column inches of listings for currently active titles: Canadian books, 8 inches; British books, 17 inches; American books, 125 inches. The titles range from comprehensive tomes with detailed notes on sources through specialized compilations to slender gift booklets of "inspirational thoughts."

The present compiler has already published four collections of quotations: *Colombo's Canadian Quotations* (1974), *Colombo's Concise Canadian Quotations* (1976), *Colombo's New Canadian Quotations* (1987), *The Dictionary of Canadian Quotations* (1991). Aside from the first compilation, which was arranged by contributor, they all share the popular subject arrangement of quoted matter. There are two other Canadian books of quotations organized by subject: David Strickland's *"Quotations" from English-Canadian Literature* (1973) and *The Dictionary of Canadian Quotations and Phrases* (1952; revised and enlarged edition, 1979), edited by Robert M. Hamilton and Dorothy Shields. Most users of such books are also users of the standard British and American quote books. Organized by contributor are both *The Oxford Dictionary of Quotations* (1941; 4th edition, 1992), edited by Angela Partington, and *Bartlett's Familiar Quotations* (1855; 16th edition, 1992), compiled by Justin Kaplan. The amount of Canadian material in these tomes has been estimated to be in the neighbourhood of zero point one percent. But there is evidence that foreign compilers are catching on and catching up. For instance, a reasonable number of Canadian quotations appears among the "quotables by notables" in the finest of the international compilations: *Simpson's Contemporary Quotations* (1964; revised and enlarged edition, 1988), edited by James B. Simpson. (That volume enjoys a unique topical arrangement: The World, Humankind, Communication and the Arts.) What does globalization hold for quote-worthy Canadians? Imperial preference of the 1900s failed to bring Canadians into British quote books. Will the FTA and NAFTA similarly fail to bring Canadians into American—and Mexican—quote books in the 2000s?

The present compilation represents French Canada to the degree that it impinges on a daily basis upon the consciousness of English Canadians. *Canada français* has yet to produce a national quote book. Three compilations—*Dictionnaire de Citations de la Littérature Québécoise* (1974), edited by David Strickland; *Citations Québécoises Modernes* (1976), edited by Claude Janelle; *Petit Dictionnaire Héritage des Citations* (1980), edited by Gilbert Forest—are limited to passages from Quebec fiction. Robert Prévost's *Petit Dictionnaire de Citations Québécoises* (1988) includes passages from literature and remarks made in real life.

The contents of the present work are largely drawn from non-fiction books, journals, magazines, and especially daily newspapers. The result is that half the quotes are concerned with the country ("The twentieth century belongs to Canada"); the other half refer to other matters ("The medium is the message"). Of all the entries, perhaps 200 of these quotations should be familiar to the average Canadian. It is hoped that presenting them here, with commentaries, will help make them all more familiar than they are today.

One feature of the present book that should be noted is the arrangement of the quotations. The arrangement is chronological, to be sure, but it is chronological by contribution rather than by contributor. What is significant is the date of the quotation rather than its originator's birth date. Thus, Pierre Elliott Trudeau's quotations—more than one dozen—cover the years from 1944 to 1991; they are not concentrated in a group, following 1919, his year of birth, as they would be had Trudeau been treated as a major contributor by the editors of the *Oxford Dictionary* and *Bartlett's*.

Colombo's All-Time Great Canadian Quotations should appeal to three groups of people: the reader, the browser, and the user. The reader will find that working through the entries from cover to cover will offer an unusually short history of the country punctuated by lightning flashes of wit and thunderbolts of wisdom. The browser will find treasures and trivia aplenty, a box of all-sorts from which to pick and choose at will. The user will observe that the book yields not only some of the standard facts but also a few eccentric fancies.

For whatever purpose the book is used—interest, instruction, information—it should add to one's knowledge of Canada, one's appreciation of Canadiana, and one's self-knowledge. Self-knowledge is the basis of all other knowledge. An important component of self-knowledge is national knowledge, knowledge of one's roots and branches. As one contributor to this collection attested in 1901, "Canada only needs to be known in order to be great."

ACKNOWLEDGEMENTS

I began to collect quotations connected with Canada in the Centennial Year 1967. Since then I have benefited from advice and assistance from people in all walks of life in this country and elsewhere in the world. Often without even meaning to, they have helped me evolve this collection's form and content. The quoted material in the present work has been so selected, so arranged, and so augmented with original commentary as to constitute a "selected quotations." Yet the work is entirely new, so I am ever aware of the contributions of other people—not to mention the contributors whose words I repeat with such delight!

I wish to acknowledge by name a few of the men and women who have rendered signal service. As in the past, I was assisted by my regular researcher, Alice Neal. Research was conducted at the Metropolitan Toronto Reference Library, North York Public Library, John P. Robarts Reference Library of the University of Toronto, Cinémathèque Ontario, CBC Reference Library, Hockey Hall of Fame, and the reference libraries of *The Globe and Mail*, *The Toronto Star*, and Canadian Press.

Nelson Doucet, Vice-President, Stoddart Publishing Co. Limited, Toronto, expressed gratifying interest in the undertaking; Donald G. Bastian, Stoddart's Managing Editor, contributed insights and ideas that unquestionably improved the work. Carlotta Lemieux, of London, Ont., did a fine editorial job, as usual.

Important contributions to the text were made by Edith Fowke and Philip Singer. Equally valued contributors include Dick Beddoes, Kamala Bhatia, Joel Bonn, Cecelia Carter-Smith, Nathan Cohen, Craig Ertl, Northrop Frye, Walter L. Gordon, David A. Gotlib, William Gough, George P. Grant, Cyril Greenland, Anthony M. Hawke, M.T. Kelly, William Kilbourn, Jon Lomberg, Marshall McLuhan, Alberto Manguel, W. Edward Mann, Judith Merril,

Thomas M. Paikeday, Alan Rayburn, Anna Sandor, Robert J. Sawyer, William Sherk, James B. Simpson, William Toye, and Dwight Whalen. (No distinction has been made between the quick and the dead; I am grateful to all, as they are all alive and well in my consciousness.) As ever, I remain indebted to my wife Ruth Colombo.

THE VEDAS 1000 B.C.

> How great is the interval that lies between the dawns which have arisen
> and those which are yet to rise?

The Vedas of India consist of the sacred hymns of the Aryan and Hindu peoples. The question that is asked here comes from the *Taittiriya Samhita* (Origin of the Chants, 1, 113, 10), one of the scriptures that composes the *Rig-Veda*, the sacred cycle of poems preserved in ancient Sanskrit for some three thousand years and chanted to this day on the subcontinent. The Indian scholar B.G. Tilak maintained that the passage from which the line was taken refers to the Arctic cycle of day and night and that other references in the Vedas establish beyond doubt that "the home of the ancestors of the Vedic people was somewhere near the North Pole before the Glacial epoch." He also maintained that the Aryan people had an intimate and detailed knowledge of the geography of the northern regions of North America, including the region of the Great Lakes. Tilak advanced his thesis in his scholarly study *The Arctic Home in the Vedas* (1903, 1925, 1971).

HUEI SHAN 499 B.C.

> When I came down from Ku Su Terrace, in the East,
> I had already arranged for a vessel to float on the sea:
> And until now resentment lingers in my mind
> That I did not succeed in exploring Fu Sang.

Fu Sang may well be a reference to North America, specifically to the Pacific coast and the British Columbia interior, which the Chinese Buddhist monk Huei Shan is said to have explored in 499 B.C. The lines above come from "Poem of Fu Sang," written by the Chinese poet Tu Fu in A.D. 726, translated by Florence Ayscouth, quoted by Hendon Mason Harris in *The Asiatic Fathers of America* (1980). Huei Shan—his name is also given as Hwui Shan or Hoei

Shin—is believed to have left the court of China for "the West" (which to him was "the East") and sailed across a Pacific-like sea to explore a land of mountains and fir-trees. The translation of *Fu Sang* is "Fir-tree," and it is sometimes argued that this text—which confirms details in an earlier text, "Classic of Mountains and Sea," which was compiled by Yu at the request of Emperor Shun and is traditionally dated to 2250 B.C.—describes the coast of British Columbia and the interior lands as far east as Writing-on-Stone Provincial Park, Alberta, according to Henriette Mertz in *Pale Ink: Two Ancient Records of Chinese Exploration in America* (1953, revised 1972).

HERODOTUS 430 B.C.

> The whole region I have been describing has excessively hard winters; for eight months of the year the cold is intolerable; the ground is frozen iron-hard, so that to turn earth into mud requires not water but fire . . . even apart from the eight months' winter, the remaining four months are cold.

Is winter, even in the Arctic, as intolerable as the description suggests? The passage is taken from the writings of the ancient Greek historian Herodotus and dates from about 430 B.C. Herodotus is certainly describing the polar north. Some anthropologists are of the opinion that the description, which comes from *Herodotus: The Histories* (1954), translated by Aubrey de Selincourt, refers to the Canadian Arctic.

VIRGIL 30 B.C.

Ultima Thule.

The Roman poet Virgil composed his long poem *Georgics* in Latin between 37 and 30 B.C. In one of its verses he referred to the Arctic region as *Ultima Thule*, "farthest Thule." The Danish-Eskimo explorer Knud Rasmussen took the name Thule for the base in Greenland from which he launched his famous Fifth Thule Expedition across Arctic America in 1921-24.

STRABO A.D. 20

Pytheas . . . describes Thule and other neighbouring places, where, according to him, neither earth, water, nor air exist, separately, but a sort of concretion of all these, resembling marine sponge, in which the earth, the sea, and all things were suspended, thus forming, as it were, a link to unite the whole together. It can neither be travelled over nor sailed through. As for the substance, he affirms that he has beheld it with his own eyes; the rest, he reports on the authority of others.

This account of the northern regions of the world, including Thule, was written by the Greek geographer and historian Strabo; it comes from his book *The Geography* written about A.D. 20. Strabo based his account on the writings of the earlier Greek geographer Pytheas of Marseilles, who lived about 300 B.C. Pytheas's writings have not survived. The English version given here is from Strabo's work *The Geography* (1854), translated by H. Hamilton and W. Falconer.

LEIF ERICSSON 1000

Now we have done better than Bjarni where this country is concerned—we at least have set foot on it. I shall give this country a name and call it *Helluland.*

Helluland? What a name for a country! It means "slab-land" in Old Icelandic. The words come from the *Greenlander's Saga* and are attributed to the explorer and colonist Leif Ericsson, also known as Leif the Lucky. He likely landed on Baffin Island in the Eastern Arctic about 1000 A.D. The passage is quoted from *The Vinland Sagas* (1965), translated from the Old Icelandic by Magnus Magnusson and Hermann Palsson. Ericsson, a Viking, made two other landfalls—on the Labrador coast, which he called *Markland* (or "forest-land"), and at L'Anse aux Meadows at the northeastern tip of Newfoundland, which he called *Vinland* (or "wine-land").

MARCO POLO 1298

It is also on islands in that sea (north of Bargu at Lake Baikal) that the Gerfalcons are bred. You must know that the place is so far to the north that you leave the North Star somewhat behind you towards the south! The Gerfalcons are so abundant there that the Emperor of China can have as many as he likes to send for.

The Venetian traveller Marco Polo had indirect knowledge of Baffin Island in the Eastern Arctic as the breeding ground of the prized falcon. He dictated his memoirs in 1298; the passage comes from *The Book of Marco Polo* (1903), edited by Sir Henry Yule. "Only the Canadian archipelago can be meant, and this identification is greatly strengthened if Bargu is rightly believed to lie south of Lake Baikal, for the meridian through the lake would strike Ellesmere Island in the Canadian Arctic," wrote Tryggvi J. Oleson in *Early Voyages and Northern Approaches 1000-1632* (1963).

ABU'L-HASAN 'ALI IBN SA'ID 1400s

The island Harmsa, which lies in the northernmost part of the inhabited world, is almost twelve days' journey in length, and at the centre, about four days' journey in breadth. From it, men get the good falcons . . . and to the little northern island, men go to obtain the white falcons which are brought thence to the Sultan of Egypt, and the price of them, which is usually entered among the expenditures of the treasury, is a thousand denarii, but if they bring dead falcons, they get five hundred denarii.

Abu'l-Hasan 'ali Ibn Sa'id was an Arab writer of the thirteenth century who in his writings preserved a reference to Baffin Island in the Eastern Arctic, the source of the white falcons that were so highly prized in the Arab world; he is quoted by Tryggvi J. Oleson in *Early Voyages and Northern Approaches: 1000-1632* (1963). Like Marco Polo's comment, this reference shows that there was knowledge of the northern part of the North American continent in the pre-Columbian and pre-Cartier period.

DEKANAHWIDEH   1450s

I, Dekanahwideh, and the Confederated Chiefs, now uproot the tallest pine tree, and into the cavity thereby made we cast all weapons of war. Into the depth of the earth, deep down into the underwater currents of water flowing to unknown regions, we cast all weapons of strife. We bury them from sight and we plant again the tree. Thus shall the Great Peace be established.

One of the oldest constitutions in the world is that of the Six Nations Confederacy. Dated as early as the 1450s, it was established by the Iroquois statesman Dekanahwideh, a chief of mythic stature, who, with the assistance of the Ojibwa chief Hiawatha, founded the Great League of the Iroquois (the Five, later, Six Nations Confederacy) near the present-day site of Kingston, Ont. Paul A.W. Wallace, in *The White Roots of Peace* (1946), reproduces the traditional words of the Great Peace, as well as Dekanahwideh's final words to his people: "If the Great Peace should fail, call on my name in the bushes, and I will return."

MARTIN BEHAIM   1492

Here one catches white falcons.

Navigator and geographer Martin Behaim inscribed these words on the Nuremberg Terrestrial Globe, the earliest globe extant, which he constructed in 1492. He was referring to Baffin Island, the breeding ground of the white falcon, so valued in Europe and the East in the late Middle Ages. The inscription was noted by E.G. Ravenstein in

Martin Behaim (1908) and quoted by Tryggvi J. Oleson in *Early Voyages and Northern Approaches 1000-1632* (1963).

JOHN CABOT 1497

> This land he called Prima vista, that is to say, First seen.

This is a contemporaneous account of the discovery of Newfoundland by John Cabot in 1497, included by Richard Hakluyt in *The Principal Navigations, Voyages, Traffiques and Discoveries of the English Nation* (1598). The key words are sometimes given as *Terra Primum Vista*, Latin for "first-seen land"; they refer to the historic landfall made by Cabot, the Genoese navigator, at Cape Bonavista, Nfld., June 24, 1497. John Quinpool, in *First Things in Acadia* (1936), ranks this "three-word account of the discovery of America" with such gems of brevity as Julius Caesar's "Veni, vidi, vici."

LEONARDO DA VINCI 1519

> Of the beaver one reads that when it is pursued, knowing this to be on account of the virtue of its testicles for medicinal uses, not being able to flee any farther it stops, and in order to be at peace with its pursuers bites off its testicles with its sharp teeth and leaves them to its enemies.

No one is going to argue that the great Italian painter Leonardo da Vinci is a Canadian, but everyone will agree that he put on early record the tradition that the beaver is cowardly to the point of self-castration. This notion goes back to a Latin bestiary of the twelfth century; it inspired the Latin name for the beaver (*castor*). *Castor canadensis* has been identified with Canada for centuries, but official recognition was extended only in 1975. Leonardo da Vinci's description of the beaver comes from a manuscript called "Peace," which was unpublished at the time of his death in 1519. The text

appears in *The Notebooks of Leonardo da Vinci* (1954), edited by
Edward MacCurdy.

JACQUES CARTIER 1534

In fine I am rather inclined to believe that this is the land God gave to
Cain.

These arresting words were written by the navigator and explorer
Jacques Cartier in his journal as he sailed past the bleak northern
shore of the Gulf of St. Lawrence, today's Labrador and Quebec, in
the summer of 1534. Cartier's image of the desolate region is the
earliest (and most powerful) image associated with the new land
based on personal experience. The words appear in *Première Relation*
in *The Voyages of Jacques Cartier* (1924), translated by H.P. Biggar.
In the King James version of the Bible, the accursed Cain wandered
into the land of Nod that was "east of Eden." Cartier's reference gave
rise to the false etymology for the country's name "Cain-ada." The
historian Laurier LaPierre asks a good question in *Canada My
Canada* (1992): "If Canada is the land of Cain, what, on earth, did
Abel inherit?"

JACQUES CARTIER 1535

And amidst these fields is situated the town of Hochelaga, near to and
touching a mountain, which is around it, very fertile and cultivated, from
the summit of which one can see far off. We called this mountain *"le Mont
Royal."*

Thus did the navigator Jacques Cartier describe the site of the
Iroquois village of Hochelaga and the future site of the city of
Montreal, 1535, quoted from *Jacques Cartier and His Four Voyages to
Canada* (1890), edited by Hiram B. Stephens.

JACQUES CARTIER 1535

The sayd men did moreover certify unto us, that there was the way and beginning of the great river of Hochelaga and ready way to Canada, which river the further it went the narrower it came, even into Canada.

These lines feature the first recorded use of the word "Canada," Algonkian for "huts." In this passage, the navigator and explorer Jacques Cartier is describing what would be found on the banks of the St. Lawrence River if he sailed upriver past Hochelaga, the native settlement on the future site of Montreal. Cartier's account is dated July 26, 1535, and it appeared in "A Shorte and Briefe Narration" (1535), *The Principal Navigations, Voyages, Traffiques and Discoveries of the English Nation* (1598), edited by Richard Hakluyt.

NOSTRADAMUS 1555

Du Mont Royal naistra d'une casane,
Qui duc, & compte viendra tyranniser,
Dresser copie de la marche Millane,
Favence, Florence d'or & gens espuiser.

This is the so-called Canadian prophecy of Nostradamus, the most celebrated prophet of all time. The physician, astrologer, and seer wrote his obscure verses in Old French and published them in a collection called *Centuries* (1555). Literally translated, Century VII, no. 32, runs like this: "Out of Montreal shall be born in a cottage, / One that shall tyrannize over duke and earl, / He shall raise an army in the land of the rebellion, / He shall empty Favence and Florence of their gold." Interpreted by Henry C. Roberts in *The Complete Prophecies of Nostradamus* (1947), the verses signify that "a Canadian leader, of lowly birth, shall be raised to great power and eventually assume command over men of the nobility." Commentators in Quebec interpreted the dark words to refer to the rise of Pierre Elliott Trudeau (except that he was not cottage-born) and then to the appearance of Brian Mulroney (except that he was not Montreal-born). Perhaps they fit Bloc Québécois leader Lucien Bouchard. Maybe it is best to assume that all prophecies are always about to be fulfilled, rather than having been fulfilled.

RICHARD HAKLUYT 1582

> For there is no doubt but that there is a straight and short way open into the West, even unto Cathay.

The British geographer Richard Hakluyt expressed the wisdom of the day, held by many a merchant seaman, when he stated his belief about the existence of a Northwest Passage to the East in *Divers Voyages Touching the Discovery of America* (1582). The "passage" exists, but it was found to be neither straight nor short, nor an opening to the riches of the East.

SIR HUMPHREY GILBERT 1583

> We are as near to heaven by sea as by land!

Sir Humphrey Gilbert, the English mariner, claimed Newfoundland as England's first overseas colony on Aug. 5, 1583. On the voyage home, he was aboard the frigate *Squirrel* when, encountering rough weather and icebergs near the Azores, it sank and Gilbert and all hands were lost. "We are as near to heaven by sea as by land!" he yelled to his crew as the frigate went down. His words, it is said, were overheard by the crew aboard his companion ship, the *Golden Hind*. Gilbert's last words—his stirring exhortation to his men—are among the most famous lines in the literature of exploration.

JOHN DAVIS 1595

> The loathsome view of the shore, and irksome noise of the ice, was such, as that it bred strange conceits among us, so that we supposed the place

to be waste and void of any sensible or vegetable creatures, whereupon
I called the same Desolation.

Desolation was the description given by the English navigator and
explorer John Davis, who conducted three searches for the Northwest Passage in 1585, 1586, and 1587, to the coasts of what is now
known as Davis Strait. The description appears in his mariner's
handbook, *The Worldes Hydrographical Description* (1595).

SAMUEL DE CHAMPLAIN   1603

Along the shores of the said Quebec are diamonds in the slate rocks which
are better than those of Alençon.

The explorer Samuel de Champlain was on the lookout for pre-
cious minerals and metals like those found in the vicinity of
Alençon in Normandy. The line comes from "Of Savages" (1603),
The Works of Samuel de Champlain (1922-36), translated by H.P.
Biggar. Alas, the "diamonds" found in Quebec on June 22, 1603,
proved to be quartz.

MARC LESCARBOT   1606

Pledge to us, great god Neptune,
Against thy ocean arrogance;
Grant us all, as highest boon
That we may meet again in France,
Grant us all, as highest boon
That we may meet again in France.

This is the last verse and chorus of the poetic masque written by
lawyer Marc Lescarbot and staged at the French settlement of
Port-Royal, in present-day Nova Scotia, on Nov. 14, 1606. The first
non-native theatrical presentation in the New World, it was published

by Lescarbot as "Le Théâtre de Neptune" (1618) and translated by Harriette T. Richardson as *The Theatre of Neptune in New France* (1928).

ROBERT HAYMAN 1628

The Aire in Newfound-land is wholesome, good;
The Fire, as sweet as any made of wood;
The Waters, very rich, both salt and fresh;
The Earth more rich, you know it is no lesse.
Where all are good, *Fire, Water, Earth,* and *Aire,*
What man made of these foure would not live there?

These charming lines descriptive of Newfoundland come from *Quodlibets* (1628), the first book of original verse written on the continent of North America. It was composed by Robert Hayman, Governor of the Colony at Harbour Grace, Conception Bay, Nfld.

JOHN DONNE 1633

O my America! my new-found-land.

These words are a direct literary reference to Newfoundland, which Sir Humphrey Gilbert had claimed for England in 1583. The words were written by the English poet John Donne and come from his "Elegie XIX" (1633), *Complete Poetry and Selected Prose* (1932), edited by John Hayward. The elegy was written much earlier, perhaps as early as 1590, seven years after Sir Humphrey Gilbert's landfall.

JEAN DE BRÉBEUF 1641

'Twas in the moon of wintertime
When all the birds had fled,

11

That Mighty Gitchi Manitou
Sent angel choirs instead.
Before their light the stars grew dim,
And wand'ring hunters heard the hymn:
"Jesus, your King, is born:
Jesus is born; In excelsis gloria!"

The Jesuit missionary Jean de Brébeuf composed the first Canadian Christmas carol, writing it in the Huron tongue at Sainte-Marie-among-the-Hurons (near present-day Midland, Ont.) in 1641. The Huron lyrics were translated into French before the year 1800; the French lyrics go like this: "Chrétiens, prenez courage, / Jésus Saveur est né! / Du malin les ouvrages / A jamais sont ruinés. / Quand il chante merveille, / A ces troublants appas / Ne prêtez pas l'oreille: / Jésus est né: In excelsis gloria!" The familiar English version is an interpretation made by J.E. Middleton in 1926.

SIEUR DE MAISONNEUVE 1642

You are a grain of mustard seed that shall rise and grow until its branches overshadow the earth. You are few, but your work is the work of God. His smile is on you, and your children shall fill the land.

Sieur de Maisonneuve, French colonist, delivered a sermon-like speech on the founding of the settlement of Ville-Marie, today's Montreal, May 18, 1642, quoted by Francis Parkman in *The Jesuits of North America in the Seventeenth Century* (1867).

JÉRÔME LALEMANT 1660

They come like foxes through the woods. They attack like lions. They take flight like birds, disappearing before they have really appeared.

The Iroquois engaged in a form of fighting that centuries later would be described as "guerrilla warfare." The Jesuit missionary Jérôme

Lalemant expressed admiration but also fear of the Iroquois in his "Relation" (1660), *The Jesuit Relations and Allied Documents* (1954), edited by Edna Kenton.

PIERRE-ESPRIT RADISSON 1661

We were Caesars, being nobody to contradict us.

This gloating line about social conditions in the Northwest in the seventeenth century was penned by the *coureur de bois* Pierre-Esprit Radisson in "Lake Superior Voyage" (1661), which can be found in *The Explorations of Pierre Esprit Radisson* (1961), edited by Arthur T. Adams. Radisson helped to found the Hudson's Bay Company in 1670. Peter C. Newman titled the second volume of his HBC history *Caesars of the Wilderness* (1987) with Radisson's boast in mind.

CHARLES II 1670

The Governor and Company of Adventurers of England trading into Hudson's Bay.

Charles II, King of Great Britain and Ireland, signed the letters-patent of the Hudson's Bay Company on May 2, 1670. It is often claimed that the HBC is the world's oldest continuing corporation.

COMTE DE FRONTENAC 1690

I have no reply to make to your general other than from the mouths of my cannon and muskets. He must learn that it is not in this fashion that one summons a man such as I. Let him do the best he can on his side as I will do on mine.

This defiant reply was made by the Comte de Frontenac, defender of Quebec, to Major Thomas Savage, envoy of Admiral Phips, the commander of the English forces, who was demanding the surrender of Quebec, Oct. 15, 1690. Phips was forced to withdraw. The reply appears in W.J. Eccles's *Canada under Louis XIV: 1663-1701* (1964).

MADELEINE DE VERCHÈRES 1692

> Let us fight to the death. We are fighting for our country and our religion. Remember that our father has taught you that gentlemen are born to shed their blood for the service of God and the King.

This rallying cry is said to have issued from the lips of Madeleine de Verchères, a bold young woman then in her fourteenth year, and to have inspired her two younger brothers and three family retainers, when their seigneury on the St. Lawrence River was attacked by the Iroquois, Oct. 22, 1692. Of such fighting words is history written! The speech was quoted by Francis Parkman in *Count Frontenac and New France under Louis XIV* (1877).

JEAN CADIEUX 1701

> Little rock on the high mountain,
> I come here to end this campaign.
> Ah, sweet echoes, hear my sighs!
> Languishing, I am soon going to die.

This is the first verse in English translation of the French-Canadian folk song "Petit Rocher" (Little Rock), the lament of Jean Cadieux. A legendary voyageur, he was mortally wounded in a battle against the native people in the Ottawa Valley. He dug his own grave, composed this lament, and wrote it in his own blood on birchbark. According to Edith Fowke in *Folklore of Canada* (1976), it is the earliest folk song of Canadian origin.

BARON DE LA HONTAN 1703

Ha! Long live the *Hurons*; who without Laws, without Prisons, and without Torture, pass their Life in a State of Sweetness and Tranquility, and enjoy a pitch of Felicity to which the *French* are utter Strangers. We live quietly under the Laws of Instinct and innocent Conduct, which wise Nature has imprinted upon our Minds from our Cradles.

The notion of the Noble Savage has influenced much of Western thought from Voltaire and the encyclopedists to the hippies and the New Age. There was an original Noble Savage, a Huron chief known to the French as "the Rat," who died in 1701. His outspoken opinions caught the ear of the French traveller Baron de La Hontan, who harboured a few unorthodox opinions of his own. In the third volume of his memoirs, published in 1703, La Hontan created a fictional chief named Adario, who speaks out on behalf of the inherent nobility of the native. In La Hontan's work, Adario wins all arguments against his European inter-rogators because he speaks eloquently on behalf of natural values as distinct from the artificial trappings of the world of man. La Hontan's work appeared as *New Voyages to North America* (1905), translated by R.G. Thwaites. The ideal of the Noble Savage has survived into the 1990s in the notion of the traditional wisdom of the world of nature and of the native people, the intuitive knowledge of shamans, etc.

JONATHAN SWIFT 1726

On the 16th Day of *June* 1703, a Boy on the Top-mast discovered Land. On the 17th we came in full View of a great Island or Continent, (for we knew not whether) on the South-side whereof was a small Neck of Land jutting out into the sea, and a Creek too shallow to hold a Ship of above one hundred Tuns.

This is the fictional account of how Captain Lemuel Gulliver came to Brobdingnag in Jonathan Swift's classic *Travels into Several*

Remote Nations of the World (1726), better known as "Gulliver's Travels." Swift located Brobdingnag, the land of the giants, off the west coast of North America somewhat north of the conjectured Strait of Anian. "This vast Tract of Land to the North-west Parts of *America*" shares its geographical locale with Vancouver Island, the largest island on the west coast of America. There is little doubt that Swift had Vancouver Island in mind when he described the physical characteristics of Brobdingnag.

LOUIS XV 1740s

Are the streets being paved with gold over there? I fully expect to awake one morning in Versailles to see the walls of the fortress rising above the horizon.

This complaint is attributed to Louis XV, who was King of France from 1715 to 1774. Construction of the Fortress of Louisbourg continued through most of his long reign. It is said that the exasperated monarch made his complaint to his military architect, Sébastien de Vauban, who continually pressed for further funds. Its reconstruction, undertaken by Parks Canada and underway since 1961, has proven to be even more costly than its original construction. The sight of Louisbourg rising over the curve of the Atlantic and visible to the courtiers in their castles at Versailles is a vision worthy of the surrealist painter Magritte.

ROYAL ANTHEM 1744

God save our gracious Queen,
Long live our noble Queen,
God save the Queen!
Send her victorious,
Happy and glorious,

Long to reign over us,
God save the Queen!

The words and music of "God Save the Queen" constitute the national anthem of the United Kingdom and, unofficially, the royal anthem of Canada. The first verse of "God Save the Queen" appears above. As Percy A. Scholes noted in *The Oxford Companion to Music* (9th ed., 1956), "This must be the best-known tune in the world." He added, "If any attribution is necessary in song-books, the word 'traditional' seems to be the only one possible, or, perhaps *'Traditional; earliest known version by John Bull, 1563-1628.'*"

JOSEPH ROBSON 1752

The Company have for eighty years slept at the edge of a frozen sea; they have shown no curiosity to penetrate further themselves, and have exerted all their art and power to crush that spirit in others.

This criticism of the Hudson's Bay Company for its action—and inaction—on behalf of trade and settlement in its vast territory was levelled at it by Joseph Robson, one of its supervisors, in *An Account of Six Years' Residence in Hudson's-Bay, from 1733 to 1736, and 1744 to 1747* (1752). Thereafter, the company's unwillingness to establish inland posts to compete with French and English traders was said to be "the sleep by the frozen sea."

ANTHONY HENDAY 1754

Behold the Shining Mountains.

This phrase is associated with the traveller and trader Anthony Henday, the first European who was known to view the Rocky Mountains, which he did near present-day Innisfail, Alta., Oct. 17, 1754. According to James G. MacGregor in *Behold the Shining*

Mountains: Being an Account of the Travels of Anthony Henday, 1754-55 (1954), the native people of the foothills region knew the Rockies as "Mountains of Bright Stones." The phrase "a sea of mountains" appears in George M. Grant's *Ocean to Ocean* (1873).

VOLTAIRE   1759

> You know that these two nations have been at war over a few acres of snow near Canada, and that they are spending on this fine struggle more than Canada itself is worth.

The French author Voltaire cast a cold eye on his country's foreign adventures, especially its struggle with the English over the mastery of Quebec. His classic novel *Candide, ou l'Optimisme* (1759) appeared the year of the British conquest of New France. The sting of Voltaire's phrase "a few acres of snow" is felt to this day. The translation above comes from *Candide, or Optimism* (1966) by Robert A. Adams.

WILLIAM PITT   1759

> Some are for keeping Canada, some Guadaloupe. Who will tell me what I shall be hanged for not keeping?

It may be hard to believe today, but at one time the British government gave equal value to two of its possessions, Canada and Guadaloupe. At the time, the name Canada meant principally Quebec; Guadaloupe referred to a chain of islands in the Lesser Antilles in the Caribbean Sea. (Guadaloupe is now spelled La Guadeloupe; since 1816 it has been a French overseas *département*.) It is said that in 1759, after Britain won both Quebec and Guadaloupe, William Pitt the Elder, Prime Minister of Great Britain, rose in the House of Commons to reply to questions concerning the future of Britain's military acquisitions. Pitt's remark was quoted by Hilda Neatby in *Quebec: The Revolutionary Age 1760-1791* (1966).

JAMES WOLFE 1759

> Gentlemen, I would rather have written those lines than take Quebec tomorrow.

Tradition holds that Major-General James Wolfe, commander of the British forces at Quebec, on board his ship the night before he led the famous assault of Sept. 13, 1759, recited Thomas Gray's "Elegy, Written in a Country Churchyard" (1749). It is said that Wolfe lingered over the fourth line in this stanza: "The boast of heraldry, the pomp of power, / And all that beauty, all that wealth e'er gave, / Awaits alike th'inevitable hour: / The paths of glory lead but to the grave." Eighteen hours later he lay dead on the Plains of Abraham. The authority for the description of the impromptu recital of the poem, described by Francis Parkman in *Montcalm and Wolfe* (1884), derives from the testimony of John Robison, who was aboard the ship with Wolfe at the time; Robison later taught natural philosophy at Edinburgh University and related the remark to one of his students, W.T. Waugh, who committed it to print in *James Wolfe: Man and Soldier* (1928). Waugh pointed out that "tomorrow" should be "today," because the remark would have been made in the early morning of the eventful day. C.P. Stacey, in *Quebec, 1759* (1959), added a caveat: "Did this really happen? The answer seems to be that the tale has more foundation than most of the Quebec legends, but that the incident did not take place as the boats moved down the river in the early morning of the 13th. Wolfe had issued orders enjoining strict silence." Nevertheless, it is a great story. Wolfe's association with Gray's "Elegy" will be recalled as long as Thomas Gray's poem is read and remembered.

JAMES WOLFE 1759

> Now, God be praised, I will die in peace!

These are the dying words of General James Wolfe, victorious commander of the British forces at the Battle of the Plains of

Abraham, Sept. 13, 1759. He uttered them upon being informed that Quebec had been taken. Wolfe died on the battlefield as a result of his wounds, as reported by Francis Parkman in *Montcalm and Wolfe* (1884).

MARQUIS DE MONTCALM 1759

I am happy that I shall not live to see the surrender of Quebec.

These are among the last words spoken to his aides by the Marquis de Montcalm, unsuccessful defender of Quebec in the Battle of the Plains of Abraham, Sept. 13, 1759. Montcalm died the following day of wounds sustained in battle, according to Francis Parkman in *Montcalm and Wolfe* (1884).

FRANCES BROOKE 1769

I no longer wonder the elegant arts are unknown here; the rigour of the climate suspends the very powers of the understanding; what then must become of those of the imagination? Those who expect to see "A new Athens rising near the pole," will find themselves disappointed. Genius will never mount high, where the faculties of the mind are benumbed half the year.

This explanation for the condition of the arts in Quebec in the eighteenth century appears in Frances Brooke's classic work, *The History of Emily Montague* (1769), the first novel set in today's Canada. In her 1985 annotated edition of the epistolary novel, critic Mary Jane Edwards traced the source of the line "A new Athens rising near the pole" to the poem "Two Choruses to the Tragedy of Brutus" (1717) by Alexander Pope, who equated the "new Athens" with Britain, not Canada. Mrs. Brooke soon left Quebec and rejoined the literary circle of Dr. Samuel Johnson. According to one biographer, "When Mrs. Brooke upon her Return to England from Quebec told Mr. Johnson that the Prospect *up* the River Saint Lawrence was the finest in the World—but Madame says he, the Prospect *down* the River St. Lawrence is I have a Notion the finest you ever saw."

PETER KALM 1770

We can enjoy none of these pleasures in *America*. The history of the country can be traced no further than from the arrival of the Europeans; for every thing that happened before that period is more like a fiction or a dream than any thing that really happened.

Peter Kalm was a Swedish botanist and traveller who spent the years 1748-49 in North America. He kept a journal which he later published as *Travels into North America* (1770-71), translated from the Swedish by J.R. Forster. Kalm contrasted Europe's antiquity with the few facts that were then known about what America was like before the arrival of the Europeans. Typically, he paid scant attention to the native inhabitants and their rich social and cultural life.

MATONABBEE 1770

"Women," added he, "were made for labour; one of them can carry, or haul, as much as two men can do. They also pitch our tents, make and mend our clothing, keep us warm at night; and, in fact, there is no such thing as travelling any considerable distance, or for any length of time, in this country, without their assistance. Women," said he again, "though they do every thing, are maintained at trifling expense; for as they always stand cook, the very licking of their fingers in scarce times, is sufficient for their subsistence."

This view of the significance and status of women was expressed by Matonabbee, the Chipewyan guide who led explorer Samuel Hearne across the Barren Lands in Oct. 1770. As Hearne noted in *A Journey from Prince of Wales's Fort in Hudson's Bay, to the Northern Ocean* (1795), Matonabbee never left home base without his wives, all eight of them.

SAMUEL HEARNE 1771

Ask a Northern Indian, what is beauty? he will answer, a broad flat face, small eyes, high cheek-bones, three or four broad black lines a-cross each cheek, a low forehead, a large broad chin, a clumsy hook-nose, a tawny hide, and breasts hanging down to the belt. Those beauties are greatly heightened, or at least rendered more valuable, when the possessor is capable of dressing all kinds of skins, converting them into the different parts of their clothing, and able to carry eight or ten stones in Summer, or haul a much greater weight in Winter. These, and other similar accomplishments, are all that are sought after, or expected of a Northern Indian woman.

Samuel Hearne, the explorer of the Barrens, wrote this passage on April 18, 1771, to illustrate the fact that standards of beauty vary from group to group and from culture to culture. It appears in Hearne's narrative, *A Journey from Prince of Wales's Fort, on Hudson's Bay, to the Northern Ocean* (1795), edited by Richard Glover.

RICHARD MONTGOMERY 1775

Push on, brave boys, Quebec is ours!

This famous battle cry was the last command of Richard Montgomery, Brigadier-General in the Continental Army, issued before he was killed attempting to scale the ramparts of Quebec, New Year's Eve, 1775; quoted by John Codman in *Arnold's Expedition to Quebec* (1901). Failing to take Quebec from the English, the American forces fell back to Montreal and then retired to the Thirteen Colonies.

JOHN ADAMS 1776

The Unanimous Voice of the Continent is "Canada must be ours; Quebec must be taken."

This rousing continentalist cry echoed throughout the American colonies in 1776, following Brigadier-General Richard Montgomery's death while attempting to storm the ramparts of Quebec on New Year's Eve, 1775. John Adams was then serving as a delegate to the Continental Congress; later he was elected the second President of the United States (1797-1801). The lines appear in *The Works of John Adams* (1854) by Charles Francis Adams.

SIR GUY CARLETON 1776

As to my opinion of the Canadians, I think there is nothing to fear from them, while we are in a state of prosperity, and nothing to hope from them in distress; I speak of the people at large; there are some among them who are guided by sentiments of honour, but the multitude is influenced only by hopes of gain, or fear of punishment.

Sir Guy Carleton, the future Lord Dorchester, had the French Canadians in mind when he gave this opinion in a letter of 1776, reproduced by Adam Shortt and Sir Arthur Doughty in *Documents Relating to a Constitutional History of Canada: 1759-1828* (1907-35).

TRADITIONAL 1780s

She's like the swallow that flies so high,
She's like the river that never runs dry,
She's like the sunshine on the lee shore,
I love my love and love is no more.

Here is one verse of "She's Like the Swallow," a traditional British folk song; it accompanied the settlers to their new home in Nova Scotia in the late eighteenth century. Maud Karpeles collected the song in 1929, publishing it in *Folk Songs from Newfoundland* (1934). Northrop Frye commented on it: "The unpredictable genius of oral transmission occasionally turns into a breathtaking beauty, as in the last line."

DAVID THOMPSON 1784

Hudson's Bay is certainly a country that Sinbad the Sailor never saw, as he makes no mention of mosquitoes.

This amusing observation was made by the geographer David Thompson while resident at Prince of Wales's Fort (now Churchill, Man.) in 1784-85. It appears in his book *Travels in Western North America, 1784-1812* (1971), edited by Victor G. Hopwood. Mosquitoes and black flies remain a problem to this day.

JAMES MONROE 1784

In the mean time the acquisition *of Canada is not an object with us*, we must make valuable what we have already *acquired* and at the same time take such measures as to *weaken it as a British province*.

The expression of the spirit of American continentalism may require the fabled "forked tongue." James Monroe was a U.S. Congressman when he wrote slyly about the British colonies in North America in a letter to Thomas Jefferson, Nov. 1, 1784, which is included by Julian P. Boyd in *The Papers of Thomas Jefferson* (1953). As U.S. President in 1823, he enunciated the Monroe Doctrine, which defined the Americas as falling within the sphere of influence of the United States.

INSCRIPTION 1789

They Sacrificed Everything Save Honour.

This inscription appears on the cairn dedicated to the memory of the

United Empire Loyalists, Tusket, N.S. The historian Robert B. Blauveldt chose the words for the monument, which was unveiled in 1964. The designations "United Empire Loyalist" and "U.E." for "Unity of Empire" were the work of Lord Dorchester, Governor-in-Chief of British North America, who chose them on Nov. 9, 1789, as "a Marke of Honour" for the families of the immigrants who left the Thirteen Colonies between 1776 and 1783 and settled in British North America.

WOLFGANG AMADEUS MOZART 1790

But as to merit, I know
For sure, yes, yes, I swear . . .
The likes of us you will not find
From Paris to Canada,
From Paris to Canada,
From Paris to Canada.

There is a reference to Canada in the opera *Così Fan Tutte*. Wolfgang Amadeus Mozart composed the music to the Italian lyrics contributed by Lorenzo da Ponte. The popular opera was first produced in Vienna in 1790. The reference occurs in "Guglielmo's Aria," which is seldom performed abroad but always performed in Canada. It appears as K. 384 in Mozart's *Sämtliche Werke*. The second act of Mozart's next opera, *The Magic Flute* (1791), commences with four notes that uncannily recall the opening notes of "O Canada," which was composed by Calixa Lavallée some ninety years later.

EDWARD AUGUSTUS, DUKE OF KENT 1791

Let me hear no more of the invidious distinction of French and English. You are all his Britannic Majesty's beloved Canadian subjects.

The "invidious distinction" is still with us in the 1990s, even though Edward Augustus, Duke of Kent, said he wanted to "hear no more" of such thoughts in the address he delivered upon the passage of the Constitutional Act in 1791. The fourth son of George III, he served as Commander-in-Chief of the British forces in North America from 1791 to 1800. His daughter was Queen Victoria.

JOHN LONG   1791

One part of the religious superstition of the Savages, consists in each of them having his *totam*, or favourite spirit, which he believes watches over him. This *totam* they conceive assumes the shape of some beast or other, and therefore they never kill, hunt, or eat the animal whose form they think this *totam* bears. . . . This idea of destiny, or, if I may be allowed the phrase, *"totamism,"* however strange, is not confined to the Savages; many instances might be adduced from history, to prove how strong these impressions have been on minds above the vulgar and unlearned.

This is the first recorded use in any language of the word *totam*, or *totem* as it is commonly spelled. The usage comes from *Voyages and Travels of an Indian Interpreter and Trader* (1791), an account kept by John Long, English-born interpreter of the Chippewa in the region of the Albany River of present-day northern Ontario. The editor of the 1904 reprint edition of this book noted, "Long was the first to apply the word 'totamism' to that system of beliefs and family relationships, now recognized as the basis of primitive society."

JOHN GRAVES SIMCOE   1792

This province is singularly blest, not with a mutilated constitution, but with a constitution which has stood the test of experience, and which is the very image and transcript of that of Great Britain; by which she has long established and secured to her subjects as much freedom and happiness as is possible to be enjoyed under the subordination necessary to civilized society.

These noble sentiments come from the address delivered by John Graves Simcoe, Lieutenant-Governor of Upper Canada, at the closing of the first session of the first Parliament of Upper Canada, Fort George, Niagara, Oct. 15, 1792.

GEORGE VANCOUVER 1792

To describe the beauties of this region will, on some future occasion, be a very grateful task to the pen of a skilled panegyrist. The serenity of the climate, the innumerable pleasing landscapes, and the abundant fertility that unassisted nature puts forth, requires only to be enriched by the industry of man with villages, mansions, cottages, and other buildings to render it the most lovely country that can be imagined; whilst the labour of the inhabitants would be amply rewarded, in the bounties which nature seems ready to bestow on cultivation.

This description of the area around the future city of Vancouver was written in the spring of 1792 by the English navigator Captain George Vancouver and was published in *A Voyage of Discovery to the North Pacific Ocean and Round the World* (1798).

SIR ALEXANDER MACKENZIE 1793

I now mixed up some vermilion in melted grease, and inscribed, in large characters, on the South-East face of the rock on which we had slept last night, this brief memorial—"Alexander Mackenzie, from Canada, by land, the twenty-second of July, one thousand seven hundred and ninety-three."

Sir Alexander Mackenzie became the first explorer to cross the American continent north of Mexico. He did so in 1793, mostly on foot, from Montreal to Dean Channel, Bella Coola River, B.C., where he left this memorial, the most historic graffiti in Canadian history. Mackenzie then published *Voyages from Montreal on the River St. Lawrence, through the Continent of North America, to the Frozen and Pacific Oceans* (1801).

THOMAS MOORE   1804

Faintly as tolls the evening chime
Our voices keep tune and our oars keep time.
Soon as the woods on shore look dim,
We'll sing at St. Ann's our parting hymn.
Row, brothers, row, the stream runs fast,
The Rapids are near and the daylight's past.

The songs of the Anglo-Irish poet Thomas Moore were once on
everyone's lips; sadly, they are now forgotten, found only in old books.
Among the most popular of his lyrics was "Canadian Boat Song:
Written on the River St. Lawrence"; its popularity has gone the way
of the voyageurs who inspired its lines. Moore wrote the poem in the
summer of 1804, a guest of the explorer Simon Fraser in his home at
Ste-Anne-de-Bellevue, outside Montreal. "Canadian Boat Song" first
appeared in Moore's collection *Epistles, Odes and Other Poems* (1806).

DAVID THOMPSON   1811

Thus I have fully completed the survey of this part of North America
from sea to sea, and by almost innumerable astronomical observations
have determined the positions of the mountains, lakes, and rivers, and
other remarkable places on the northern part of this continent, the maps
of all of which have been drawn, and laid down in geographical position,
being now the work of twenty-seven years.

David Thompson, explorer and surveyor, made this entry in his
journal, July 14, 1811, at Fort Astoria. The passage appears in
Travels in Western North America, 1784-1812 (1971), edited by Victor
G. Hopwood. In the words of *The Canadian Encyclopedia*, "The maps,
based primarily on his own explorations and observations, were the
first to provide a comprehensive view of the vast western territories
that became part of Canada in 1870." Thompson died at Longueuil,
Canada East, in 1857, a pauper.

WILLIAM HULL 1812

Inhabitants of Canada. . . . The army under my command has invaded your country, and the standard of UNION now waves over the territory of Canada. To the peaceable unoffending inhabitant, it brings neither danger nor difficulty. I come to *find* enemies, not to *make* them. I come to protect, not to injure you.

Brigadier-General William Hull, as Commander of the Northwestern Army of the United States, issued this proclamation as a poster in Sandwich, Lower Canada, July 12, 1812. It appears in Robert Christie's *History of the Late Province of Lower Canada, Parliamentary and Political* (1854).

THOMAS JEFFERSON 1812

The acquisition of Canada this year, as far as the neighbourhood of Quebec, will be a mere matter of marching, and will give us experience for the attack of Halifax the next, and the final expulsion of England from the American continent.

The American statesman Thomas Jefferson, who served as President of the United States from 1801 to 1809, expressed this opinion in a letter to Colonel William Duane, Monticello, Virginia, Aug. 4, 1812, which appears in *The Writings of Thomas Jefferson* (1903), edited by Andrew A. Lipscomb.

SIR ISAAC BROCK 1812

Push on, brave York Volunteers!

Celebrated in story and song, the dying command of Sir Isaac Brock, commander of the British and militia forces in the War of 1812, is recalled to this day. Brock issued the command to the militia who had been brought to the Niagara Peninsula from York, Upper Canada (later, Toronto, Ont.), and pressed into the Battle of Queenston Heights, Oct. 13, 1812. Upon issuing the command, Brock fell to an American sniper's bullet. Some historians have expressed scepticism about the dying command, but military historian C.P. Stacey found it credible in "Brock's Muniments," *Books in Canada*, Aug.-Sept. 1980. Sir Isaac Brock and Laura Secord have emerged respectively as the "hero" and "heroine" of the War of 1812.

JAMES LAWRENCE 1813

> Tell the men to fire faster and not to give up the ship; fight her till she sinks.

This was the last command of James Lawrence, Captain of the U.S. ship *Chesapeake*. Usually shortened and quoted as "Don't give up the ship," it was adopted as the motto of the U.S. Navy. Alas, after a fifteen-minute sea battle outside Boston Harbour, June 1, 1813, the *Chesapeake* was taken by the HMS *Shannon*, commanded by Sir Philip Bowes Vere Broke.

LAURA SECORD 1813

> Did at great Risk peril & danger travelling on foot & partly in the Night by a circuitous route, through woods mountains, and enemys lines & Indian Encampments to give important intelligence of a meditated attack of the Americans upon our troops & by which circumstance has laid the foundation of a disease from which she has never recovered. . . .

Thus did Laura Secord describe (in the third person) her celebrated trek of some thirty kilometres by night from Queenston to Beaver Dams, June 22, 1813, to warn of an impending American attack in the Niagara Peninsula. Her account took the form of a petition written for monetary and other considerations in 1840 and addressed to the Lieutenant-Governor; it failed, as noted by Ruth

McKenzie in *Laura Secord: The Legend and the Lady* (1971). It was not until 1860 that Laura Secord received some compensation for her war work. A lame joke made the rounds in the 1960s: "If it weren't for this brave act, we'd be eating Martha Washington's chocolates today."

SIR GEORGE PREVOST 1814

We consider that the destruction of the Public Buildings at Washington are a just retribution for the outrages committed by an American force at the seat of Government of Upper Canada.

Sir George Prevost, commander of the British forces, explained that the burning of the Capitol building and the presidential mansion in Washington, D.C., Aug. 24, 1814, was the direct consequence of the sacking and burning of public and private buildings in York (later Toronto), April 30, 1813. The presidential mansion was then white-washed and became known as the White House. Prevost's explanation was quoted by Henry Scadding in *Toronto of Old* (1873). John Strachan, Anglican rector of York, wrote as follows in a letter addressed to former U.S. President Thomas Jefferson, Jan. 30, 1815: "Can you tell me, Sir, the reason why the public buildings and library at Washington should be held more sacred than those at York?" The letter is quoted by William F. Coggin in *1812; the War, and Its Moral* (1864). A century and a half after the War of 1812, comedian Don Harron quipped, "Canadians beat the Americans in this War—18 to 12."

NAPOLEON BONAPARTE 1817

England would be better off without Canada; it keeps her in a prepared state for war at great expense and constant irritation.

This was the opinion of Napoleon Bonaparte, one-time Emperor of the French, who spent his last years in exile on the island of Saint

Helena; it comes from the entry of Jan. 11, 1817, *A Diary at St. Helena: The Journal of Lady Malcolm (1816, 1817) Containing the Conversations of Napoleon with Sir Pulteney Malcolm* (1899, 1929), edited by Sir Arthur Wilson.

SIR CHARLES BAGOT   1817

And His Royal Highness agrees, that all other armed vessels, on these lakes shall be forthwith dismantled, and that no other vessels of war shall be there built or armed.

This is the "arms-limitation" clause of the Rush-Bagot Agreement between Great Britain and the United States, April 28-9, 1817. This clause, drafted by the British envoy Sir Charles Bagot, governs arms on the Great Lakes to this day.

SIR GEORGE SIMPSON   1821

It has occurred to me however that Philanthropy is not the exclusive object of our visits to these Northern Regions, but that to it are coupled interested motives, and that Beaver is the grand bone of contention.

This masterpiece of understatement about the purpose of the "company of traders" of the Hudson's Bay Company among the native population was made in a letter written from Fort Weddeburn in the Northwest on May 18, 1821, by the company's Governor, Sir George Simpson. It comes from Simpson's *Journal of Occurrences in the Athabasca Department* (1931), edited by E.E. Rich.

WILLIAM WARREN BALDWIN   1828

Responsible Government.

The notion of responsible government for the colonies of British North America was first proposed by reformer William Warren

Baldwin. Advocating the election rather than appointment of Cabinet Ministers, he expressed his views in a letter to the Duke of Wellington in 1828. His son, the reformer Robert Baldwin, recommended responsible government in a memorandum to the Colonial Secretary in 1836. He also corresponded with Lord Durham, who made the implementation of governors responsible to the electorate one of the recommendations in his influential *Report* (1839).

JOHN CHARLTON FISHER   1828

MORTEM VIRTUS COMMUNEM

FAMAM HISTORIA

MONUMENTUM POSTERITAS DEBIT

This inspired Latin inscription graces the Wolfe and Montcalm Monument, which was erected in the Governor's Garden next to today's Château Frontenac in Quebec City, Sept. 8, 1828. The inscription, composed by Quebec journalist John Charlton Fisher, translates: "Valour gave them a common death / history a common fame / posterity a common monument." Unique among the monuments of the world, it honours not only the victorious General Wolfe but also the vanquished Marquis de Montcalm, Battle of the Plains of Abraham, Sept. 13, 1759.

DAVID MACBETH MOIR   1829

Listen to me, as when ye heard our father
Sing long ago the song of our shores—
Listen to me, and then in chorus gather
All your deep voices, as ye pull your oars:
Fair these broad meads—these hoary woods are grand;
But we are exiles from our fathers' land.

These lines come from the poem called "Canadian Boat-Song (from the Gaelic)." It expresses a Highland Scot's lament at his

33

exile in the New World. Although it appeared anonymously in *Blackwood's*, Sept. 1829, its authorship has been ascribed to a Scots versifier, David Macbeth Moir, who never visited North America but who corresponded with the Scots-Canadian colonist and novelist John Galt. Its lines are strong in stoicism and suggest the determination and endurance of the Scots who settled Canada.

JOSIAH HENSON 1830

It was the 18th of October, 1830, in the morning, when my feet first touched the Canadian shore. I threw myself on the ground, rolled in the sand, seized handfuls of it and kissed them, and danced around, till, in the eyes of several who were present, I passed for a madman.

Josiah Henson, the most famous of the fugitive slaves and the model for the fictional Uncle Tom in Harriet Beecher Stowe's novel *Uncle Tom's Cabin; or, Life Among the Lowly* (1852), thus described, in *An Autobiography* (1881), his joy and relief upon reaching freedom from slavery in Upper Canada (present-day Ontario). His cabin still stands at Dresden, north of Chatham, Ont.

ETIENNE PARENT 1831

Nos Institutions, Notre Langue, Nos Lois.

"Our institutions, our language, our laws" was the motto chosen by publisher Etienne Parent when he resumed publication of the newspaper *Le Canadien* in Quebec City, Que., May 7, 1831.

WILLIAM LYON MACKENZIE 1831

There are those doubtless who fear the ignorance of the people of Upper Canada; I, on the other hand, stand more in dread of rulers like ours who are virtually independent of them. The people have an interest in good government, but the rulers have a gain by misrule.

These remarks come from an editorial written by the political reformer William Lyon Mackenzie and published in his newspaper the *Colonial Advocate*, July 14, 1831; reproduced by Margaret Fairley in *The Selected Writings of William Lyon Mackenzie* (1960). Six years after his editorial appeared, "the little rebel" led the Rebellion of 1837 in Upper Canada (present-day Ontario).

JOHN STRACHAN 1835

Nobody would ask for the vote by ballot but from gross ignorance; it is the most corrupt way of using the franchise.

This was the anti-democratic opinion of John Strachan, the influential Torontonian who became the first Bishop of Toronto in 1839, quoted by W.L. Mackenzie, chairman of *The Seventh Report from the Select Committee of the House of Assembly of Upper Canada on Grievances* (1835).

JOSEPH HOWE 1835

Yes, gentlemen, come what will, while I live, Nova Scotia shall have the blessing of an open and unshackled press.

Freedom of the press became a reality in early Canada following Joseph Howe's impassioned address to the jury in a courtroom in Halifax in May 1835. Charged with publishing libel in his newspaper *The Novascotian*, he defended himself so ably in a two-day address that he was acquitted. News of the acquittal marked a turning point in the history of the press in British North America. Known as the Tribune of Nova Scotia, Howe became Premier and then Lieutenant-Governor of his native province. The speech appears in *The Speeches and Public Letters of The Hon. Joseph Howe* (1858), edited by William Annand.

CATHARINE PARR TRAILL 1836

> As to ghosts or spirits they appear totally banished from Canada. This is too matter-of-fact a country for such supernaturals to visit. Here there are no historical associations, no legendary tales of those that came before us. Fancy would starve for lack of marvellous food to keep her alive in the backwoods.

Catharine Parr Traill, pioneer settler and writer, wrote at some length about the lack of "historical associations" in the backwoods area around Peterborough, Ont. "No Druid claims our oaks," she continued, sharing with many European settlers an indifference or ignorance of the native traditions of the original inhabitants of the land. The passage, dated May 9, 1833, comes from Traill's classic work, *The Backwoods of Canada* (1836).

CATHARINE PARR TRAILL 1836

> It is a good country for the honest, industrious artisan. It is a fine country for the poor labourer who, after a few years of hard toil, can sit down in his own log-house and look abroad on his own land and see his children well settled in life as independent freeholders. It is a grand country for the rich speculator who can afford to lay out a large sum in purchasing land in eligible situations; for if he have any judgement he will make a hundred per cent as interest for his money after waiting a few years. But it is a hard country for the poor gentleman whose habits have rendered him unfit for manual labour.

Things have not changed all that much since this opinion was expressed by the pioneer settler and writer Catharine Parr Traill in *The Backwoods of Canada* (1836).

ANONYMOUS 1837

Remember the *Caroline*.

These words became the rallying cry of the Patriots in the Rebellion of 1837. The *Caroline*, an American-owned steamer used by the Patriots on Navy Island in the Niagara River as a supply boat, was cut adrift by the British, set on fire, and sent flaming over Niagara Falls, Dec. 29, 1837. Its American owners considered a lawsuit, threatening to turn the Rebellion in Upper Canada into an international incident.

SIR GEORGE-ETIENNE CARTIER 1837

Before all I am a Canadian.

This line is the title and also the final line of a moving song composed by Sir George-Etienne Cartier during the Rebellion of 1837 in Lower Canada. At the time, Cartier was a student; in later years, he was a Father of Confederation, expressing patriotism for both Quebec and Canada. The original French runs "Avant tout je suis Canadien."

ANTOINE GÉRIN-LAJOIE 1838

Un Canadien errant,
Banni de ses foyers,
Parcourait en pleurant
Des pays étrangers.

This is the first verse of "Un Canadien Errant" (1838), the moving lament for the exiles of the Rebellion of 1837, composed by Antoine Gérin-Lajoie. John Boyd's English translation appeared in *Canadian Poetry in English* (1954): "Weeping sorely as he journeyed / Over many a foreign strand, / A Canadian exile wandered, / Banished from his native land."

LORD DURHAM 1839

I expected to find a contest between a government and a people: I found two nations warring in the bosom of a single state: I found a struggle, not of principles, but of races; and I perceived that it would be idle to attempt any amelioration of laws or institutions until we could first succeed in terminating the deadly animosity that now separates the inhabitants of Lower Canada into the hostile divisions of French and English.

The phrase "two nations warring in the bosom of a single state" first appeared in Lord Durham's famous *Report on the Affairs of British North America* (1839). Hardly a year has passed that a political commentator has not recalled these ten words and pressed them into service to reflect on the relations between the French and English in Canada. Durham was sent from England to report on the causes of the Rebellion of 1837. In 1839, having determined the reasons for the insurrections in both Lower and Upper Canada, today's Quebec and Ontario, he completed his comprehensive *Report*, which apportioned the blame. Had more attention been paid to his findings, there might have been less friction between the French and English in Quebec and Canada over the last century and a half.

LORD DURHAM 1839

There can hardly be conceived a nationality more destitute of all that can invigorate and elevate a people, than that which is exhibited by the descendants of the French in Lower Canada, owing to their retaining their peculiar language and manners. They are a people with no history, and no literature.

This appraisal of their past and their culture did not sit well with educated French Canadians. No sooner did Lord Durham make this point in his famous (or infamous) *Report* (1839), reprinted from Sir Charles P. Lucas's edition of *Lord Durham's Report on the Affairs of*

British North America (1912), than the Quebec City lawyer, François-Xavier Garneau, devoted his efforts to researching and writing his influential three-volume *Histoire du Canada* (1845-48), thus providing evidence of a history and a literature. Garneau vowed: "I shall write the history which you do not even know exists. You will see that our ancestors yielded only when outnumbered. There are defeats which are as glorious as victories."

FREDERICK MARRYAT 1839

You are at once struck with the difference between the English and the American population, system and ideas. On the other side of the lake, you have much more apparent property, but much less real solidarity and security. The houses and stores of Toronto are not to be compared with those of the American towns opposite. But the Englishman has built according to his means—the American according to his expectations.

This astute observation was made by Captain Frederick Marryat, the popular novelist and sea captain. He travelled in the eastern United States and in Upper and Lower Canada, and he compared the sights he saw, describing and discussing them in *Diary in America, with Remarks on Its Institutions* (1839). The reference to "Englishman" should be taken to mean a settler from Britain or a native-born person living in that region of North America that was then still known as British North America.

WILLIAM ALLEN 1844

Fifty-four Forty, or Fight!

U.S. Senator William Allen is credited with first uttering the rallying cry "Fifty-four Forty, or Fight!" Thereafter, it was adopted as the slogan of the Democratic Party in the federal election of 1844. The fighting words are said to derive from a speech Allen delivered on the Oregon boundary question in the U.S. Senate in that year. The dispute was between Britain and the United States over the border between British North America and the United States west of the Rocky Mountains. The Americans wanted the boundary to extend as far north as Russian Alaska (54°40′ N) as well as including the Columbia River mouth; the American government compromised (and did not fight) when it signed the Oregon Treaty of June 15, 1846, which accepted the forty-ninth parallel (49° N), although some details were not resolved until 1872, one year after British Columbia joined Confederation.

SIR ETIENNE-PASCHAL TACHÉ   1846

> Be satisfied we will never forget our allegiance till the last cannon which is shot on this continent in defence of Great Britain is fired by the hand of a French Canadian.

The French formed an alliance with the British in Canada that time would not diminish, in the opinion of Sir Etienne-Paschal Taché, a future Father of Confederation, in his address in the Quebec Assembly, April 24, 1846; quoted by Jacques Monet in *The Last Cannon Shot* (1969). Governor General Lord Elgin asked the following question in a letter of May 4, 1848: "Who will venture to say that the last hand which waves the British flag on American ground may not be that of a French Canadian?"

HENRY WADSWORTH LONGFELLOW   1847

> Still stands the forest primeval; but under the shade of its branches
> Dwells another race, with other customs and language.
> Only along the shore of the mournful and misty Atlantic
> Linger a few Acadian peasants, whose fathers from exile
> Wandered back to their native land to die in its bosom.
> In the fisherman's cot the wheel and the loom are still busy;
> Maidens still wear their Norman caps and their kirtles of homespun,
> And by the evening fire repeat Evangeline's story,

While from its rocky caverns the deep-voiced, neighbouring ocean
Speaks, and in accents disconsolate answers the wail of the forest.

These are the opening lines of *Evangeline: A Tale of Acadie* (1847), the narrative poem written by American versifier Henry Wadsworth Longfellow. The long poem, with its melancholy lines, is a moving account of the expulsion of the Acadians in 1755 from their traditional habitat in "the little village of Grand-Pré" on "the shores of the Basin of Minas." It tells the tale of Acadian lovers, Evangeline and Gabriel, who are separated by the English but eventually meet again in Louisiana. Evangeline Bellefontaine is a fictional character, but Longfellow based his account of her experiences on a real-life Acadian woman named Emmeline Labische (who died of shock when she finally met her long-lost lover only to find him engaged to another woman). Unlike their real-life counterparts, the characters in the poem remain true to one another. In Nova Scotia's Grand Pré National Park, Longfellow is honoured with a plaque; Evangeline is remembered with a unique statue, sculpted by Henri Hébert to show the youthful Acadian from one angle and the aged Acadian from another. Silent film star Dolores del Rio posed for the statue of Evangeline erected in St. Martinville, Louisiana.

THOMAS CHANDLER HALIBURTON 1849

The Nova Scotian . . . is the gentleman known throughout America as Mr. Blue Nose, a *sobriquet* acquired from a superior potato of that name, for the good qualities of which he is never tired of talking, being anxious, like most men of small property, to exhibit to the best advantage the little he had.

The word *bluenose* refers to someone from Nova Scotia and it was first used in print by T.C. Haliburton, Nova Scotia-born author, judge, and member of the British Parliament. It appears in his novel *The Old Judge, or, Life in a Colony* (1849).

ABRAHAM GESNER 1849

It is in vain to suppose that a free trade system will be beneficial to a new and struggling colony, which has nothing to export but raw materials; it is rather calculated to enrich an old commonwealth, whose people by their skill and labour make such raw materials valuable, and then return them for consumption. The result of the system alluded to has been that the suppliers of the raw material at last become hewers of wood and drawers of water to the manufacturers.

Abraham Gesner is remembered as the scientist who devised a method of producing kerosene in Halifax in 1846. He is also remembered as a critic of reciprocity, a form of free trade, who expressed his views in *The Industrial Resources of Nova Scotia* (1849).

SUSANNA MOODIE 1853

Has Canada no poet to describe the glories of his parent land—no painter that can delineate her matchless scenery of land and wave? Are her children dumb and blind, that they leave to strangers the task of singing her praise? The standard literature of Canada must be looked for in the newspapers.

Pioneer settler and writer Susanna Moodie made this argument in the introduction to her novel *Mark Hurdlestone, The Gold Worshipper* (1853). The situation has improved somewhat in the last century and a half, but the same criticisms are sometimes sounded in the 1990s!

HENRY WADSWORTH LONGFELLOW 1855

Should you ask me, whence these stories?
Whence these legends and traditions,
With the odours of the forest,
With the dew and damp of meadows,
With the curling smoke of wigwams,

With the rushing of great rivers,
With their frequent repetitions,
And their wild reverberations,
As of thunder in the mountains?
I should answer, I should tell you,
"From the forests and the prairies,
From the great lakes of the Northland."

These are the heavily accented opening lines of *The Song of Hiawatha* (1855), written by the American poet and versifier Henry Wadsworth Longfellow. The book-length narrative poem tells the story of the Ojibwa brave Hiawatha, and much of its action is set in the region north of Lake Superior. Longfellow based his account on the writings of the Indian agent H.R. Schoolcraft; ethnologists have argued that he confused the legendary figure of Hiawatha with the mythical figure of Nanabozho. Hiawatha was the chief who assisted Dekanahwideh in the founding of the Iroquois Confederacy; Nanabozho is the principal Algonkian "culture hero." But the supposed confusion—the poet's amalgamation perhaps—may well be one factor that accounted for the work's great popularity, which lasted for over one hundred years.

JOSEPH SCRIVEN 1857

What a Friend we have in Jesus,
All our sins and griefs to bear!
What a privilege to carry
Everything to God in prayer!

The well-loved Protestant hymn "What a Friend We Have in Jesus" was based on the poem "Pray without Ceasing," which was written about 1857 by Joseph Scriven, a resident of the Port Hope area of Ontario. The text appeared in Scriven's *What a Friend We Have in Jesus and Other Hymns* (1895), edited by Jas. Cleland.

SIR EDMUND HEAD   1857

On the whole, therefore, I believe that the least objectionable place is
the city of Ottawa. Every city is jealous of every other city except Ottawa.

One reason why Ottawa was chosen to be the capital of the new
Dominion was given in the confidential memorandum addressed to
the British Colonial Secretary by Governor General Sir Edmund
Head, Oct. 1857, reprinted by James A. Gibson in *Canadian Historical Review*, Dec. 1935. The essayist Goldwin Smith groaned that
"Ottawa is a sub-arctic lumber-village converted by royal mandate
into a political cockpit."

LORD MONCK   1858

A careful consideration of the general position of British North America
induced the conviction that the circumstances of the times afforded the
opportunity, not merely for the settlement of a question of personal
politics, but also for the simultaneous creation of a new nationality.

Lord Monck, in his Throne Speech, Parliament of Canada, Quebec,
Jan. 19, 1865, addressed the notion that the provinces should be
united into a confederation. Confederation came about two years
later, and Lord Monck was appointed the first Governor General
of Canada. The concept of "a new nationality" (as distinct from
the American ideal of "a new nation") originated in 1858 with the
Montreal lawyer Alexander Morris, who was later appointed
Lieutenant-Governor of Manitoba; the notion was popularized by
Father of Confederation Thomas D'Arcy McGee.

PAUL KANE   1859

But the face of the red man is now no longer seen. All traces of his
footsteps are fast being obliterated from his once favourite haunts, and
those who would see the aborigines of this country in their original state,

or seek to study their native manners and customs, must travel far through the pathless forest to find them.

It was through the "pathless forest" that the painter Paul Kane travelled from his studio in Toronto, venturing across the West, to the Pacific Coast, sketching the land and its native inhabitants, and describing their society in *Wanderings of an Artist among the Indians of North America* (1859). He preserved images, in words and oil paintings, of a fast-receding (but not vanishing) native way of life.

JAMES H. RICHARDSON 1860

Resolved: that all Native Canadians joining in the procession, whether identified with the National Societies or not, should wear the maple leaf as the emblem of the land of their birth.

Businessman and patriot James H. Richardson drafted this resolution, which was adopted at the joint meeting of the National Societies, Toronto, Aug. 21, 1860. The resolution concerned the impending visit of the Prince of Wales, and it marks the date of the adoption of the maple leaf as the quasi-official emblem for Canada.

WILLIAM H. SEWARD 1861

So I look upon Prince Rupert's Land and Canada, and see how an ingenious people, and a capable, enlightened government, are occupied with bridging rivers and making railroads and telegraphs to develop, organize and create and preserve the great British provinces of the north; by the Great Lakes, the St. Lawrence and around the shores of Hudson's Bay, and I am able to say, "It is very well; you are building excellent states to be hereafter admitted to the American Union."

American continentalist aspirations were given vigorous expression by William H. Seward, Republican politician and future U.S.

Secretary of War. That Seward had a good sense of North American geography is shown in the above passage from a campaign speech delivered at St. Paul, Min., as reported in *The New York Herald*, Jan. 25, 1861. Mounting tensions among the American states prevented any immediate American continentalist adventures.

IMRE MADÁCH 1861

There are too many Eskimos and not enough seals.

This is an explanation of why life seems to be so difficult. It was once widely quoted in central Europe, for it comes from the Hungarian poetic drama *The Tragedy of Man* (1861). In this philosophical work in fifteen acts composed by the Hungarian poet Imre Madách, two characters are living at the North Pole and one is explaining life's difficulties to the other. According to the Hungarian-American composer Miklós Rózsa in *Double Life* (1982), the remark "has gone into the language as a catchphrase and sums up life in Budapest at that time very well: in other words, too many talents and not enough opportunities."

SIR JOHN WILLIAM DAWSON 1863

Canada has two emblems which have often appeared to some to point out its position in these respects,—the *Beaver* and the *Maple*. The beaver in his sagacity, his industry, his ingenuity, and his perseverance, is a most respectable animal; a much better emblem for our country than the rapacious eagle or even the lordly lion; but he is also a type of unvarying instincts and old-world traditions. He does not improve, and becomes extinct rather than change his ways. The maple, on the other hand, is the emblem of the vitality and energy of a new country; vigorous and stately in its growth, changing its hues as the seasons change, equally at home in the forest, in the cultivated field, and stretching its green boughs over the dusty streets, it may well be received as a type of the progressive and versatile spirit of a new and growing people.

This mini-essay on the two national emblems was written by the educator Sir John William Dawson and appeared in *The Duties of Educated Young Men in British America* (1863). It did much to establish the beaver and the maple leaf as quasi-national emblems.

GEORGE WASHINGTON JOHNSON 1864

I wandered today to the hill, Maggie,
   To watch the scene below,
The creek and the creaking old mill, Maggie,
   As we used to long ago.
The green grove is gone from the hill, Maggie,
   Where first the daisies sprung,
The creaking old mill is still, Maggie,
   Since you and I were young.

This is the first verse of the love ballad "When You and I Were Young," which was written by the teacher George Washington Johnson, who included it in his book of verse *Maple Leaves* (1864). Two years later, J.A. Butterfield, an English composer then resident in Chicago, read it and set it to music. It became popular throughout the English-speaking world. The ballad celebrated the love Johnson felt for his student Maggie Clark, as noted by the plaque that marks her childhood home on Nebo Road outside Burlington, Ont.

THOMAS D'ARCY MCGEE 1865

One individual chooses Tuponia and another Hochelaga, as a suitable name for the new nationality. Now I would ask any hon. member of this House how he would feel if he woke up some fine morning and found himself, instead of a Canadian, a Tuponian or a Hochelagander. I think, sir, we may safely leave for the present discussion of the name as well as the origin of the new system proposed.

The Dominion of Canada may sound all right today, but in the 1860s the name for the new country was the subject of much discussion and debate in Parliament. Thomas D'Arcy McGee, a Father of Confederation, tired of the wrangling and memorably ridiculed some of the suggestions in the Legislative Assembly, Quebec, Feb. 9, 1865; from *Parliamentary Debates on the Subject of the British North American Provinces* (1865).

SIR HENRI-GUSTAVE JOLY DE LOTBINIÈRE 1865

Since we cannot find a comparison on the poor earth emblematic of our future greatness, let us borrow one from the heavens at the risk of losing ourselves in the clouds with the advocates of Confederation; I propose the adoption of the rainbow as our emblem. By the endless variety of its tints the rainbow will give an excellent idea of the diversity of races, religions, sentiments and interests of the different parts of the Confederation. By its slender and elongated form, the rainbow would afford a perfect representation of the geographical configuration of the Confederation. By its lack of consistence—an image without substance—the rainbow would represent aptly the solidity of our Confederation. An emblem we must have, for every great empire has one; let us adopt the rainbow.

It is charming to think that the rainbow could have been chosen as the emblem of Confederation. Whether in the spirit of jollity or jest, the proposal was made by Sir Henri-Gustave Joly de Lotbinière, politician and writer, in the Legislative Assembly, Quebec, Feb. 20, 1865; from *Parliamentary Debates on the Subject of the British North American Provinces* (1865).

SIR JOHN A. MACDONALD 1865

In the Upper House, the controlling and regulating, but not initiating
branch, we have the sober second thought in legislation.

The view that the Senate, the Upper House of Parliament, should offer
legislators time for a "sober second thought" was advanced by Sir John
A. Macdonald on April 6, 1865, and was quoted by Sir Joseph Pope in
Confederation (1895). Elsewhere, Pope quotes Macdonald as saying less
elegantly, "The Senate is the saucer into which we pour legislation to cool."

HENRY DAVID THOREAU 1866

I fear that I have not got much to say about Canada, not having seen
much; what I got by going to Canada was a cold.

Henry David Thoreau was a fine writer and thinker (and the author
of *Walden* in 1854) but not much of a traveller. He left Concord,
Mass., for Quebec on Sept. 25, 1850, returning on Oct. 2, 1850. He
was not very impressed. *A Yankee in Canada* (1866) is the dyspeptic
account of his experiences. He explained, "In Canada you are
reminded of the government every day."

LOUIS-FRANÇOIS LAFLÈCHE 1866

My brethren, I will hide nothing of my thoughts on this point: the
heaviest tax resulting from the Conquest has been the necessity of
knowing English. It is quite proper, I admit, that some people should
acquire a knowledge of English, but of this tax let us not pay any more
than is strictly necessary.

This was the advice given to his French-Canadian parishioners by
Louis-François LaFlèche, Bishop of Trois-Rivières, Saint-Jean-
Baptiste Day, 1866, as quoted by Dominique Clift in *The Secret Kingdom:*

Interpretations of a Canadian Character (1989). "Speak English, but speak it badly" is what he meant, according to Télésphore-Damien Bouchard, speaking in the House of Commons, June 21, 1944.

SIR SAMUEL LEONARD TILLEY 1866

His dominion shall be from sea to sea.

It was the suggestion of Sir Samuel Leonard Tilley, a Father of Confederation, at the pre-Confederation conference in London, England, Dec. 1866, that the working title of the new country should be the Dominion of Canada, based on a passage found in the King James version of the Bible: "His dominion shall be from sea to sea" (Zechariah 9:10). Up to this point, there had been a move to call it the Kingdom of Canada or the Vice-royalty of Canada, to affirm its monarchical nature. In the end, the designation "dominion" was chosen so as not to offend the republican feelings of the United States.

OFFICIAL MOTTO 1866

A mari usque ad mare.

The official motto of the Dominion of Canada is the Latin phrase *A mari usque ad mare.* The official translations are "From Sea to Sea" and "D'un océan à l'autre." The motto is based on Sir Samuel Leonard Tilley's quotation from the King James version of the Bible (Zechariah 9:10), "His dominion shall be from sea to sea," at the pre-Confederation Conference in London, England, Dec. 1866. The notion that Canada extends from sea to sea is repeated in the national anthem "O Canada"; in the 1908 English version by R. Stanley Weir, the second and third verses refer to the land extending "from East to Western Sea." Since the late 1950s and the Northern Vision of Prime Minister John G. Diefenbaker, it has been fashionable to speak of Canada as a country extending "from sea to sea to sea"—from the Atlantic to the Pacific to the Arctic. A sea is a sea in Canada; in the United States, it is a "shining" sea.

The popular U.S. anthem "America the Beautiful" requests God to "crown thy good with brotherhood / From sea to shining sea." It was written by Katherine Lee Bates, who was inspired by the sight of Pikes Peak in 1893 and set the words to the tune of Samuel Ward's song "O Mother Dear, Jerusalem." A reference to "the sea" turns up in the introductory verse to another popular U.S. anthem "God Bless America," composed by Irving Berlin, which begins as follows: "While the storm clouds gather / Far across the sea." The second verse includes these lines: "From the mountains to the prairies/ To the oceans white with foam." Seas seem to be in season in North America.

THE BRITISH NORTH AMERICA ACT 1867

It shall be lawful for the Queen, by and with the Advice of Her Majesty's Most Honourable Privy Council, to declare by Proclamation that, on and after a Day therein appointed, not being more than Six Months after the passing of this Act, the Provinces of Canada, of Nova Scotia, and New Brunswick shall form and be One Dominion under the name of Canada; and on and after that Day those Three Provinces shall form and be One Dominion under that Name accordingly.

This is Article 3 of the British North America Act, 1867, commonly called the BNA Act, passed in the British Parliament on March 29, 1867; it became effective on July 1, 1867.

THE BRITISH NORTH AMERICA ACT 1867

It shall be lawful for the Queen, by and with the Advice and Consent of the Senate and House of Commons, to make Laws for the Peace, Order, and good Government of Canada.

This is a key section from the British North America Act, 1867, which came into effect on July 1, 1867. It became part of the Constitution Act, 1982.

HENRI-RAYMOND CASGRAIN 1867

We live at two opposite poles; you at the pole of naturalism; I at that of supernaturalism; but there is one point on which we meet: that is the love of humanity.

This remarkable and magnanimous tribute is an attempt to bridge the chasm that divides the French and the English in Canada. It was tendered by Henri-Raymond Casgrain, priest and historian, acknowledging receipt of a gift from Francis Parkman of a copy of the Boston historian's newly published volume, *The Jesuits in North America in the Seventeenth Century* (1867). It was quoted by Howard Doughty in his biography, *Francis Parkman* (1962).

OCTAVE CRÉMAZIE 1867

The more I reflect on the destiny of Canadian literature, the less chance I find for its leaving a mark in history. Canada lacks its own language. If we spoke Iroquois or Huron, our literature would live.

*

The cause of this inferiority lies not in the rarity of men of talent, but in the disastrous environment provided for the writer by the indifference of a population which has as yet no taste for letters, at least for works produced by native sons.

*

Are we not a million Frenchmen forgotten by the mother country on the shores of the St. Lawrence? It is not enough to encourage all those who hold a pen to know that this little people will grow great, and that it will always guard the name and memory of those who aided it to conserve intact the most precious of all treasures, the tongue of its fathers?

Despairing of opportunities for poets and writers in his native Quebec, the poet Octave Crémazie left and settled in France in 1862. Yet he expressed considerable faith in Quebec's future, as is shown by these passages from the letter he wrote to Abbé Henri-Raymond

Casgrain, Jan. 29, 1867, included in *Les Oeuvres Complètes d'Octave Crémazie* (1882), edited by Casgrain.

ALEXANDER MUIR 1867

In days of yore, from Britain's shore,
   Wolfe, the dauntless hero, came,
And planted firm Britannia's flag
   On Canada's fair domain.

Here may it wave, our boast and pride,
   And, joined in love together,
The Thistle, Shamrock, Rose entwine
   The Maple Leaf forever!

The Maple Leaf, our emblem dear,
   The Maple Leaf forever;
God save our Queen, and Heaven bless
   The Maple Leaf forever.

"The Maple Leaf Forever" is not sung much these days, but at one time it was lustily sung by every English-speaking Canadian. Yet the words stuck in the craw of every Québécois—not for everybody was General Wolfe a "dauntless hero"! Alexander Muir, a Toronto school teacher, composed the words and music of the popular anthem in 1867.

FOLK SONG 1869

Then hurrah for our own native isle, Newfoundland!
Not a stranger shall hold one inch of its strand!
Her face turns to Britain, her back to the Gulf.
Come near at your peril, Canadian Wolf!

Newfoundlanders resisted the appeal of Confederation from 1867 to April 1, 1949, when Newfoundland became Canada's tenth province.

(Some commentators maintain that there are Newfoundlanders who resist its appeal to this day!) "An Anti-Confederation Song" was sung during the election of 1869, when Newfoundlanders voted against Confederation with Canada. The full text appears in *Old-Time Poetry and Songs of Newfoundland* (1940), edited by Gerald S. Doyle.

THOMAS D'ARCY MCGEE 1869

In the seaport of Saint Malo, 'twas a smiling morn in May,
When the Commodore Jacques Cartier to the westward sail'd away.

There was a time in this strange land when the school children memorized lines of verse, and one of the poems they committed to memory was the ballad "Jacques Cartier," which celebrated the exploits of the French navigator and explorer, the Canadian Columbus. The ballad was written by patriot and politician Thomas D'Arcy McGee, and it appears in *The Poems of Thomas D'Arcy McGee* (1869), edited by Mrs. J. Sadlier. The first two lines of the poem (reproduced here) are still recalled with pleasure, generally by those readers who also remember the first line of Winifred Sackville Stoner's "The History of the U.S." which was written in the twentieth century. It begins, "In fourteen hundred ninety-two, Columbus sailed the ocean blue."

LOUIS RIEL 1869

You go no farther!

Louis Riel, leader of the Métis in the Red River and Northwest rebellions, issued this warning to the British surveyors, Oct. 11, 1869. "The métis simply stood on the chain while Riel declared that the territory south of the Assiniboine belonged to the people of the Red River and not to Canada, and that the métis would not allow the survey to proceed any farther," wrote George F.G. Stanley in *Louis Riel* (1963).

FOLK SONG 1870

Come and sit by my side if you love me,
    Do not hasten to bid me adieu,
But remember the Red River Valley
    And the girl who has loved you so true.

This is the chorus of the perennially popular western folk song, "The Red River Valley." According to folklorist Edith Fowke, in *Singing Our History* (1984), it was probably composed in Manitoba at the time of the Red River Rebellion of 1870.

SIR WILLIAM FRANCIS BUTLER 1870

REMEMBER BUTLER, 69TH REGIMENT.

This is the entire text of the famous cable sent to Colonel Garnet Wolseley, who was organizing the Red River Expedition in 1870. It was sent by the British officer Sir William Francis Butler, then resident in England; Wolseley remembered Butler and agreed to his presence on the expedition against the Métis uprising, according to Viscount Wolseley's memoirs, *The Story of a Soldier's Life* (1903).

QUEEN VICTORIA 1871

Her Majesty hopes that this new colony on the Pacific may be but one step in the career of steady progress by which Her Majesty's dominions in North America may ultimately be peopled, in an unbroken chain from the Atlantic to the Pacific, by a loyal and industrious population of subjects of the British Crown.

With these words did Queen Victoria address the British House of Commons in 1871, according to Alexander Morris in *Nova Britannia; or Our New Canadian Dominion Foreshadowed* (1884).

JOSEPH HOWE 1871

A wise nation preserves its records, gathers up its muniments, decorates the tombs of its illustrious dead, repairs its great public structures, and fosters national pride and love of country, by perpetual references to the sacrifices and glories of the past.

Canada has been notably lax in preserving its records. For instance, eighty-six years of nationhood were allowed to lapse before an act was passed that established the National Library of Canada in 1953. Joseph Howe, the journalist and then statesman, who fought successfully to ensure a free press, delivered an address at Framingham, Mass., Aug. 31, 1871, in which he pointed out the need to preserve records and muniments (documents kept as evidence of rights or privileges). The address is included in his *Poems and Essays* (1874).

WILLIAM A. FOSTER 1871

As between the various Provinces comprising the Dominion, we need some cement more binding than geographical contact; some bond more uniting than a shiftless expediency; some lodestar more potent than a mere community of profit. Temporizing makeshifts may suit a futureless people.

William A. Foster, a leading nationalist in the immediate post-Confederation period, feared that the newly created Dominion of Canada would remain little more than a "geographical expression" unless its leaders endorsed a set of ideals or goals. The passage above comes from his influential tract *Canada First* (1871).

SIR GEORGE-ETIENNE CARTIER 1872

All aboard for the West!

The Pacific Railway Act, passed by the House of Commons, June 1, 1872, created the Canadian Pacific Railway. On that occasion,

Father of Confederation Sir George-Etienne Cartier rose from his seat and shouted, "All aboard for the West!"

ALFRED LORD TENNYSON 1873

And that true North, whereof we lately heard.

The words "true North" have a remarkable ring to them and the ring is poetical. It was first sounded in the poem "O Loyal to the Royal in Thyself," which is part of *Idylls of the King* (1873) by Alfred Lord Tennyson. The poet laureate composed the lines that include the words "true North" immediately after reading an editorial in *The Times,* Oct. 30, 1872, which advised Canada to seek its independence from Britain. Tennyson felt this advice to be gratuitous and patronizing if not unpatriotic. Stanley Weir worked the words into his version of "O Canada," composed in 1908: "With glowing hearts we see thee rise, / The True North, strong and free."

GEORGE MONRO GRANT 1873

Travel a thousand miles up a great river, more than another thousand along great lakes and a succession of smaller lakes, a thousand miles across rolling prairies, and another thousand through woods and over three great ranges of mountains, and you have travelled from Ocean to Ocean through Canada. All this Country is a single Colony of the British Empire; and this Colony is dreaming magnificent dreams of a future when it shall be the "Greater Britain," and the highway across which the fabrics and products of Asia shall be carried, to the East as well as the Western sides of the Atlantic.

This famous peroration was written by George Monro Grant for his nationalistic work *Ocean to Ocean* (1873). Grant served as secretary to Sir Sandford Fleming on the latter's exploratory expedition "through Canada" in 1872. Grant's account captures the excitement of that experience. Known and revered as Principal Grant of Queen's, he was the father of W.L. Grant of Upper Canada College, and the grandfather of the philosopher George P. Grant.

JOHN WILSON BENGOUGH   1873

> These hands are clean!

This is the caption that appears below the most famous of all Canadian political cartoons, called "Whither Are We Drifting?" It was drawn by the noted artist J.W. Bengough for the Toronto comic weekly *Grip*, Aug. 6, 1873. In the cartoon, Prime Minister Sir John A. Macdonald is shown absolving himself of all charges of corruption in connection with the Pacific Scandal. Yet in his left hand he holds a sign that says "Send me another $10,000," and in his right, a charter for the "Prorogation and Suppression of the Investigation."

CORNELIUS HOWATT   1873

> Elect me and I will keep you out of Confederation.

This was the campaign promise made by politician Cornelius Howatt while campaigning for election in 1873. He was elected to the Legislative Assembly of Prince Edward Island (which later that year voted to join with Canada). His promise appeared in *Cornelius Howatt: Superstar!* (1974) by Harry Baglole and David Weale; apparently, the biographers established an association, called the Brothers and Sisters of Cornelius Howatt, to reconsider the island's future.

LORD DUFFERIN   1873

> I found the Island in a high state of jubilation and quite under the
> impression that it is the Dominion that has been annexed to Prince

Edward; and in alluding to the subject I had adopted the same tone.

Prince Edward Island joined Confederation on July 1, 1873. Governor General Lord Dufferin spoke in Charlottetown three weeks later, and thereafter sent a letter to Prime Minister Sir John A. Macdonald with the above observation; quoted by D.C. Harvey in "Confederation and Prince Edward Island," *Canadian Historical Review*, June 1933.

EDWARD BLAKE 1873

The time will come when that national spirit which has been spoken of will be truly felt among us, when we shall realize that we are four million Britons who are not free, when we shall be ready to take up that freedom, and to ask what the late prime minister of England assured us we should not be denied—our share of national rights.

These words come from the so-called Aurora Speech on the need for a national spirit, delivered by the politician Edward Blake at Aurora, Ont., Oct. 3, 1873. The speech was edited by W. Stewart Wallace and published in the *Canadian Historical Review*, Sept. 1921.

MAWEDOPENAIS 1873

Now you see me stand before you all: what has been done here today has been done openly before the Great Spirit and before the nation, and I hope I may never hear any one say that this treaty has been done secretly: and now in closing this council, I take off my glove, and in giving you my hand I deliver over my birthright and lands: and in taking your hand I hold fast all the promises you have made, and I hope they will last as long as the sun rises and the water flows, as you have said.

Mawedopenais was the chief spokesman of the Ojibwa tribes at Fort Francis when Treaty Number 3 (North-West Angle Treaty) was signed, Oct. 1873. The speech, which included the formulaic refrain "as long as the sun rises and the water flows," appeared in Alexander Morris's volume, *The Treaties of Canada with the Indians of Manitoba and the North-West Territories* (1880).

RCMP MOTTO 1873

Maintiens le droit.

This is the official motto of the Mounties: the North-West Mounted Police (1873-1904), Royal North-West Mounted Police (1904-1920), Royal Canadian Mounted Police (from 1920). The French phrase is officially translated as "Uphold the Right." Proposed in 1873, the motto came into use two years later. The RCMP's oath of office requires recruits to attend to their duties "without fear, favour or affection"—another vivid phrase. The unofficial motto, "They always get their man," dates from 1877.

SAMUEL BUTLER 1874

Stowed away in a Montreal lumber room
The Discobolus standeth and turneth his face to the wall;
Dusty, cobweb-covered, maimed, and set at naught,
Beauty crieth in the attic and no man regardeth:
    O God! O Montreal!

The English satirist Samuel Butler visited the old Montreal Museum of Natural History in 1874, where he saw that the plaster cast of Myron's Discobolus was relegated to the storage room. The act of curatorial prudery inspired him to write the satiric verse "A Psalm of Montreal"—with its refrain "O God! O Montreal!"—published in *The Spectator,* May 18, 1878. Some four decades later, in 1913, the poet Rupert Brooke wrote: "I made my investigations in Montreal. I have to report that the Discobolus is very well, and, nowadays, looks the whole world in the face, almost quite unabashed." Would that this were so in the 1990s! The Discobolus, part of the permanent collection of the Montreal Museum of Fine Arts, was loaned for display purposes in the 1960s and disappeared from view. Perhaps it languishes to this day in some Montreal "lumber room."

ALFRED LORD TENNYSON 1875

> Not here; the White North has thy bones,
>   And thou, heroic sailor soul,
> Are passing on thy happier voyage now
>   Toward no earthly pole.

This moving verse was composed by Alfred Lord Tennyson, the British poet laureate, and inscribed on the monument erected in Westminster Abbey in 1875 to the memory of Sir John Franklin, the explorer who disappeared in the Arctic in 1847. Franklin's fate has yet to be determined, for his remains have yet to be found in "the White North."

PIERRE-JOSEPH-OLIVIER CHAUVEAU 1876

> English and French, we climb by a double flight of stairs toward the destinies reserved for us on this continent, without knowing each other, without meeting each other, and without even seeing each other, except on the landing of politics. In social and literary terms, we are far more foreign to each other than the English and French of Europe.

This image of the "double flight of stairs" is an arresting one and was minted by Pierre-Joseph-Olivier Chauveau, first Premier of Quebec following Confederation. It appeared in *L'Instruction Publique au Canada* (1876) as quoted by Mason Wade in the introduction to *Canadian Dualism* (1960).

MELVILLE BELL 1876

Yes, Alec, it is I, your father, speaking.

Melville Bell was a noted language instructor and an innovator in the field of language instruction for the deaf. He was also the father of Alexander Graham Bell, the inventor of the telephone. The world's first long-distance telephone call was placed by the instructor to the inventor on Aug. 10, 1876, when Melville spoke into a primitive transmitter in Brantford and was heard by Alexander in a shoe store in Paris, Ont., thirteen kilometres away. This first long-distance call lasted three hours. Alexander called it "the first transmission of speech to a distance," but it was one-way communication, with Alexander replying in Morse code by telegraphy. Canada can lay a claim to long-distance telephone communication, but what about the telephone itself? In 1917, Alexander declared, "The telephone was conceived in Brantford in 1874, and born in Boston in 1875." Like microwave ovens and fax machines, the telephone was popular from the first. In 1935, Mohandas K. Gandhi informed a group of school children in Wardha, central India, "The telephone is a most useful invention. We can discuss important matters, spread peace and love by persuading others as we talk. It was invented in Canada by Alexander Bell."

WILLIAM KIRBY 1877

Je suis un chien qui ronge lo
En le rongeant je prends mon repos
Un temps viendra qui n'est pas venu
Que je morderay qui maura mordu.

This is Quebec City's famous "Golden Dog" inscription which features, in addition to four lines of old French, the gilded figure of a dog gnawing on a bone. Carved in stone and placed over the lintel of a private residence on Rue Baude, the inscription was later affixed to the portal of the Quebec City post office, where it may be seen today. The lines recall a tale of vengeance dating back to 1737, and they inspired William Kirby's historical novel *The Golden Dog* (1877, 1896). They may be translated: "I am a dog that gnaws his bone / I crouch and gnaw it all alone / The time will come which is not yet / When I'll bite him by whom I'm bit."

SIR JOHN A. MACDONALD 1878

Until this great work is completed, our Dominion is little more than a "geographical expression." We have as much interest in B. Columbia as in Australia, and no more. The railway once finished, we become one great united country with a large interprovincial trade, and a common interest.

Prime Minister Sir John A. Macdonald wrote about the need for the Canadian Pacific Railway in order to prevent Canada remaining little more than a "geographical expression." The railway would link the East with the new Province of British Columbia. The remark comes from his letter to Sir Stafford Northcote, Chancellor of the Exchequer in Disraeli's government, May 1, 1878, included in *The Correspondence of Sir John Macdonald* (1921), edited by Sir Joseph Pope.

SIR JOHN A. MACDONALD 1878

I move: That the Speaker do not now leave the Chair, but that this House is of the opinion that the welfare of Canada requires the adoption of a National Policy, which, by a judicious readjustment of the Tariff, will benefit and foster the agricultural, the mining, the manufacturing and other interests of the Dominion; that such a policy will retain in Canada thousands of our fellow countrymen now obliged to expatriate themselves in search of the employment denied them at home, will restore prosperity to our struggling industries, now so sadly depressed, will prevent Canada from being made a sacrifice market, will encourage and develop an active inter-provincial trade, and moving (as it ought to do) in the direction of reciprocity of tariffs with our neighbours, so far as the varied interests of Canada may demand, will greatly tend to procure for this country, eventually, a reciprocity of trade.

Sir John A. Macdonald, as leader of the Opposition, moved this amendment to the government's budget speech, and thereby declared the principles of his protectionist National Policy in the House of Commons, March 7, 1878. It is intriguing to note that the speech neatly addresses issues that remain important and contentious for Canada, especially in the 1990s with the anti-protectionist provisions of the Free Trade Agreement with the United States and the North American Free Trade Agreement that includes Mexico.

GOLDWIN SMITH 1878

Canadian nationality being a lost cause, the ultimate union of Canada with the United States appears now to be morally certain; so that nothing is left for Canadian patriotism but to provide that it shall be a union indeed, and not an annexation.

Not all annexationists were Americans; some, like Goldwin Smith, were Canadians. A British-born lecturer and writer, Smith preferred the New World to the Old, lecturing at Cornell University in New York State and then settling in Toronto, where from The Grange he lost no occasion to advance the cause of continentalism. The passage comes from his political study, *The Political Destiny of Canada* (1878).

MARK TWAIN 1881

This is the first time I was ever in a city where you couldn't throw a brick without breaking a church window.

The American humorist Mark Twain addressed a large group of well-wishers at a banquet held in his honour at the Windsor Hotel, Montreal, Dec. 7, 1881. He had taken up temporary residence in

Montreal to establish British Empire copyright on his books, so he was in a good position to make many amusing observations about Montreal, the French language, the Catholic Church, and human nature.

OSCAR WILDE 1882

I am having charming audiences, you will be glad to hear; the Canadians are very appreciative people, but it is a great fight in this commercial age to plead the cause of Art. Still the principles which I represent are so broad, so grand, so noble that I have no fear for the future.

Oscar Wilde, wit and playwright, toured central and eastern Canada in 1882, speaking on esthetic matters in opera houses, concert halls, Mechanics' Institutes, etc. He appreciated the acclaim of Canadians but not their materialism and philistinism. The excerpt above comes from a letter he wrote from Halifax, Oct. 8, 1882, which was included in *The Letters of Oscar Wilde* (1962), edited by Rupert Hart-Davis. Wilde was no snob when it came to popular attractions and natural wonders. He visited Niagara Falls in Feb. 1882 and marvelled at the cataract. He duly noted that the Falls were being promoted, then as now, as the Honeymoon Capital of the World, according to Kevin O'Brien in *Oscar Wilde in Canada* (1982). Wilde memorably quipped, "Niagara Falls must be the second major disappointment of American married life."

MARQUIS OF LORNE 1882

In token of the love which thou hast shown
For this wide land of freedom, I have named
A province vast, and for its beauty famed,
By thy dear name to be hereafter known.
      Alberta shall it be!

These are the first five lines of the fourteen-line *verse d'occasion* composed by Governor General Lord Lorne on the subject of why he chose the name Alberta for the former District of Assiniboia in 1882. Lorne named "a province vast" after his wife, Louise Caroline Alberta, fourth daughter of Queen Victoria. The full text is found in Lorne's *Yesterday and Today in Canada* (1910). Lord Lorne served as Governor General from 1878 to 1883. Although not renowned for his wit, now and then he made a light comment, such as this one quoted by W. Stewart MacNutt in *Days of Lorne* (1955): "It is no easy thing to be Governor General of Canada. You must have the patience of a saint, the smile of a cherub, the generosity of an Indian prince, and the back of a camel."

SIR CHARLES G.D. ROBERTS 1882

O Child of Nations, giant limbed,
    Who stand'st among the nations now
Unheeded, unadorned, unrhymed,
    With unanointed brow,—

How long the ignoble sloth, how long
    The trust in greatness not thine own?
Surely the lion's brood is strong
    To front the world alone!

Sir Charles G.D. Roberts was a member of the generation of writers and artists who found inspiration in the creation of the Dominion of Canada in 1867. The group is loosely called the Poets of Confederation. In poems such as "Canada" (1882) and "An Ode for the Canadian Confederacy" (1882), both included in the *Selected Poems* (1939), Roberts urged his fellow Canadians to respond to the challenge of nation building with national thoughts and patriotic feelings. His "Ode" begins: "Awake, my country, the hour is great with change!" The new national mood found political expression in the Canada First movement.

UNKNOWN 1882

The climate of Manitoba consists of seven months of Arctic weather and five months of cold weather.

This description of Manitoba's weather sounds like a poor joke, but it was offered as the unvarnished truth to the readers of *Settler's Guide to the North-West* (1882), issued in New York by the Northern Pacific Railway Company.

EUGÈNE TACHÉ 1883

Je me souviens.

The motto of the Province of Quebec is "Je me souviens." The three words mean "I remember." Being recalled are the glories of the Ancien Régime—the language, laws, and religion of Quebec before the Conquest of 1759. What is interesting is the origin of the motto. It was selected to be inscribed beneath the coat of arms of the National Assembly in Quebec City, Feb. 9, 1883. The architect Eugène Taché took the words from a three-line poem, which runs like this: "Je me souviens / Que né sous le lys, / Je crois sous la rose." The poem is of unknown origin; the words mean: "I remember / That while under the fleur de lys [of France], / I grow under the rose [of England]." The lines implied co-existence; but in the motto the words suggest separate existence. In 1978, "Je me souviens" replaced "La Belle Province" as the inscription on Quebec's automobile licence plates.

TIMOTHY EATON 1884

Goods Satisfactory or Money Refunded.

This famous guarantee comes from Eaton's Catalogue and was once a byword in households across the country. The T. Eaton Co. was founded by Timothy Eaton in Toronto in 1869. The company's mail-order catalogue, found in most Canadian households, was issued annually from 1884 to 1976. The terms of sale were established early on, but the wording that appears above was not used in print in the catalogue until 1913. C.L. Burton of The Robert Simpson Co. Ltd., Eaton's principal competitor, exceeded Eaton's promise in 1928 by ensuring not just goods but also a psychological state: "Satisfaction Guaranteed."

Unidentified Well-Wisher 1884

You'll never die, John A.!

An unidentified well-wisher delivered this cry at a gathering in Toronto to celebrate Prime Minister Sir John A. Macdonald's forty years in Parliament, Dec. 17, 1884. He had a tendency to procrastinate in political matters, so he was dubbed "Old Tomorrow" by the editors of the English comic weekly *Punch,* who published the following verse as his 1891 obituary notice: "Canada's 'Old Tomorrow' lives today / In unforgetting hearts, and nothing fears / The long tomorrow of the coming years."

George Stephen 1884

Stand fast, Craigellachie!

These words, as no other words, symbolize the determination of the great railroad builders of Canada. A cablegram carried these words from George Stephen, President of the Canadian Pacific Railway, who was in London to raise last-minute capital, to his cousin, Donald Smith, Lord Strathcona, in Montreal, Nov. 1884. They signalled that Smith was not to lose faith and that the needed capital would be raised in the nick of time. It was, and the railway went through. Lord Strathcona had the honour of driving in the "last spike" at Craigellachie, Eagle Pass, B.C. A plaque marks the spot with this inscription: "Here on November 7, 1885, a plain iron spike welded

East to West." Craigellachie is the name of a rocky prominence in Northern Scotland; in Gaelic, the word means "the rock of alarm."

SIR WILLIAM CORNELIUS VAN HORNE 1885

All I can say is that the work has been done well in every way.

Asked to speak at the "last spike" ceremony, Craigellachie, Eagle Pass, B.C., Nov. 7, 1885, Sir William Cornelius Van Horne, the engineer who oversaw the construction of the Canadian Pacific Railway, made this impromptu remark. Immodest in public manner and achievement, he was personally a modest man. It was Pierre Berton who referred to the construction of the CPR as the realization of "the national dream" in his two-volume history *The National Dream: 1871-1881* (1970) and *The Last Spike: 1881-1885* (1971). It was the playwright Bernard Slade who added, "There has to be something wrong with a country whose National Dream is a railroad."

LOUIS RIEL 1885

I say humbly, through the grace of God I believe I am the prophet of the New World.

Louis Riel, the Métis leader, spoke with messianic fervour when he addressed the jury, Regina, July 31, 1885; *The Queen vs. Louis Riel, Accused and Convicted of the Crime of High Treason* (1886).

SIR WILFRID LAURIER 1885

Had I been born on the banks of the Saskatchewan, I would myself have shouldered a musket to fight against the neglect of governments and the shameless greed of speculators.

The Sunday following the hanging of Louis Riel for treason, Sir Wilfrid Laurier, the future Prime Minister, thus addressed a demonstration in the Champ de Mars, Montreal, Nov. 22, 1885; quoted by O.D. Skelton in *Life and Letters of Sir Wilfrid Laurier* (1921).

GOLDWIN SMITH 1888

Rich by nature, poor by policy.

This comment on the social and economic condition of the Dominion of Canada was made by the essayist Goldwin Smith in *Handbook of Commercial Union* (1888). In *Canada and the Canadian Question* (1891), he wrote, "'Rich by nature, poor by policy,' might be written over Canada's door. Rich she would be if she were allowed to embrace her destiny and be part of her own continent; poor, comparatively at least, she is in striving to remain a part of Europe."

WILLIAM WILFRED CAMPBELL 1889

Along the line of smoky hills
    The crimson forest stands,
And all the day the blue-jay calls
    Throughout the autumn lands.

This is the first verse of the poem "Indian Summer" written by the poet William Wilfred Campbell and published in *Lake Lyrics and Other Poems* (1889). It used to appear in textbooks and was memorized by generations of high-school students.

CROWFOOT 1890

A little while and I will be gone from among you, whither I cannot tell. From nowhere we came, into nowhere we go. What is life? It is a flash of a firefly in the night. It is a breath of a buffalo in the winter time. It is as the little shadow that runs across the grass and loses itself in the sunset.

These are said to be the last words of Crowfoot, the Blackfoot chief, who uttered them as he lay dying in his teepee which overlooked the Bow River, April 25, 1890. The poetic words were credited to Crowfoot by the historian John Peter Turner in *The North-West Mounted Police: 1873-1893* (1950). But as Turner cited no source, Hugh Dempsey ignored the speech in his biography of Crowfoot. Historian Robert S. Carlisle, in "Crowfoot's Dying Speech" in *Alberta History*, Summer 1990, established a prior source: *King Solomon's Mines* (1885), a once-popular novel written by Sir Henry Rider Haggard. In the novel, the African chieftain Umbopa speaks these words: "What is life? . . . It is the glow-worm that shines in the night-time and is black in the morning; it is the white breath of the oxen in winter, it is the little shadow that runs across the grass and loses itself in sunset." Did Turner Canadianize the African references and ascribe the fictitious Umbopa's words to the real-life Crowfoot? Certainly, Haggard was one of the most popular novelists of the time. Ayesha Peak, west of Alberta's Bow Lake, was named after the immortal Ayesha in Haggard's lost-race novel *She* (1887).

ARCHIBALD LAMPMAN 1891

One May evening somebody lent me *Orion and Other Poems*, then recently published. Like most of the young fellows about me I had been under the depressing conviction that we were situated hopelessly on the outskirts of civilization, where no art and no literature could be, and that it was useless to expect that anything great could be done by any of our companions, still more useless to expect that we could do it ourselves. I sat up all night reading and rereading *Orion* in a state of the wildest excitement and when I went to bed I could not sleep. It seemed to me a wonderful thing that such a work could be done by a Canadian, by a young man, one of ourselves. It was like a voice from some new paradise of art, calling to us to be up and doing.

Archibald Lampman was a student at Trinity College in Toronto and not yet an outstanding poet when he chanced upon Sir Charles G.D. Roberts's first book, *Orion* (1880). Eleven years later, in a lecture Lampman delivered in Ottawa, Feb. 19, 1891 (published in the *University of Toronto Quarterly,* July 1944), he recalled the galvanizing effect the poems in it had on him when he first came across them.

JAMES GAY   1891

Hail our great Queen in her regalia;
One foot in Canada, the other in Australia.

This remarkable couplet, complete with unintentional humour, has been attributed to James Gay (1810-1891), the poetaster and resident of Guelph, Ont., who described himself as "Poet Laureate of Canada and Master of All Poets." William Arthur Deacon wrote about Gay in his serio-comic study, *The Four Jameses* (1927).

SIR JOHN A. MACDONALD   1891

As for myself, my course is clear. A British subject I was born—a British subject I will die.

Sir John A. Macdonald, Canada's first Prime Minister, was born a British subject in Scotland in 1815; he died a British subject in Canada in 1891. Macdonald made his appeal to the British connection in his final address in the House of Commons, Feb. 7, 1891. At that time, to be born in Britain or in Canada was to be born a British subject, and not a citizen; one was a subject of the Crown. It was not until the Canadian Citizenship Act in 1947 that

Canadians officially became citizens of Canada all the while retaining the status of British subjects. With the Citizenship Act of 1977, Canadian citizens ceased to be "British subjects," becoming "citizens of the Commonwealth."

SIR JOHN A. MACDONALD 1891

Canada is a hard country to govern.

This sentiment is attributed to Prime Minister Sir John A. Macdonald, who conducted his third and last campaign in 1891 and died in office three months later. Although it has yet to be located in Macdonald's letters or *obiter dicta,* the sentiment has been echoed by at least three of his successors in office. Sir Wilfrid Laurier noted in 1905, "This is a difficult country to govern." Lester B. Pearson informed an interviewer in 1965, "It has been said that Canada is the most difficult country in the world to govern. I am perhaps more aware of that than I used to be." Brian Mulroney agreed, telling an interviewer in 1986, "This is a difficult country to govern." As Richard Gwyn opined in *The 49th Paradox* (1985), "Lastly, while Canada is not in any way the 'difficult country to govern' it is often claimed to be, since it is inherently orderly, democratic, and affluent, it is an almost impossible country to lead."

SALTATHA 1892

To the man who is not a lover of Nature in all her moods the Barren Ground must always be a howling, desolate wilderness; but for my part, I can understand the feeling that prompted Saltatha's answer to the worthy priest, who was explaining to him the beauties of Heaven. "My father, you have spoken well; you have told me that Heaven is very beautiful; tell me now one thing more. Is it more beautiful than the country of the musk-ox in summer, when sometimes the mist blows over the lakes, and sometimes the water is blue, and the loons cry very often? That is beautiful; and if Heaven is still more beautiful, my heart will be glad, and I shall be content to rest there till I am very old."

The nature of beauty and how it relates to faith is the subject of this passage. Saltatha was a native of the Yellowknife tribe and served as the guide of the English traveller Warburton Pike, who wintered in the Barren Lands of the Northwest Territories in 1889-90 and wrote about the experience in *The Barren Ground of Northern Canada* (1892).

BLISS CARMAN 1893

Was it a year or lives ago
We took the grasses in our hands,
And caught the summer flying low
Over the waving meadow lands,
And held it there between our hands?

These moving lines appear in the poem "Low Tide on Grand Pré" (1893), written by Bliss Carman about his native New Brunswick and collected in *Bliss Carman's Poems* (1929).

L.M. MONTGOMERY 1895

Elderly couple apply to orphan asylum for a boy. By mistake a girl is sent them.

The young teacher inscribed this entry in "a faded notebook" in 1895. The teacher was L.M. Montgomery. The entry blossomed into the children's classic, *Anne of Green Gables* (1908).

SIR GEORGE E. FOSTER 1896

Splendid isolation.

The phrase "splendid isolation" to refer to standing all alone with one's principles against an unprincipled horde was used by Sir

George E. Foster, Laurier's Minister of Finance, in the House of Commons, Jan. 16, 1896: "But he [the patriot] would read the signs of the times not aright in these somewhat troublesome days, when the great mother Empire stands splendidly isolated in Europe, with interest stretching over the wide world." Thereafter, the phrase "splendid isolation" received wide use.

SIR CLIFFORD SIFTON 1896

> I think a stalwart peasant in a sheep-skin coat, born on the soil, whose forefathers have been farmers for ten generations, with a stout wife and a half-dozen children, is good quality.

Sir Clifford Sifton, Minister of the Interior from 1896 to 1905, encouraged the immigration to western Canada of Ukrainian and Doukhobor farmers and labourers. Consequently, this period of the development of the West is associated with the image of the "stalwart peasant in a sheep-skin coat," who would settle and work "The Last Best West." The "peasant" phrase itself appeared only years later in Sifton's article "The Immigrants Canada Wants," *Maclean's*, April 1, 1922.

G.W. CARMACK 1896

> TO WHOM IT MAY CONCERN
> I do, this day, locate and claim, by right of discovery, five hundred feet, running up stream from this notice. Located this 17th day of August, 1896.
> G.W. Carmack.

Prospector G.W. Carmack struck gold in the Yukon and staked his claim on Aug. 17, 1896. The Klondike Gold Rush was the result. According to Pierre Berton, writing in *Klondike* (1958), "Carmack blazed a small spruce tree with his hand axe, and on the upstream side wrote with a pencil" the words that appear above.

JOSEPH-ISRAËL TARTE 1896

Elections are not won by prayers alone.

This sardonic observation dates from the victory of the Liberal Party in the election of 1896. It was made by one of that victory's begetters and beneficiaries, Joseph-Israël Tarte, controversial Minister of Public Works, Quebec "bagman," master of patronage, etc. In the 1940s, Quebec Premier Maurice Duplessis always spoke about "good patronage." Historian Michel Brunet was philosophical about political corruption. "There's always corruption," he explained. "It's bad when it's more than fifteen percent."

RUDYARD KIPLING 1897

A Nation spoke to a Nation,
 A Throne sent word to a Throne:
"Daughter am I in my mother's house,
 But mistress in my own.
The gates are mine to open,
 As the gates are mine to close.
And I abide by my Mother's House,"
 Said our Lady of the Snows.

The independent yet subordinate relation of the Dominion of Canada to Great Britain, the "mother country," was given dramatic expression by Rudyard Kipling, an Imperialist, in the final stanza of the verse "Our Lady of the Snows." The verse was subtitled "Canadian Preferential Tariff, 1897" upon its initial publication in the London *Times*, April 27, 1897. The tariff was denounced as an impediment to tourism and immigration. The third and fourth lines were widely quoted as an expression of filial gratitude until the outbreak of World War I.

ANONYMOUS 1898

There's a dusky, husky maiden in the Arctic,
   And she waits for me but it is not in vain,
For some day I'll put my mukluks on and ask her
   If she'll wed me when the ice worms nest again.

"When the Ice Worms Nest Again" is a traditional folk song of the North. No one is sure where or when it originated. Robert W. Service, the Bard of the Yukon, always denied that he wrote it, publishing his own version in *Twenty Bath-Tub Ballads* (1938). The original folk song may be associated with the Klondike Gold Rush of 1898. The traditional version appears in G.E. Gillham's *Raw North* (1947). According to *The Canadian Encyclopedia* there is a species of worm that nests in the melting ice of glaciers.

MRS. CLEMENTINA FESSENDEN 1898

The twenty-fourth of May
   Is the Queen's Birthday;
If you don't give us a holiday,
   We'll all run away.

This traditional ball-bouncing rhyme has been known to generations of Canadian children. It was quoted in this form by Sara Jeannette Duncan in her novel *The Imperialist* (1904), which is based on life at the time in Brantford, Ont. The idea of setting aside a day each year to celebrate the British Empire and then of selecting Queen Victoria's birthday, May 24, occurred to Mrs. Clementina Fessenden, a schoolteacher in Hamilton, Ont. Her notion was taken up by George W. Ross, Ontario Minister of Education, and within a few years "the Queen's Birthday" was the focus of Imperial celebrations throughout the British Empire. The rhyme has outlasted the British Empire, and so has the observation of the statutory holiday that is still observed on the Monday closest to the 24th of May.

SIR WILLIAM MULOCK 1898

WE HOLD A VASTER EMPIRE THAN HAS BEEN.

These imperial-sounding words appeared on Canada's first commemorative postage stamp, which was issued in 1898 to honour the "Imperial penny postage." The two-cent stamp was the first Canadian stamp to be printed in multiple colours, red and black; it bore the above legend in English only. The use of the words was authorized by Sir William Mulock, Laurier's Postmaster General, who took the eight imposing and impressive words from the poem "Song of Empire" (which includes the lines "We hold a vaster Empire than has been! / Nigh half the race of man is subject to our Queen!"), composed by the English versifier Sir Lewis Morris to celebrate Queen Victoria's Jubilee, June 20, 1887. It was never certain who the "we" identified.

EMILE BERLINER 1900

His Master's Voice.

This world-famous slogan of RCA Victor Records was first used in Montreal in 1900 by the German-American inventor Emile Berliner. He employed it along with the equally famous painting of the dog hearing "his master's voice" emerge from the horn of an old-fashioned phonograph. The painting was done by the French artist François Barraud of his dog Nipper, as noted by Edward B. Moogk in *Roll Back the Years: A History of Canadian Recorded Sound and Its Legacy* (1975).

MARGARET MURRAY 1900

One Flag, One Throne, One Empire.

This is the motto of the IODE (Imperial Order Daughters of the Empire), a women's patriotic and philanthropic organization. Dr. Margaret Murray formed the first provincial chapter in Fredericton, N.B., Feb. 13, 1900. Some ninety years later the IODE boasts ten thousand members in chapters from coast to coast.

RICHARD E.W. TURNER 1900

Never let it be said the Canadians had let their guns be taken!

This was the cry of Lieutenant Richard E.W. Turner of the Royal Canadian Dragoons, who was awarded the Victoria Cross for valour shown at Leliefontein, Union of South Africa, Nov. 7, 1900, as quoted by John Swettenham in *Valiant Men* (1973).

JOSHUA SLOCUM 1900

I sprang from the oars to my feet, and lifted the anchor above my head, threw it clear just as she was turning over. I grasped her gunwale and held on as she turned bottom up, for I suddenly remembered that I could not swim.

Joshua Slocum, the master mariner from Nova Scotia, was the first person to sail solo around the world. It took from April 1895 to July 1898. In his memoir *Sailing Alone around the World* (1900) he described the feat—including the fact that he could not swim.

HENRY FULLER DAVIS 1900

H.F. Davis,
Born Vermont, 1820,

Died, Slave Lake, 1893.
Pathfinder, Pioneer, Miner, Trader.
"He was everyman's friend
and never locked his cabin door."

This is one of the famous pioneer epitaphs. The gravestone in question is said to overlook the town of Peace River, Alta. The inscription is a testimonial to the friendliness of the Old Northwest. The prospector Henry Fuller Davis was nicknamed "Twelve-Foot" for the fact that he once staked a claim so narrow that it was only twelve feet wide. The historian Hugh Dempsey has noted that Davis died in 1900, not 1893.

REGINALD A. FESSENDEN   1900

One, two, three, four. Is it snowing where you are, Mr. Thiessen? If so telegraph back and let me know.

These are the first words spoken on the first radio broadcast of the human voice, Dec.23, 1900. They were uttered by the Canadian-born inventor Reginald A. Fessenden at his laboratory on Cobb Island, Potomac River, near Washington, D.C., over a primitive radio device, and were heard by his assistant Thiessen in Arlington, Virginia, eighty kilometres away, according to Sandy Stewart in *A Pictorial History of Radio in Canada* (1975).

J. CASTELL HOPKINS   1901

Canada only needs to be known in order to be great.

This aphorism ought to be better known. It served as the maxim of the Toronto-based editor J. Castell Hopkins, who included it in the preface to his study *The Story of the Dominion* (1901).

RICHARD MAURICE BUCKE 1901

Cosmic Consciousness, then, is a higher form of consciousness than that possessed by the ordinary man.

The term *Cosmic Consciousness* refers to an ecstatic or mystical state of awareness and is identified with the psychiatrist Richard Maurice Bucke, who served as superintendent of the mental hospital in London, Ont. Bucke first used the words in the title of the paper he read before the American Medico-Psychological Association, Philadelphia, May 18, 1894. He went on to distinguish among levels of consciousness in his opus *Cosmic Consciousness: A Study in the Evolution of the Human Mind* (1901). Bucke's friendship with the American poet Walt Whitman is the subject of the feature film *Beautiful Dreamers* (1990), written and directed by John Kent Harrison, starring Colm Feore as the young physician and Rip Torn as the poet.

JULES-PAUL TARDIVEL 1902

It is not necessary that we possess industry and money. We will no longer be French Canadians but Americans almost like the others. Our mission is to possess the earth and spread ideas. To cling to the soil, to raise large families, to maintain the hearths of intellectual and spiritual life, that must be our role in America.

This declaration of faith in the national vocation of the French-Canadian people was made in a speech in 1902 delivered by Jules-Paul Tardivel, novelist and nationalist. Although born in Kentucky, Tardivel hitched his wagon to three Quebec causes: Catholicism, nationalism, and separatism.

LOUIS-ADOLPHE PÂQUET 1902

We are not only a civilized race, we are the pioneers of civilization; we are not only a religious people, we are the messengers of the religious idea; we are not only submissive sons of the Church, we are, we ought to be, numbered among its zealots, its defenders, and its apostles. Our mission is less to manipulate capital than to change ideas; it consists less in lighting the fires of factories than in maintaining and radiating afar the hearthlight of religion and thought.

Louis-Adolphe Pâquet, priest and theologian, defined for the French-Canadian people a national vocation, in his inspirational address in Quebec City, St-Jean-Baptiste Day, 1902.

SIR ERNEST RUTHERFORD 1902

I would like to take this opportunity to emphasize that the credit for the first definite proof of atomic transformation belongs to McGill University. It was in the Macdonald Building in the years 1902-1904 that Soddy and I accumulated the experimental evidence that the radioactive elements were undergoing spontaneous transformations.

Sir Ernest Rutherford conducted ground-breaking research at McGill University in Montreal from 1902 to 1904 on the nature of radioactivity for which he was awarded the Nobel Prize, as was his assistant Frederick Soddy. Rutherford's tribute came from a letter written in 1932 quoted by Edgar Andrew Collard in *Montreal: The Days that Are No More* (1976).

PAULINE JOHNSON 1903

The Dutch may have their Holland, the Spaniard have his Spain,
The Yankee to the south of us must south of us remain;
For not a man dare lift a hand against the men who brag
That they were born in Canada beneath the British flag.

These rousing lines come from the final stanza of Pauline Johnson's poem "Canadian Born" (1903), included in *Flint and Feather* (1912).

SIR WILFRID LAURIER 1904

The twentieth century belongs to Canada.

Here is the most celebrated of all Canadian aphorisms. It is identified with Prime Minister Sir Wilfrid Laurier, who made the affirmative remark during the course of an address to the Canadian Club of Ottawa, Jan. 18, 1904. According to the printed text of the address, Laurier used these words: "The nineteenth century was the century of the United States. I think we can claim that it is Canada that shall fill the twentieth century." Immediately thereafter, the words took the neat form of this aphorism: "The twentieth century belongs to Canada." Since that time, the remark has been seen to be a touchstone of national aspiration measured against national achievement. In the 1900s it was regarded as prophecy; in the 1990s, as irony.

The aphorism has occasioned much commentary. Over two dozen variations on the words and theme appear in *Colombo's Canadian Quotations* (1974), four more in *Colombo's New Canadian Quotations* (1987), and four additional ones in *The Dictionary of Canadian Quotations* (1991). Here are some highlights: "I remember a Toronto in which the admirably true phrase . . . was accepted as the general watchword; only nobody had begun to realize what a rotten century the twentieth was going to be." (B.K. Sandwell, 1924) / "The twentieth century, as Laurier prophesied, may yet be ours. (Whatever that means.)" (A.M. Klein, 1946) / "The twentieth century *did* belong to Canada." (Brian Moore, 1963) / "The twentieth century really belongs to those who will build it. The future can be promised to no one." (Pierre Elliott Trudeau, 1968) / "The twenty-first century belongs to Japan." (Herman Kahn, 1970) / "Twentieth-Century still belongs to Fox (whoever he is). (Don Harron, 1972) / "The twentieth century belongs to the Moon." (Earle Birney, 1973) / "The nineteenth century was an age of hardware, the twentieth century is that of software—that is, of information." (Marshall McLuhan, 1977) / "The real question is whether Canada will belong to the twenty-first century." (Peter C. Newman, 1988) / "As was the case with reciprocity, Laurier was wrong. Let's assure that it will be the twenty-first century that belongs to Canada." (Mel Hurtig, 1990)

JOHN E. KENNEDY 1904

Advertising is salesmanship in print.

This formulation is one of the most famous definitions in the world of advertising and the principal contribution to the "reason why" school of advertising. It was devised by John E. Kennedy, a one-time RCMP officer who found fame and fortune on Madison Avenue. In 1904, he sent the Chicago advertising executive Albert D. Lasker the following note: "I am in the saloon downstairs, and I can tell you what advertising is. I know what you don't know. It will mean much to me to have you know what it is and it will mean much to you. If you wish to know what advertising is, send the word 'Yes' down by messenger." "Word went down to Kennedy, who then appeared in Lasker's office. After an hour they went down to the saloon together, and emerged at midnight." John Gunther added in *Taken at the Flood: The Story of Albert D. Lasker* (1960), "From that time on, Lasker knew what advertising was. First Kennedy asked him what his own ideas were, and Lasker mentioned news. Kennedy said, 'No. News is a technique of presentation, but advertising is a very different thing. I can give it to you in three words.' Lasker said, 'I am hungry. What are those three words?' Kennedy said, 'Salesmanship in print.'" Lasker hired Kennedy on the spot and together they promoted the "reason why" concept.

HARRY WILLIAMS 1905

In the shade of the old apple tree,
Where the love in your eyes I could see,
    When the voice that I heard,

Like the song of a bird,
Seem'd to whisper sweet music to me.

The popular song "In the Shade of the Old Apple Tree" (1905) has given pleasure to millions. A tree on Glen Edith Drive in Toronto inspired Harry Williams to write the lyrics. The melody was contributed by the American composer Egbert Van Alstyne.

SIR WILLIAM OSLER 1905

One of the first duties of the physician is to educate the masses not to take medicine.

This is one of the celebrated maxims of Ontario-born Sir William Osler, famous physician, professor of medicine, and influential diagnostician, who was appointed to the Regius Chair of Medicine at Oxford in 1905. It comes from *Sir William Osler: Aphorisms from His Bedside Teachings and Writings* (1950), edited by W.B. Bean.

ROBERT W. SERVICE 1907

A bunch of the boys were whooping it up in the Malamute saloon;
The kid that handles the music-box was hitting a rag-time tune;
Back of the bar, in a solo game, sat Dangerous Dan McGrew,
And watching his luck was his light-o-love, the lady that's known as Lou.

*

There are strange things done in the midnight sun
    By the men who moil for gold;
The Arctic trails have their secret tales
    That would make your blood run cold;
The Northern Lights have seen queer sights,
    But the queerest they ever did see

> Was that night on the marge of Lake Lebarge
> I cremated Sam McGee.

These lines will be recognized as the opening verses of two of the most popular ballads of the twentieth century. "The Shooting of Dan McGrew" and "The Cremation of Sam McGee" were composed by Robert W. Service, the Scots-born bank clerk who came to be recognized as the Poet of the Yukon. They were published in his first collection, *Songs of a Sourdough* (1907). More than any other literary work, they convey the spirit of the Klondike Gold Rush of 1898.

HOWARD ANGUS KENNEDY 1907

> New Canadians.

The words "New Canadians" to identify recent immigrants came into favour around the turn of the century, and it was employed by journalist Howard Angus Kennedy in his sociological work *New Canada and the New Canadians* (1907). After World War II, the majority of immigrants were called Displaced Persons. Around 1967 the word "ethnics" began to be applied to immigrants and the words "ethnic groups" to minority groups. The buzz-word of the 1990s is "multicultural groups" and sometimes "multinational groups."

MRS. HUMPHRY WARD 1908

> So, in a swallow's flight from sea to sea, I saw the marvellous land wherein,
> perhaps, in a far, hidden future, lies the destiny of our race.

British sentiment and Imperial oratory influenced generations of Canadians. This expression of a hope and a wish and a prayer appeared in the novel titled *Canadian Born* (1908), written by the popular English author Mrs. Humphry Ward, who travelled across the Dominion at the expense of the Canadian Pacific Railway and wrote up her experiences. The passage was given some currency by British Prime Minister Stanley Baldwin, addressing the Canadian Club of Ottawa, Aug. 15, 1932. He quoted the words, noting, "That is a pregnant sentence. And one asks oneself, belonging to an old country, what preparation Canada is making for that day, what ideals she is keeping before herself; for by ideals alone a nation lives."

SIR ADAM BECK 1908

We must deliver power to such an extent that the poorest working man will have electric light in his home.

Sir Adam Beck, founder and first chairman from 1906 to 1925 of the Ontario Hydro-Electric Power Commission (now Ontario Hydro), made this commitment two years after assuming the chairmanship. He made good on his pledge, electrifying both urban and rural Ontario.

JOSEPH-ELZÉAR BERNIER 1909

I took possession of Baffin Island for Canada in the presence of several Eskimo, and after firing nineteen shots I instructed an Eskimo to fire the twentieth, telling him that he was now a Canadian.

The mariner Joseph-Elzéar Bernier claimed the Arctic archipelago for Canada on July 1, 1909. He did so in an imaginative little ceremony of his own devising, recalling the occasion in an address to the Empire Club of Canada in 1926.

LIONEL GROULX 1910

Our Master, the Past, that is to say, the past, master of the future.

"Our Master, the Past" (*Notre maître, le passé*) was the personal maxim of Lionel Groulx, priest and historian. It became the slogan of the Association de la Jeunesse, a religious-nationalist group that Groulx headed in the 1910s. Quebec Premier Joseph-Adélard Godbout in the 1930s played on Groulx's maxim when he declared "*Notre maître, l'avenir*" ("Our master, the future").

RUDYARD KIPLING 1910

Believe me, the very name is an asset, and as years go on will become more and more of an asset. It has no duplicate in the world; it makes men ask questions.

A group of businessmen led the movement to change the name of their town from Medicine Hat to Progress. The movement was derailed by other Albertans, who wrote to Rudyard Kipling, addressing him as the "Father Confessor of the Empire" and asking him to lead the retentionist cause. Kipling recalled his happy visit to Medicine Hat in 1892, and he rallied to the cause, writing a strong letter (including the sentences above) on Dec. 9, 1910. Kipling suggested that if the name had to be changed the only appropriate substitute would be "Judasville."

OLIVIA SMITH 1910

There is one thing you have forgotten in your deliberations and that is justice to women. I hope that at your future meetings you will give more attention to the cause of women. That is all I have to say.

Olivia Smith, a militant suffragette, rose from the Visitor's Gallery of the Ontario Legislature and made this statement just as the Lieutenant-Governor was about to prorogue the legislature, March 19, 1910. Smith made a quick exit and was never heard from again. A description of the incident appeared in *The Canadian Annual Review of Public Affairs, 1910* (1911), edited by J. Castell Hopkins.

DUKE OF CONNAUGHT 1911

Keep yer fork, Duke, the pie's acomin'.

The story is frequently told that Prince Philip, Duke of Edinburgh, dining in a rural area, was told by an over-friendly waitress who was removing the main-course plates, "Keep yer fork, Duke, the pie's acomin'." It never happened to the Duke of Edinburgh, but it apparently did happen to Governor General the Duke of Connaught at a Board of Trade dinner in a small community in the Peace River district of British Columbia between 1911 and 1916. In 1986, Peter Gzowski, host of CBC Radio's "Morningside," spent some time tracking down the amusing story.

JOE CAPILANO 1911

We may paddle many moons on the sea, but our canoes will never enter the channel that leads to the yesterdays of the Indian people.

This is the lament of the Squamish chief Joe Capilano, who recounted his people's tales and traditions to the poet Pauline Johnson, who published them in her book *Legends of Vancouver* (1911).

SIR GEORGE E. FOSTER 1911

No Truck Nor Trade with the Yankees!

These words served as the slogan of the Conservative Party for the election of 1911, which was fought over the issue of reciprocity, a form of free trade. The slogan was effective, for the electorate rejected the free-trade agreement reached by Prime Minister Sir Wilfrid Laurier and U.S. President William Howard Taft. The Liberals were replaced by the Conservatives, who favoured Imperial preference in trade and were led by Sir Robert Borden, whose

Minister of Trade and Commerce, Sir George E. Foster, had devised the winning slogan.

STEPHEN LEACOCK 1911

> Lord Ronald said nothing; he flung himself from the room, flung himself upon his horse and rode madly off in all directions.

This sentence is vintage Leacock, and it comes from his sketch "Gertrude the Governess: or, Simple Seventeen," which appeared in his self-published collection of parodies called *Nonsense Novels* (1911). It is said that "riding madly off in all directions" entered the language when former U.S. President Theodore Roosevelt made use of it in a political address, giving credit to Leacock for these words which so dramatically convey the idea of a state of confusion. Leacock's sentence is one of the few internationally quoted expressions of Canadian origin.

JOE HILL 1912

> Where the Fraser River flows, each fellow worker knows,
> They have bullied and oppressed us, but still our Union grows.
> And we're going to find a way, boys, for shorter hours and better pay, boys!
> And we're going to win the day, boys; where the River Fraser flows.

Mention the name Joe Hill and a unionist's eyes will grow misty or bright. Hill, the martyred labour hero and singer-songwriter, composed "Where the Fraser River Flows" to the tune of "Where the River Shannon Flows" to support the striking construction workers laying track for the Canadian Northern Railroad in British Columbia. The strike broke out on March 27, 1912; Hill wrote the song at Yale, B.C., shortly thereafter. The strikers, supported by the Wobblies, won the battle, according to Gibbs M. Smith in *Labour Martyr* (1969).

HENRI BOURASSA 1912

A free Anglo-French Confederacy, in the northern part of America, united by bonds of amity and kinship with Great Britain and France, of two great nations from which it had derived its races, its civilization and its thoughts, and offering to the trade and the intellectuality of the world a friendly rival and counterpoise to the expanding civilization of the United States, would become one of the greatest contributions to humanity.

This mission for an inwardly united and outward-looking Canada was defined by Henri Bourassa, the French-Canadian nationalist and publisher in his address titled "Imperialism and Nationalism" delivered before the Canadian Club of Ottawa, Dec. 18, 1912. Bourassa's vision was quite close to that of Prime Minister Lester B. Pearson and that of the economic nationalists of the 1960s.

STEPHEN LEACOCK 1912

Mariposa is not a real town. On the contrary, it is about seventy or eighty of them. You may find them all the way from Lake Superior to the sea, with the same square streets and the same maple trees and the same churches and hotels, everywhere the sunshine of the land of hope.

Stephen Leacock was frequently accused of modelling his fictional Mariposa on the Ontario town of Orillia, where he spent his summers in a residence that is now a museum dedicated to his life and work. But Mariposa was the quintessential small Ontario town of the time, populated with lovable eccentrics who were faced with "happy problems." Leacock's amusing defence against the charge appears as the preface to his classic work, *Sunshine Sketches of a Little Town* (1912).

BOB EDWARDS 1913

One can always tell when one is getting old and serious by the way that holidays seem to interfere with one's work.

Only people who are over thirty or self-employed will fully appreciate Bob Edwards's insight into the connection between work and play. Edwards was a prairie newspaperman who published the tabloid called *Eye Opener*. This comment dates from the issue of Dec. 20, 1913.

T.E. HULME 1914

Speaking of personal matters, the first time I ever felt the necessity or inevitableness of verse was in the desire to reproduce the peculiar quality of feeling which is induced by the flat spaces and wide horizons of the virgin prairie of western Canada.

The literary movement known as Imagism was established in England by the British philosopher T.E. Hulme. He had been much influenced by the sight of the prairies, which he encountered as an agricultural labourer in western Canada in 1906. Hulme's acknowledgement appeared in "Lectures on Modern Poetry" (1914), quoted by Michael Roberts in *T.E. Hulme* (1938).

SIR ARTHUR CONAN DOYLE 1914

Great deeds are better than great sonnets, and Canada's call to her sons is a stirring one to action; for the poetry of action exists just as does the poetry of words and the great deed that is accomplished is more glorious than the great sonnet.

These lines come from a stirring address delivered by Sir Arthur Conan Doyle, British author, creator of Sherlock Holmes, who travelled widely through the British Empire and spoke with enthusiasm on Imperial themes and subjects. This sentence comes from his address titled "The Future of Canadian Literature," delivered before the Canadian Club of Montreal, June 4, 1914. Doyle meant to console Canadians on the relative poverty of national literary expression, extolling the enduring merit of "great deeds" in lieu of "great sonnets" (especially in wartime). World War I brought forth both great deeds and one great sonnet (John McCrae's "In Flanders Fields").

SIR WILFRID LAURIER 1914

It would be seen by the world that Canada, a daughter of Old England, intends to stand by her in this great conflict. When the call comes our answer goes at once, and it goes in the classical language of the British answer to the call of duty: "Ready, aye, ready."

"Ready, aye, ready," the traditional British response to the call of arms as well as the motto of the Marlboroughs, has echoed throughout English Canada from the outbreak of the Crimean War to the Suez Crisis. It was voiced by Sir Wilfrid Laurier, Leader of the Opposition, during the special war session of the House of Commons, Aug. 19, 1914. Arthur Meighen, when Leader of the Opposition, used the words in a Toronto speech, Sept. 22, 1922, at the time of the Chanak Affair. The belief that Canada would follow Britain's lead received a deadly blow when Canada issued its own declaration of a state of war in 1939.

HARRY WILLIAMS 1914

It's a long way to Tipperary, it's a long way to go;
It's a long way to Tipperary, to the sweetest girl I know!
Good-bye, Piccadilly, farewell, Leicester Square,
It's a long, long way to Tipperary, but my heart's right there!

The words to this popular marching song were written by the Canadian lyricist Harry Williams in 1908 and set to music composed by the British musician Jack Judge. "It's a Long Way to Tipperary" came into its own when it was adopted by the British army as its marching song in the 1914-18 war. Tipperary is a town in Ireland.

WILLIAM WILFRED CAMPBELL   1914

Vaster Britain.

Imperialists such as the poet William Wilfred Campbell, who aspired to be the first poet laureate of the British Empire (an office that was never created), thought of Canada in terms of a "vaster Britain." The concept was expressed in the verse "Vaster Britain" in *Sagas of Vaster Britain: Poems of the Race, the Empire, and the Divinity of Man* (1914). The book was published the year of the outbreak of World War I; the carnage put an end to such conceptions.

SIR SAM HUGHES   1914

I'll be damned if I will.

Lord Kitchener, British Secretary of State for War, ordered Sir Sam Hughes, Minister of Militia and Defence, to divide the First Canadian Division among British formations. "You have your orders, carry them out," ordered Kitchener. "I'll be damned if I will," replied Hughes, marching out of the meeting that took place on Aug. 26, 1914. The First Canadian Division was never broken up.

SIR ROBERT BORDEN   1914

Continuous consultation leading to concerted action.

This mouthful of words is associated with Sir Robert Borden, who served as Prime Minister from 1911 to 1920. The words characterized his attitude to the divisive issue of conscription that arose during World War I.

JOHN MCCRAE 1915

In Flanders fields the poppies blow
Between the crosses, row on row,
    That mark our place; and in the sky
    The larks, still bravely singing, fly
Scarce heard amid the guns below.

We are the Dead. Short days ago
We lived, felt dawn, saw sunset glow.
    Loved, and were loved, and now we lie
    In Flanders fields.

Take up our quarrel with the foe:
To you from failing hands we throw
    The torch; be yours to hold it high.
    If ye break faith with us who die
We shall not sleep, though poppies grow
    In Flanders fields.

"In Flanders Fields" is probably the most famous poem occasioned by the Great War. It was written on May 3, 1915, during the Second Battle of Ypres, Belgium, by Major John McCrae, First Brigade surgeon in the Canadian Field Artillery. It appeared anonymously in *Punch*, Dec. 8, 1915. McCrae died in France on Jan. 28, 1918, and is buried at the Wimereux Cemetery, Boulogne, France. Since that year, "In Flanders Fields" has been recited as part of the official Armistice Day program on Nov. 11 and has become an integral part of all Remembrance Day ceremonies in Canada. The text used here appears in *In Flanders Fields and Other Poems* (1919), published posthumously, edited by Sir Andrew Macphail.

GITZ RICE 1915

Oh, Mademoiselle from Armentières,
    Parlez-vous,

Oh, Mademoiselle from Armentières,
   Parlez-vous,
She hasn't been kissed in forty years,
   Hinky-dinky, par-lee-voo.

"Mademoiselle from Armentières" is one of the most widely performed songs associated with the Great War. It was composed by
Gitz Rice, a Nova Scotia-born Sergeant in the Canadian Army who
wrote it in 1915 in the small French town of Armentières, near Lille.
He composed the words while he sat in a café, watching a pretty
barmaid. He sang the composition a few days later before the Fifth
Battery, Montreal, then stationed in France. It has been endlessly
parodied.

NELLIE L. MCCLUNG 1915

"No woman, idiot, lunatic, or criminal shall vote."

In her lively speeches, the pioneer writer and suffragette leader Nellie
L. McClung used to cite this passage from the Election Act of the
Dominion of Canada, as she mentions in her memoirs *In Times Like
These* (1915). The problem is that the phrase does not appear in the
Revised Statutes of Canada, 1906, which remained unrevised until
1927.

CARL GUSTAV JUNG 1916

There are indeed people who lack a developed persona—"Canadians
who know not Europe's sham politeness"—blundering from one
social solecism to the next, perfectly harmless and innocent, soulful
bores or appealing children, or, if they are women, spectral
Cassandras dreaded for their tactlessness, eternally misunderstood,
never knowing what they are about, always taking forgiveness for
granted, blind to the world, hopeless dreamers. From them we can

see how a neglected persona works, and what one must do to remedy the evil.

An unexpected but explicit reference to the character or the personality of Canadians occurs in the midst of a description of personality disorders in an essay written by the Swiss psychoanalyst Carl Gustav Jung. It appears in "The Relations between the Ego and the Unconscious" (1916), *Two Essays on Analytic Psychology* (1966), translated from the German by R.F.C. Hull. The line about Canadians appears in quotation marks because Jung was quoting the opening line of a poem which at the time was known to every educated European. The poem was a narrative work titled "The Wild One." It was written by the German poet Johann Gottfried Seume who, impressed by the Hessians, served as a British soldier in British North America in the 1780s. "Der Wilde" in *Sämmutliche Werke* (1839) records the thoughtless ingratitude of a European whose life is saved by one of the native people.

LOUIS HÉMON 1916

> Strangers have surrounded us whom it is our pleasure to call foreigners; they have taken into their hands most of the rule, they have gathered to themselves much of the wealth; but in this land of Quebec nothing has changed. Nor shall anything change, for we are the pledge of it ... These people are a race which knows not how to perish. . . . In this land of Quebec naught shall die and naught change. . . .

This is the profound peroration of the novel *Maria Chapdelaine* (1916), written by the French journalist and traveller Louis Hémon about life in the farming communities of the Lac Saint-Jean region of Quebec. It was translated in 1921 by W.H. Blake and has thrice been filmed. Young Maria is offered a choice between the virtues of farm life and the temptations of city life in Boston. Hémon was right about mood, less right about mores. Times change, though some things in Quebec may not. As the sociologist Jean-Charles Falardeau noted in 1953, "The daughter of Maria Chapdelaine who was an ammunition-factory worker at Valcartier during the war now lives with her own family of five children in the Rosemount ward of Montreal. Maria's married brothers are employees of the Aluminum Company at Arvida and Shipsaw, after having been workers at the Jonquière pulp plant."

J.S. WOODSWORTH 1917

> Last century made the world a neighbourhood; this century must make it a brotherhood.

This well-known aphorism, dated Feb. 1917 and quoted by Margaret Fairley in *Spirit of Canadian Democracy* (1945), was coined by J.S. Woodsworth, who later became leader of the CCF party.

INSCRIPTION 1917

> In the Hearts and Minds of the
> Delegates Who Assembled
> In This Room on September 1, 1864
> Was Born the Dominion of Canada
>
> Providence Being Their Guide
> They Builded Better Than They Knew.

This inscription appears on the bronze plaque erected in 1917 (but not unveiled until July 1, 1927) outside the Legislative Chamber, Province House, Charlottetown, P.E.I. Here the basis was established for the confederation of the colonies of British North America. The inscription's last two lines are taken from English and American poetry. "Providence being their guide" comes from *Paradise Lost* (1667), in which John Milton described the expulsion of Adam and Eve from the Garden of Eden. "They builded better than they knew" comes from "The Problem," *Poems* (1847), in which Ralph Waldo Emerson wrote about the need for belief. The lines remain a powerful pastiche of British thought and American sentiment, and as such are completely Canadian.

J.E.H. MACDONALD 1917

He lived humbly but passionately with the wild. It made him brother to all untamed things of nature. It drew him apart and revealed itself wonderfully to him. It sent him out from the woods only to show these revelations through his art. And it took him to itself at last.

Thus runs the inscription on the cairn erected to the memory of Tom Thomson, identified as "artist, woodsman, and guide," who drowned in Canoe Lake, Algonquin Park, Ont., July 8, 1917. The inscription was the work of fellow artist J.E.H. MacDonald, and the memorial was erected on the shore of Canoe Lake on Sept. 27, 1917.

SIR ARTHUR CURRIE 1917

Truly magnificent . . . the sight was awful and wonderful.

This is the entry for Easter Monday, April 9, 1917, concerning the Battle of Vimy Ridge, France, written in the war diary kept by Sir Arthur Currie, the general who commanded the Canadian Division; as reproduced in *Historical Documents of Canada: Volume 5* (1972), edited by C.P. Stacey.

RUDYARD KIPLING 1917

They are too near
To be great
But our children

Shall understand
When and how our
Fate was changed
And by whose hand.

These solemn words were composed by the British author Rudyard Kipling for the stately inscription that appears on one wall of
the Memorial Chamber in the Peace Tower of the Centre Block
of the Parliament Buildings on Parliament Hill in Ottawa. It is a
reference to the men and women who fought and died in the Great
War and by extension all earlier and later wars. As a member of
the Imperial War Graves Commission, which came into existence
in May 1917, Kipling chose the following inscription for the head-
stones of unknown Canadian soldiers who died in the Great War:
"A Canadian Soldier of the Great War / Known Unto God." The
centrepiece of many Commonwealth war cemeteries is an imposing cenotaph with the inscription "Their Name Liveth for Ever-
more / Leur Nom Vivra à Jamais." Kipling chose the words from
Ecclesiastes, one of the apocryphal books of the Bible, according
to Herbert Fairlie Wood and John Swettenham in *Silent Witness*
(1974).

LIONEL GROULX   1918

The "revenge of the cradle" should naturally lead to thinking about "the
protection of the cradle."

Here is an instance of the use of the catch-phrase *revanche de berceau*
or "revenge of the cradle" with respect to the birthrate of French
Canadians overtaking that of other Canadians. It was used by the
nationalist historian Abbé Lionel Groulx in an address at the Monument National, Montreal, April 10, 1918, and was included in *Dix
Ans d'Action Française* (1926).

JEAN BRILLIANT 1918

Take me to the rear, that my men might not see me suffer, not that I fear
to suffer, but that I fear it might affect and discourage them.

This was the last command of Lieutenant Jean Brilliant of the 22nd
Canadian Infantry Division who, twice wounded, led his men to
capture 150 enemy and 15 machine guns, Aug. 8-9, 1918, during the
Battle of Amiens, France. He died of a third set of wounds and was
posthumously awarded the Victoria Cross "for most conspicuous
bravery and outstanding devotion to duty," according to George C.
Machum in *Canada's V.C.'s* (1956).

GEOFFREY O'HARA 1918

K-K-K-Katy, beautiful Katy,
You're the only g-g-g-girl that I adore,
When the m-m-m-moon shines over the cow-shed,
I'll be waiting at the k-k-k-kitchen door.

"K-K-K-Katy," known as the "stammering song," was written by the
Chatham-born Tin Pan Alley composer Geoffrey O'Hara. He composed the words and music much earlier, but "K-K-K-Katy" did not
become a hit until 1918, when its lively spirit was identified with the
Armistice that ended the Great War.

HENRI BOURASSA 1918

Our special task, as French Canadians, is to insert into America the spirit
of Christian France.

The mission of French Canada was so defined by Henri Bourassa,
French-Canadian nationalist and publisher, in his study *La Langue,
Gardienne de la Foi* (1918). Bourassa went on to define "our religious

and national heritage" and to see it as "the refuge and anchor amid the immense sea of saxonizing Americanism." Bourassa's image of the "immense sea" was pressed into service by George P. Grant in *Lament for a Nation* (1965) with respect to conservativism in the Dominion of Canada, not just for Catholicism and the French language in the Province of Quebec.

ANDREW ROSS MCMASTER 1919

I say to the minister, and I say to this Government: Trust the people; the heart of the Canadian people is as sound as our No. 1 Hard Manitoba wheat.

For decades it was commonplace for Canadians to consider themselves "as sound as our No. 1 Hard Manitoba wheat." The comparison was used, perhaps for the first time, in a speech delivered by Andrew Ross McMaster, a prairie Member of Parliament, in the House of Commons, June 24, 1919.

DUKE OF WINDSOR 1919

And of all the information that I brought back I think what delighted him [King George V] most was the following doggerel picked up in a Canadian border town:

Four and twenty Yankees, feeling very dry,
Went across the border to get a drink of rye.
When the rye was opened, the Yanks began to sing,
"God bless America, but God save the King!"

The Duke of Windsor, later Edward VIII, toured Canada for the first time in 1919 and was received with boisterous enthusiasm. Here is what he recalled of the royal visit when thirty years later he wrote *A King's Story* (1951).

JOHN CERIDIGEON JONES 1919

All's well, for over there among his peers
A Happy Warrior sleeps.

These lines are engraved above the entranceway to the Memorial
Chamber, Peace Tower, Centre Block, Parliament Hill, Ottawa.
They were chosen by John Pearson, architect of the reconstruction
of the building following the 1916 fire, though he forgot their source.
In 1939, a Welsh-born versifier and itinerant labourer named John
Ceridigeon Jones claimed authorship; he was able to prove that these
lines were taken from his doggerel poem "The Returning Man,"
composed in 1919-20 and published in the *Calgary Albertan*. He was
paid $8.00 by the government and died in obscurity in 1950, according
to Albert and Theresa Moritz in *The Oxford Illustrated Literary Guide
to Canada* (1987).

FRED J. DIXON 1920

Grass will grow, the river will reach the sea, the boy will become a man,
and labour will come into its own.

This declaration of faith in the advancement of organized labour was
made by Fred J. Dixon, a leader of the Winnipeg General Strike.
Charged with seditious conspiracy, he made his defence to the jury
in the Winnipeg Courthouse, Feb. 13-14, 1920.

J.A. RITCHIE 1920

THE WHOLESOME SEA IS AT HER GATES... HER GATES BOTH EAST AND WEST.

These lines of verse come from the poem "There Is a Land" (1920),
written by the Ottawa barrister and poetaster J.A. Ritchie. The verse
runs as follows: "The wholesome Sea is at her gates, / Her gates both

East and West, / Then is it strange that we should love / This Land, Our Land, the best?" The first two lines were inscribed in stone over the main entrance of the Centre Block, Parliament Buildings, Ottawa.

FREDERICK G. BANTING   1920

Diabetus.
Ligate pancreatic ducts of dog. Keep dogs alive till acini degenerate leaving Islets. Try to isolate the internal secretion of these to relieve glycosuria.

These twenty-five words were scribbled by physician and researcher Frederick G. Banting in his notebook, 2:00 A.M., Oct. 31, 1920. They led to the discovery of insulin for the treatment of diabetes; documented by Michael Bliss in *The Discovery of Insulin* (1982).

ANGUS WALTERS   1921

The wood that can beat the *Bluenose* ain't been planted yet.

The *Bluenose*, the last of the great clipper ships, was launched in Lunenburg, N.S., in 1921. Under Captain Angus J. Walters, it raced and won the International Fisherman's Trophy, emblematic of the sailing championship of the fishing fleets of the North Atlantic, gaining the trophy in 1921 and for years thereafter. Walters made the above boast in 1921. The *Bluenose*'s image first appeared on the dime in 1937. The ship's replica, *Bluenose II*, was launched in 1963.

JAMES J. TOMPKINS   1921

Practise self-help.

This maxim is associated with Father James J. Tompkins, pioneer adult educator, whose six-week extension course, held at St. Francis Xavier University, Antigonish, N.S., in 1921, led to the establishment of the Antigonish Movement, a co-operative, self-help movement with world-wide influence. Since 1960, the Coady International Institute, named after fellow priest Father M.M. Coady, has trained students from foreign countries, especially those in the Third World, to be "masters of their own destiny."

LAWREN HARRIS 1921

New material demands new methods and new methods fling a challenge to old conventions. It is as impossible to depict the autumn pageantry of our northern woods with a lead pencil as it is to bind our young art with the conventions and methods of other climates and other ages.

The artist Lawren Harris was the intellectual leader of the painters who formed the Group of Seven. The group's uncompromising vision of the Canadian North and the values they found in the new subject matter were given expression by Harris in the foreword to the second "Group of Seven Catalogue Exhibition of Paintings, May 1921"; reproduced by Peter Mellen in *The Group of Seven* (1970).

GEORGE CECIL 1921

Down from Canada came tales of a wonderful beverage. . . . For years and years, visitors to Canada have come back with tales of a wonderful ginger ale. They described its exquisite flavour—they told of drinking it in the Houses of Parliament in Ottawa, in the residence of the Governor-General and in the Royal Canadian Yacht Club.

These lines of hyperbole come from the newspaper advertisement that introduced Canada Dry, "The Champagne of Ginger Ales," to the U.S. public in 1921. Canada Dry Pale Ginger Ale was devised and marketed by J.J. McLaughlin, brother of Colonel Sam McLaughlin of McLaughlin-Buick fame, in Toronto. The advertising copy was written by George Cecil of N.W. Ayer & Son, N.Y., and appears in *The 100 Greatest Advertisements* (1949) by Julian Lewis Watkins.

VILHJALMUR STEFANSSON 1921

The friendly Arctic.

Popularizing this phrase and the notion behind it was the life's work of Arctic explorer Vilhjalmur Stefansson. Personal experience and innate perversity led him to the conclusion that the North, far from being forbidding, should be viewed as a region that is generally amicable and congenial. In his book *The Friendly Arctic* (1921), he argued that the history of Canada would unfold in the upper latitudes. History has proven him right in many of his opinions and predictions, but not as yet in this one.

ESKIMO SONG 1921

And yet, there is only
One great thing,
The only thing:
To live to see, in huts and on journeys
The great day that dawns
And the light that fills the world.

These evocative words come from "a little nameless Eskimo song" that was sung by the Inuit at Kent Peninsula, N.W.T., and recorded by the Danish-Eskimo explorer Knud Rasmussen on the Fifth Thule Expedition in the Arctic, 1921-24; from *The Mackenzie Eskimos* (1942), edited by H. Ostermann.

ROBERT J. FLAHERTY 1922

Here were a people with less resources than any other people on earth, and yet they were the happiest people I have ever known.

The people are the Eskimo or Inuit of the Canadian Arctic, and the observation about their nature was made by Robert J. Flaherty, prospector turned filmmaker. After ten years of living among the Eskimo in Ungava and the Belcher Islands, Flaherty wrote, photographed, and directed *Nanook of the North* (1922), the world's first feature-length documentary film. His observation about the native people of the Far North, no doubt made in later years, was quoted by Robert Hughes in *Film* (1959).

VICTORIA HAYWARD   1922

It is indeed a mosaic of vast dimensions and great breadth.

The first use of the word "mosaic" with respect to Canada's social and cultural diversity appeared in *Romantic Canada* (1922), a travel book written by the American traveller Victoria Hayward. Sociologist John Porter examined the structure of Canadian society horizontally (to study ethnicity) and vertically (to study class) and published his findings in *The Vertical Mosaic* (1965). The ethnic composition of Canada is routinely contrasted with that of the United States, the former a "mosaic," the latter a "melting pot." This contrast was more noticeable before the 1970s with the appearance in the United States of the so-called "unmeltable ethnics."

STEPHEN LEACOCK   1922

If I were founding a university—and I say it with all the seriousness of which I am capable—I would found first a smoking room; then when I had a little more money in hand I would found a dormitory; then after that, or more probably with it, a decent reading room and a library. After that, if I still had money over that I couldn't use, I would hire a professor and get some text books.

As well as being a leading humorist and public speaker, Stephen Leacock was Professor of Economics at McGill University. He thought long and hard about education and expressed this opinion in the essay "Oxford as I See It" in *My Discovery of England* (1922). Since then, many universities and colleges have been founded in Canada, but not one of them grew out of the nucleus of a "smoking room." The imagery is dated, yet the sense of the passage is sound: Conversation, discussion, and debate lead to education.

VILHJALMUR STEFANSSON 1922

The Northward Course of Empire.

This phrase was given currency by Arctic explorer Vilhjalmur Stefansson, who wrote passionately about the prospects of the polar region in *The Northward Course of Empire* (1922). The phrase is an adaptation of Bishop Berkeley's "Westward the course of empire takes its way" from the verse titled "On the Prospect of Planting Arts and Learning in America" (1752).

ESKIMO SONG 1923

Only the Air-Spirits know
What lies beyond the hills,
Yet I urge my team farther on.
Drove on and on,
On and on!

These lines come from one of the many traditional Inuit hunter's songs collected in the central Arctic in 1923 by the explorer Knud Rasmussen, leader of the Fifth Thule Expedition. The lines appear on the plinth of the modernistic statue of Rasmussen erected in 1963 on the outskirts of Copenhagen, Denmark. Rasmussen and the lines face north.

A.H. REGINALD BULLER 1923

There was a young lady named Bright
Whose speed was far faster than light;
    She set out one day
    In a relative way
And returned on the previous night.

When this limerick was published in *Punch*, Dec. 19, 1923, it appeared anonymously under the title "Relativity." It deals with the paradox of time travel. It must be the most widely known "clean" limerick. Authorship has been claimed by A.H. Reginald Buller, Professor of Botany, University of Manitoba, a world authority on fungi. It is not known that he could prove his claim, but W.S. Baring-Gould, in *The Lure of the Limerick* (1968), recorded Buller's claim and printed Buller's rather wayward sequel: "To her friends said the Bright one in chatter, / 'I have learned something new about matter: / My speed was so great, / Much increased was my weight, / Yet I failed to become any fatter!'"

BLISS CARMAN 1923

Have little care that Life is brief,
    And less that art is long.
Success is in the silences,
    Though fame is in the song.

The lyric poem "Envoi" was written by Bliss Carman, the New Brunswick-born versifier and poet, and it appeared in his collection *Ballads and Lyrics* (1923). The lines of the lyric are reproduced on the plaque erected in Carman's honour in Poets' Corner, University of New Brunswick, Fredericton, N.B.

LEAGUE OF NATIONS 1923

> It is for the constitutional authorities of each Member to decide . . . in what degree the Member is bound to assure the execution of this obligation by employment of its military forces.

This is the so-called Canadian Resolution on Article 10, League of Nations Assembly, The Hague, Sept. 24, 1923. It permits each member country to determine the degree of its compliance with the general duty of maintaining peace. As Gwynne Dyer and Tina Viljoen noted in *The Defence of Canada: In the Arms of the Empire* (1990), the effect of Canada's interpretation of the League's resolution was to destroy the effectiveness of Article 10.

JOHN W. DAFOE 1923

> A journalist is hardly an authority upon anything—unless perhaps upon the appraisal of the drift of public opinion.

John W. Dafoe, the longtime editor of *The Winnipeg Free Press*—he was associated with the paper from 1886 to his death in 1944—made this observation in a convocation address, University of Manitoba, Winnipeg, May 1923; quoted by Murray Donnelly in *Dafoe of the Free Press* (1968). On another occasion he said, "There are only two kinds of government, the scarcely tolerable and the absolutely unbearable."

RAOUL DANDURAND 1924

> We live in a fire-proof house, far from inflammable materials.

This classic expression of Canadian isolationism comes from an address expressing precisely that sentiment delivered before the League of Nations Assembly, The Hague, Oct. 2, 1924, by Canada's delegate, Raoul Dandurand. The full text appears in *Documents on Canadian Foreign Policy: 1917-1939* (1962), edited by Walter A. Riddell.

OTTO HARBACH & OSCAR HAMMERSTEIN II 1924

Oh, Rose-Marie, I love you!
I'm always dreaming of you.
No matter what I do,
I can't forget you.

The Royal Canadian Mounted Police will ever be identified with the love song "Rose-Marie," which was the hit song of the 1924 Broadway operetta *Rose-Marie*, words by Otto Harbach and Oscar Hammerstein II with music by Rudolf Friml. Jeanette MacDonald and Nelson Eddy starred in the 1936 Hollywood movie *Rose Marie* (without the hyphen). To this day a soft assignment within RCMP ranks is known as "a Rose-Marie posting."

STEPHEN LEACOCK 1924

Advertising may be described as the science of arresting the human intelligence long enough to get money from it.

Stephen Leacock's definition of the nature of advertising has yet to be bettered. It comes from the humorist's sketch "The Perfect Salesman" in *The Garden of Folly* (1924). The definition brings to mind another remark, one made by the explorer Vilhjalmur Stefansson, which appears in the latter's autobiography, *Discovery* (1964): "What is the difference between unethical and ethical advertising? Unethical advertising uses falsehoods to deceive the public; ethical advertising uses truth to deceive the public."

AGNES MACPHAIL 1925

When I hear men talk about woman being the angel of the home I always, mentally at least, shrug my shoulders in doubt. I do not want to be the angel of any home; I want for myself what I want for other women, absolute equality. After that is secured then men and women can take turns at being angels.

Agnes Macphail was on the front lines of many progressive causes and could be called a pioneer feminist. She made the above remark in a speech in the House of Commons, Feb. 26, 1925.

D.W. GRIFFITH 1925

You in Canada should not be dependent either on the United States or on Great Britain. You should have your own films and exchange them with those of other countries. You can make them just as well in Toronto as in New York City.

It is interesting to note that D.W. Griffith, pioneer director of silent films, saw no reason why there should not be a vigorous feature-film industry in Canada. He was speaking before the Canadian Club of Toronto, Dec. 14, 1925, and was quoted in *The Toronto Star* the following day.

STEPHEN LEACOCK 1925

I never realized that there was history too, close at hand, beside my very own home. I did not realize that the old grave that stood among the brambles at the foot of our farm was *history*.

Most people know Stephen Leacock as a humorist. Some people know he was also an economist. Few appreciate the fact that he was also a historian of some standing. The autobiographical remark above comes from his address on "The Place of History in Cana-

dian Education," *Report of the Canadian Historical Association 1925* (1926).

SIR HENRY THORNTON 1926

It is essential that broadcasting be surrounded with such safeguards as will prevent the air becoming what might be described as an atmospheric billboard.

Sir Henry Thornton, pioneer of public broadcasting, had the foresight to warn the public that the commercial/advertising complex had designs on radio broadcasting. (Indeed, commercial and consumer interests took over radio broadcasting, commercialized television, and cable, and are now infecting telecommunications.) Thornton's warning came in the form of a hard-hitting address delivered before the Advertising Clubs of the World, Philadelphia, Penn., June 21, 1926, as quoted by E. Austin Weir in *The Struggle for National Broadcasting in Canada* (1965).

BALFOUR DECLARATION 1926

They [the Dominions] are autonomous Communities within the British Empire, equal in status, in no way subordinate one to another in any aspect of their domestic or external affairs, though united by a common allegiance to the Crown, and freely associated as members of the British Commonwealth of Nations.

This closely reasoned sentence was an affirmation of Canada's "equal status" with Britain and the other "dominions beyond the seas." It comes from the Balfour Declaration, named after British statesman A.J. Balfour. Its official title is "Report of Inter-Imperial Relations Committee, Imperial Conference, Nov. 18, 1926." The full document is reprinted in *Historical Documents of Canada: Volume 5* (1972), edited by C.P. Stacey.

A.J.M. SMITH 1926

This is a beauty
of dissonance,
this resonance
of stony strand. . . .

This is the beauty
of strength
broken by strength
and still strong.

These moving lines, so evocative of the Precambrian shield, come
from the poem "The Lonely Land" (1926), composed by the poet
A.J.M. Smith and reprinted in his *Poems* (1967).

A.J.M. SMITH 1928

The heart is willing, but the head is weak. Modernity and tradition alike
demand that the contemporary artist who survives adolescence shall be
an intellectual. Sensibility is no longer enough, intelligence is also
required. Even in Canada.

A.J.M. Smith, poet and critic, was a member of the group of Montreal
writers who introduced literary modernism to Canadian literature.
This passage could be Smith's critical credo. It comes from his essay
"Wanted: Canadian Criticism," *The Canadian Forum*, April 1928.

ERIC ARTHUR 1929

I believe it will take a thousand years to develop a national style in
Canada, but I do see a light in the west over a grain elevator.

The preservation of the best from the past and the promotion of a
national style in architecture were the twin concerns of architectural
writer Eric Arthur. He hazarded this remark about the emergence

of a national style in his article "Architecture in Canada" in *Yearbook of the Arts in Canada: 1928-29* (1929), edited by Bertram Brooker.

LORD SANKEY 1929

Their Lordships are of opinion that the word "persons" in s. 24 does include women, and that women are eligible to be summoned to and become members of the Senate of Canada.

This was the landmark decision in the famous "persons" case, handed down by Lord Sankey, Lord Chancellor of the Privy Council of Great Britain, Oct. 18, 1929. The case is entitled *Henrietta Muir Edwards and Others v. Attorney-General for Canada* (1929). The five women active in the "persons" case all came from Alberta: Emily Murphy, Nellie L. McClung, Louise McKinney, Irene Parlby, Henrietta Muir Edwards.

JAMES H. GRAY 1929

When the Depression came, our world stopped and we got off.

The Great Depression brought untold hardship to Canadians, particularly to prairie farmers, beginning in 1929 and lasting until the outbreak of World War II ten years later. James H. Gray, a Calgary writer, was quoted by Barry Broadfoot in *Ten Lost Years 1929-1939: Memoirs of Canadians Who Survived the Depression* (1973).

R.B. BENNETT 1930

I will end unemployment or perish in the attempt.

This is a simplification and popularization of what the Leader of the Opposition, R.B. Bennett, said in a Winnipeg address, June 9, 1930: "I propose that any government of which I am the head will at the first session of Parliament initiate whatever action is necessary to that end, or perish in the attempt." The words were inserted into the Conservative leader's speech by his brother-in-law W.H. Herridge, as noted by J.R.H. Wilbur in *The Bennett New Deal* (1968). Bennett was elected and served as Prime Minister 1930-35 but perished in the attempt to end unemployment.

GILBERT A. LABINE 1930

It's an elephant!

This was the excited cry when prospector Gilbert A. LaBine heard his geiger counter make extra-loud crackling sounds, indicating the presence of pitchblende, the ore that yields radioactive uranium. He discovered the Port Radium deposit while prospecting the south shore of Great Bear Lake, near Beaverlodge Lake, N.W.T., May 16, 1930, as quoted by D.M. LeBourdais in *Metals and Men* (1957).

FOLK SONG 1930s

Saskatchewan, Saskatchewan,
There's no place like Saskatchewan.
We sit and gaze across the plains,
And wonder why it never rains,
And Gabriel blows his trumpet sound;
He says, "The rain, she's gone around."

This is the refrain of "Saskatchewan," which was sung to the tune of "Beulah Land" in the Dirty Thirties. It is credited to someone called W. Smith in *The Penguin Book of Canadian Folk Songs* (1973), edited by Edith Fowke.

FOLK SONG 1930s

Farewell to Nova Scotia, the sea-bound coast!
Let your mountains dark and dreary be,

For when I am far away on the briny ocean tossed

Will you ever heave a sigh and a wish for me?

Folklorist Helen Creighton collected this sailor's lament in rural Nova Scotia in the 1930s. It became the theme song of the Halifax-based, CBC-TV show "Singalong Jubilee" in 1961, and it was memorably recorded by Catherine McKinnon. Edith Fowke and Richard Johnston printed it in *Folk Songs of Canada* (1954).

FOLK SONG 1930s

Les Canadiens sont là!

This is the rallying cry of the Montreal Canadiens hockey team, which played its first game on Jan. 5, 1910. Associated with the "flying Frenchmen" since the 1930s, the line is derived from a Franco-Ontarian folk song that runs: "Les canayens sont un peu là! / Ah! ah! Les canayens sont un peu là!" (The Canadiens are always ready! / Ah! ah! The Canadiens are always ready.) The words and music appear in Edith Fowke's *Folklore of Canada* (1976). "But it was in the early 1950s that *les Canadiens* really began to *sont là*," wrote Trent Frayne in *The Mad Men of Hockey* (1974). Anglophone sports fans recall the hockey club's nickname, Habitants, when they cry out, "Go, Habs, go!"

AL CAPONE 1931

I don't even know what street Canada is on.

Roy Greenaway, ace reporter for *The Toronto Star*, interviewed Al Capone in 1931, the year the Chicago mobster was sent to prison for income tax evasion. Greenaway asked Capone if Canada was the main source of supply for his lucrative bootlegging operation. Capone replied, "I don't even know what street Canada is on." The reply may be more than an amusing riposte. It is possible that Capone was punning on the nickname of Blaise Diesbourg, a Windsor-based bootlegger who was a source of supply to Capone in Chicago and to the Purple Gang in Detroit. Diesbourg's nickname was King Canada, as noted by Marty Gervais in *The Rumrunners: A Prohibition Scrapbook* (1980).

R.B. BENNETT 1931

It is perhaps one of the passing phases of our civilization that those who are of a conservative bent of thought should follow the maxim . . . "That man's the true Conservative / Who lops the moulder'd branch away." There are many mouldered branches with respect to our system of taxation.

A true Conservative, Prime Minister R.B. Bennett spoke on behalf of restraint in the House of Commons, July 2, 1931. A Depression-weary electorate identified Bennett with the image of the "moulder'd branch," which Bennett took from Alfred Lord Tennyson's poem "Hands All Round" (1852).

EARL OF BESSBOROUGH 1931

Before I left London, a friend of mine, with a great knowledge of this Dominion, gave me his views on various great cities, and when he came to Toronto he prefaced his remarks, I remember, by saying, "There are two things they understand in Toronto—the British Empire and a good horse."

At one time Toronto considered itself the bastion of the Empire. This humorous reference comes from the address delivered by Governor General the Earl of Bessborough before the Canadian Club of Toronto, Nov. 24, 1931.

STATUTE OF WESTMINSTER   1931

It is hereby declared and enacted that the Parliament of a Dominion has full power to make laws having extra-territorial operation.

Section 3 of the Statute of Westminster, 1931, affirmed Canada's autonomous status within the British Empire and Commonwealth. The statute is reprinted in *British North America Acts and Selected Statutes* (1962), edited by Maurice Olliver.

GRAHAM SPRY   1932

The question before this committee is whether Canada is to establish a chain that is owned and operated and controlled by Canadians, or whether it is to be owned and operated by commercial organizations associated or controlled by American interests. The question is, the State or the United States?

Graham Spry was Chairman of the Canadian Radio League, which was in large part responsible for the creation of the Canadian Broadcasting Corporation in 1936. In an address before the Parliamentary Committee on Broadcasting on April 18, 1932, Spry expressed the need for government intervention in cultural affairs. He saw the need in terms of positioning a state enterprise against an American enterprise. The last nine words of Spry's last sentence were widely quoted in the 1960s; even today they are sometimes heard, despite the fact that American enterprise seems to have all but engulfed Canadian state enterprise.

FAY WRAY   1932

When I'm in New York, I look at that building and feel as though it belongs to me . . . or is it vice versa?

Alberta-born movie star Fay Wray appeared as the hapless and helpless heroine Ann Darrow in the clutches of the giant ape in *King Kong* (1932), the greatest monster movie of all time. Thereafter the Empire State Building occupied a special place in her affections, or so she informed Mitchell Smyth in *The Toronto Star*, Dec. 15, 1985.

TIM BUCK 1932

I was shot at—

Assassinations—actual or attempted—are rare in Canadian public or political life. Somebody made an attempt on the life of Tim Buck, the imprisoned Communist leader, who at the time was alone in his cell at Kingston Penitentiary, Oct. 20, 1932. The first knowledge that the public had that rifle bullets were shot into his cell during a prison riot came from Buck's testimony at the trial of fellow Communist A.E. Smith in Toronto the following year. Buck's words were subsequently struck from the court's record.

FOSTER HEWITT 1933

He shoots! He scores!

This is the most famous quotation in the history of sports in Canada. The four words evoke the colourful career of veteran hockey broadcaster Foster Hewitt, who covered Maple Leaf and National Hockey League games on radio and then television from 1923 to within a few years of his death in 1985. In a radio broadcast from Toronto's Mutual Street Arena, Hewitt covered the hockey game between the Toronto Maple Leafs and the Boston Bruins. It was a long game. After five hours of play, at 1:45 A.M., April 4, 1933, Ken Doraty, the smallest player on either team, whipped the puck into the Boston net. An exhausted Hewitt murmured: "He shoots! He scores!" This was the birth of a hockey legend.

F.H. UNDERHILL 1933

No CCF Government will rest content until it has eradicated capitalism and put into operation the full programme of socialized planning which will lead to the establishment in Canada of the Co-operative Commonwealth.

Here is one of a number of controversial passages from the "Regina Manifesto," which was read before the founding convention of the Co-operative Commonwealth Federation (CCF), Regina, Sask., July 1933; reproduced in *The Anatomy of a Party* (1969) by Walter D. Young. A controversial heading in the report was three words long: "Capitalism Basically Immoral."

MITCHELL HEPBURN 1934

This is the first time in my life that I have spoken from a Tory platform.

This remark will ever be associated with Mitchell Hepburn, Liberal Premier of Ontario from 1934 to 1942. Mitch (he was also called "son of a mitch"), while campaigning among the farmers of Elgin County, stood on the seat of a manure spreader and made the above observation. One farmer roared, "Throw her in high gear, Mitch, she's never had a bigger load on," according to Neil McKenty in his biography *Mitch Hepburn* (1967).

SAMUEL BRONFMAN 1934

We who make whiskey say: "Drink Moderately."

This was the theme of the advertising campaign launched by Seagram's through the Blackman Agency in New York in Oct. 1934. It first appeared in *The New York Times*, as noted by Michael R. Marrus in *Mr. Sam: The Life and Times of Samuel Bronfman* (1991). Seagram's also owned Calvert, the division headed by William

Wachtel, who in the 1930s introduced the celebrated advertising campaign that featured the "Man of Distinction," prominent Americans announcing their preference for Lord Calvert whiskey, a premium blend. The phrase "Men of Distinction," noted Marrus, "slipped into the vocabulary of the age via newspaper columnists, script writers and even a play in New York."

MAURICE DUPLESSIS 1935

> The bishops eat from my hand.

Maurice Duplessis, who formed the Union Nationale party in 1935 and became Premier of Quebec the following year, was renowned for his witty remarks and ripostes in the two official languages. According to Conrad Black in *Duplessis* (1977), the remark quoted above is "possibly Duplessis's most famous line of all, frequently uttered in the Assembly and in conversation, but difficult to find in contemporary newspapers. Everyone who knew Duplessis remembers this." Black would have been wiser to have written "infamous" rather than "famous."

ARTHUR (SLIM) EVANS 1935

> You referred to us as not wanting work. Give any of us work and see whether we will work. This is an insidious attempt to propagandize the press on your part, and anybody who professes to be premier and uses such despicable tactics is not fit to be premier of a Hottentot village.

Arthur (Slim) Evans was a Communist labour organizer who led a delegate of striking relief-camp workers to Ottawa, where they met with Prime Minister R.B. Bennett in his East Block office, June 22, 1935. The meeting did not go well; Bennett accused Evans of being an embezzler, and Evans charged Bennett with being a liar. The full exchange is reproduced in Ronald Liversedge's *Recollections of the On to Ottawa Trek* (1961, 1973), edited by Victor Hoar.

HECTOR DE SAINT-DENYS-GARNEAU 1935

Great art consists of going beyond reality and not in evading it. One must be able to say, "That is how it is—and something more." Art lies in that "more."

Hector de Saint-Denys-Garneau, almost unique among the French-Canadian poets of his time, kept a journal in which he intermittently pondered and probed the nature of life and art. This passage, which is typical of his thought, comes from a journal entry dated April 15, 1935, *The Journal of Saint-Denys-Garneau* (1962), translated by John Glassco.

DOUGLASS DUMBRILLE 1935

We have ways to make men talk.

This chilling threat was uttered by the wicked potentate Mohammed Khan in the movie *Lives of a Bengal Lancer* (1935); the Hamilton-born, Hollywood actor Douglass Dumbrille spoke the words and gave them currency. According to Harry Purvis in *The Canadian*, Sept. 17, 1977, Dumbrille's speech continued: "Little bamboo slivers—but when they're driven under the fingernails and *lighted*, we find them *very* effective." The line is frequently parodied. Another parodied line is "Devil child have forked tongue," which was first uttered by the actor Victor Jory (who was born in Dawson, Y.T.) to child actress Shirley Temple in the 1939 Hollywood movie *Susannah of the Mounties* (based on the novel by Muriel Denison). Canada has contributed a surprising number of villains to Hollywood movies, including such "heavies" as Jack Carson, John Ireland, and John Vernon, not to mention the insidious Joseph Wiseman (Dr. No).

J. ROBY KIDD 1935

Good intentions and sentimentalism are not enough. At the first meeting of the Canadian Association for Adult Education in 1935 there was coined a slogan that, while somewhat vulgar, is worth some consideration: "Now and then forget your bleeding heart and use your bloody head!"

J. Roby Kidd, adult educator, *Education for Perspective* (1969). The slogan became a catch-phrase of the country's important adult-education movement, embodied in the Canadian Association for Adult Education, established in Toronto in 1935.

WILLIAM ABERHART 1935

The Eyes of the World Are on Alberta.

This was the campaign slogan of the Social Credit Party of Alberta in the provincial election of Aug. 22, 1935. William Aberhart led his party to victory. As John A. Irving noted in *The Social Credit Movement in Alberta* (1959), "The slogan was true: There *was* world-wide interest in the monetary theories of Major Douglas and in the Alberta 'experiment.'"

MACLEAN'S 1935

KING OR CHAOS.

This must be the most amazing headline to appear in a major Canadian publication. It spread across two pages of *Maclean's*, Oct. 15, 1935, prior to the general election of that year, in which W.L. Mackenzie King defeated Prime Minister R.B. Bennett—which led wits to conclude that Canada got both King and chaos. The story behind the headline is discussed by Floyd S. Chalmers in *A Gentleman of the Press* (1969).

PAUL MARTIN 1935

Is there anybody here from Windsor?

Paul Martin, Sr., served in public life from 1935 to 1979 as a Member of Parliament, Cabinet Minister, Senator, and Ambassador. It is said that whenever he delivered a speech in this country or abroad, he asked the above question as a way of alluding to his constituency, in and around Windsor, Ont. He was a leading member of the Liberal Party, as is his son Paul Martin, Jr.

MAURICE DUPLESSIS 1936

You know, we French Canadians are improved Frenchmen.

This remark was attributed to Maurice Duplessis, who served as Premier of Quebec (with one break) from 1936 to 1959. It was noted by Pierre Laporte in *The True Face of Duplessis* (1961).

GREY OWL 1936

I want to arouse in Canadian people a sense of responsibility, the great responsibility they have for that north country and its inhabitants, human and animal.

The pioneer naturalist known as Grey Owl was not a native person at all but an Englishman born Archibald Belaney. He wrote lyrical prose and lectured eloquently about the wonders of the natural world. He lived in national parks and dedicated his efforts to the well-being of the beaver. The remark above comes from "A Plea for the Canadian Northland," an address he delivered to the Empire Club of Canada in Toronto in 1936.

NORMAN (RED) RYAN 1936

You've got me, boys. I've had enough.

Norman (Red) Ryan, notorious bank robber, whispered these words to the policemen who shot and mortally wounded him in a gun battle after he tried to rob a liquor store in Sarnia, Ont., May 23, 1936. Ryan was on parole at the time, supposedly a "model prisoner." His recidivism inspired Morley Callaghan's novel *More Joy in Heaven* (1937).

W.L. MACKENZIE KING 1936

> We are fortunate both in our neighbours and in our lack of neighbours. It may be that this fortunate position is not due to any special virtue on our part, that it is an accident of geography and of history, but one has only to be in any European country a day to realize how relatively fortunate a position it is, and what folly it would be to throw it away. It is equally true, I should add, that if some countries have too much history, we have too much geography.

The last twelve words in this excerpt have been widely quoted. They come from a speech on Canada's international responsibilities delivered by Prime Minister W.L. Mackenzie King in the House of Commons, June 18, 1936.

ANDRÉ SIEGFRIED 1937

> I remember having breakfasted with a French Canadian in Montreal and having dined with an English Canadian family in Toronto on the same day. The contrast was quite a shock to my senses. It was like experiencing the different pressures in a diving bell. Involuntarily I thought of the uncompromising formula of Maurice Barrès: "Prayers that do not mingle."

The last line has a sting to it that has yet to lose its venom. Barrès was a well-known French politician and author whose novels often explored the effects of nationalist sentiment. Siegfried was a French historian who spent time in Quebec and Ontario in 1904 and again in 1935. He made the above observation in his study *Canada: An International Power* (1937), in which he went on to define the relationship between the French and English as "a *modus vivendi* without cordiality."

BERT PEARL 1937

Knock, knock.
Who's there?
It's the Happy Gang!
Well, com'on in!

These are the famous opening lines of "The Happy Gang," CBC Radio's daily comedy and music program that was heard across the land from 1937 to 1959. The nine-member group gave 4,890 performances under their leader Bert Pearl, who composed the music to their signature tune, "Keep Happy with the Happy Gang." The program featured the talents of Cliff McKay, Bobby Gimby, Lloyd Edwards, Joe and Bert Niosi, Jimmy Namaro, Lou Snider, and others. So popular was Pearl that the Blood Indians named him Chief Happy Voice in the Sky.

DAVID A. CROLL 1937

You know my origins; I have always been with, and one of, the workers, and I have neither the desire nor the ability to swing at this late date to the other side. In my official capacity I have travelled the middle of the road, but now that you have put the extreme alternative to me, my place is marching with the workers rather than riding with General Motors. At this late date I cannot oppose unionism and the workers and labour as a whole.

Oshawa's autoworkers were striking for union recognition when David A. Croll, Ontario Minister of Public Welfare, Labour, and Municipal Affairs, sent this letter of resignation to Ontario Premier Mitchell Hepburn, April 14, 1937. It appeared in *The Toronto Star* the following day.

NORMAN BETHUNE 1937

The function of the artist is to disturb. His duty is to arouse the sleeper, to shake the complacent pillars of the world. He reminds the world of its dark ancestry, and shows the world its present, and points the way to its new birth. He is at once the product and the preceptor of his time.

This is the credo of Norman Bethune, physician and surgeon, supporter of the Loyalists during the Spanish Civil War and champion of the Communists during the Chinese Civil War. The lines come from an impassioned letter written to the Montreal artist Marian Scott from Madrid, Spain, May 5, 1937. Bethune wrote the letter shortly before departing for war-torn China, where he joined the army of Mao Zedong and died administering to the army's medical needs in 1939.

LIONEL GROULX   1937

We carry in our very bones the mind and marrow of our forebears. No, a nation cannot separate itself from its past any more than a river can separate itself from its source, or sap from the soil whence it arises. No generation is self-sufficient. It can and does happen that a generation forgets its history, or turns its back upon it; such an act is a betrayal of History.

Abbé Lionel Groulx, a priest and historian at the University of Montreal, envisaged a conservative Catholic mission for the French-Canadian people. These remarks were made during the course of an address in Quebec City, June 29, 1937, reproduced by Susan Mann Trofimenkoff in *Abbé Groulx* (1973).

J.W. PICKERSGILL   1937

The Liberal Party is the party of government.

This adage has long been attributed to J.W. (Jack) Pickersgill who served as adviser on policy and politics to Prime Ministers Mackenzie King and St. Laurent and as grey eminence of the Liberal Party from 1937 to 1967. In a private communication, Nov. 24, 1978, Pickersgill wrote, "I do not know who said the Liberals are the party of government. It is conceivable, but unlikely, I said it in jest, but knowing how dangerous it is for Canadian politicians to jest I think it improbable." It goes without saying that if the Liberal Party is the "party of government," the Conservative Party is the "party of opposition."

DONALD G. CREIGHTON 1937

The few members who watched the British North America Act of 1867 in its speedy passage through parliament could scarcely conceal their excruciating boredom; and after the ordeal was over, they turned with lively zeal and manifest relief to the great national problem of the tax on dogs.

Thus was passed the BNA Act, 1867, which created the Dominion of Canada, as described by historian Donald G. Creighton in "The Victorians and the Empire" (1937), *Towards the Discovery of Canada* (1972).

SIR WILFRED GRENFELL 1938

The service we render to others is really the rent we pay for our room on this earth.

Sir Wilfred Grenfell administered to the medical needs of the out-porters of Newfoundland and Labrador. This quotation comes from Grenfell's *A Labrador Logbook* (1938).

FREDERICK PHILIP GROVE 1938

This lack of mental aliveness is fundamental. Canada is a non-conductor of any sort of intellectual current.

This verdict on the level of discourse in Canadian society was rendered by the novelist Frederick Philip Grove in "The Plight of

Canadian Fiction? A Reply," *University of Toronto Quarterly*, July 1938. Similar complaints were registered by other commentators, both native and foreign, throughout the 1930s, 1940s, and 1950s.

JOE SHUSTER 1938

> I never met a girl who matched up to Lois Lane.

The world's first and foremost "superhero" was Superman, the comic-book character who made his début in *Action Comics*, June 1938. Superman's originators were two high-school students, Joe Shuster and Jerry Siegel. Shuster was born in Toronto, a cousin of comedian Frank Shuster, and he worked summers for *The Toronto Star*. He moved to Cleveland with his family and there teamed up with Jerry Siegel, and together they created the costumed, caped crusader. Siegel supplied the story-line, Shuster the artwork. "No one drew skyscrapers like Shuster," observed Jules Feiffer. Together they created an American—and world—legend. Clark Kent, Superman's alter ego, originally worked for the *Daily Planet*, which was modelled on *The Toronto Star*. (In later years he worked for television.) If Canada cannot claim Superman as entirely its own, perhaps it can claim Clark Kent. Mordecai Richler has argued that "Kent is the archetypical middle-class Canadian WASP, superficially nice, self-effacing, but within whom there burns a hate-ball, a would-be avenger with superhuman power, a smasher of bridges, a breaker of skyscrapers, a potential ravager of wonder women." Joe Shuster never returned to Canada, never married, and always admired Clark Kent's girlfriend, Lois Lane.

FRANKLIN DELANO ROOSEVELT 1938

> The Dominion of Canada is part of the sisterhood of the British Empire.
> I give to you assurance that the people of the United States will not stand idly by if domination of Canadian soil is threatened by any other Empire.

We can assure each other that this hemisphere, at least, shall remain a strong citadel wherein civilization can flourish unimpaired.

The important words "the United States will not stand idly by" indicated that the Republic would support the Dominion and hence the Empire. The words were spoken by U.S. President Franklin Delano Roosevelt, Convocation Address, Queen's University, Kingston, Ont., Aug. 18, 1938,

---

CAMILLIEN HOUDE 1939

You know, Your Majesty, some of this is for you.

This wisecrack, more than any official speech, is what the public remembers of the royal visit of King George VI and Queen Elizabeth. The royal couple rode through the streets of downtown Montreal in a convertible, accompanied by their host, the irrepressible Camillien Houde, Mayor of Montreal. Hearing the crowd cheer, Houde waved his hands and made the above comment, May 18, 1939.

CBC RADIO ANNOUNCER 1939

The King, the Queen and Mr. King have now arrived at the city hall and Mr. Queen is on the steps to meet them. . . . The King is now shaking hands with Mr. Queen and now the Queen is shaking hands with Mr. Queen, and now Mr. King is shaking hands with Mr. Queen. . . . And now the King and Mr. Queen and the Queen and Mr. King are moving into the reception hall. . . . And now the King and Mr. Quing, I mean Mr. Keen and the Quing, I'm sorry, I mean, oh sh—.

The royal visit of King George VI and Queen Elizabeth was the first of its kind. By all accounts it was an impressive spectacle and a stylish exercise of imperial pomp and circumstance in the face of the oncoming war. Tens of thousands of Canadians recall to this day the sight of Their

Majesties' Royal Blue Train pulling into the station of their village, town, or city. When that train pulled into the Winnipeg station, May 24, 1939, Their Majesties and their host, Prime Minister Mackenzie King, were greeted by Mayor John Queen and Mrs. Queen. An unnamed radio announcer for the CBC covered the event for the Dominion. The rough transcript of what he said appears in Tom MacDonnell's *Daylight upon Magic: The Royal Tour of Canada—1939* (1989).

JOHN GRIERSON 1939

Art is not a mirror but a hammer.

This notion of the nature of art was held by John Grierson, the fiery Scot who coined the word "documentary" in 1926 and served as first Commissioner of the National Film Board of Canada from 1939 to 1945. Grierson defined the documentary film as "the creative treatment of actuality." Its outstanding documentary films, both shorts and features, have given the NFB an enviable world-wide reputation. Grierson's art-as-hammer notion, his personal maxim, dates from the early 1930s and is variously expressed in *Grierson on Documentary* (1946, 1966), edited by H. Forsyth Hardy.

NATIONAL FILM BOARD ACT 1939

To produce and distribute and promote the production and distribution of films designed to interpret Canada to Canadians and to other nations.

This is the key passage from the "NFB's mandate" from An Act Respecting the National Film Board, passed May 2, 1939. As John Grierson, the board's first Commissioner, noted the next year: "But when that sentence was drafted I remember thinking: Why can't we say and be done with it, the National Film Board will be the *eyes of Canada*? It will, through a national use of cinema, see Canada and see it whole—its people and its purposes."

ROSS PARKER & HUGHIE CHARLIE 1939

Red, White and Blue,
What does it mean to you?
Surely you're proud,
Shout it aloud,
Britain's awake!

This is the stirring chorus of the patriotic song "There'll Always Be an England," which was composed by two Englishmen, Ross Parker and Hughie Charlie, rejected by countless sheet music publishers, but finally accepted by the Gordon V. Thompson music-publishing company in Toronto. It was published in 1939, immediately prior to the outbreak of World War II with which it remains identified.

SIR WINSTON CHURCHILL 1939

That long frontier from the Atlantic to the Pacific oceans, guarded only by neighbourly respect and honourable obligations, is an example to every country and a pattern for the future of the world.

Sir Winston Churchill waxed eloquent about the "unguarded border" in an address delivered in honour of R.B. Bennett at the Canada Club, London, England, April 20, 1939. The length of the "unguarded border" between Canada and the United States is 6,416 km.; as well, there is the border with Alaska which extends 2,478 km. So the total length of the southern and northern borders is 8,894 km. Strictly speaking, the border is not unguarded. There are armed guards on both sides, but they are not as heavily armed as guards at many border crossings elsewhere in the world. Governor General Vincent Massey, in *On Being Canadian* (1948), noted dryly: "It has long been undefended, but realists have observed that the disparity of population has made armaments for one country futile and for the other superfluous."

FREDERICK CHARLES BLAIR 1939

No country could open its doors wide enough to take in the hundreds of thousands of Jewish people who want to leave Europe; the line must be drawn somewhere.

This sentence is taken from the letter that Frederick Charles Blair, Director of the Immigration Branch of the Department of Mines and Resources, addressed to O.D. Skelton, Undersecretary of State for External Affairs, dated June 16, 1939. It was quoted by Irving Abella and Harold E. Troper in "The Line Must Be Drawn Somewhere," *The Canadian Jewish Mosaic* (1981), edited by M. Weinfeld, W. Shaffir, and I. Cotler. The statement "None is too many" is often attributed to Blair, but it was spoken by an unnamed senior official with the Department of Immigration, who gave this reply to journalists in early 1945 when asked how many Jews would be allowed into Canada after World War II.

J.S. WOODSWORTH 1939

I take my place with the children.

J.S. Woodsworth cast the sole dissenting vote to ratify Canada's entry into World War II, House of Commons, Sept. 9, 1939. A lifelong pacifist and a Methodist clergyman, the CCF leader felt he was representing through his vote the young and the unborn.

ALBERT EINSTEIN 1939

The United States has only very poor ores of uranium in moderate quantities. There is some good ore in Canada and the former Czechoslovakia, while the most important source of uranium is Belgian Congo.

A reference to Canada appears in the most influential letter written in modern times, the one drafted by atomic scientist Leo Szilard and signed by physicist Albert Einstein on Aug. 2, 1939, addressed to

U.S. President Franklin Delano Roosevelt. It resulted in the Manhattan Project, the crash program to produce the atomic bomb. The letter is reproduced by J. Bronowski in *The Ascent of Man* (1973).

LORD TWEEDSMUIR   1940

Man, according to Aristotle, is a political animal, but there is an exception in the case of a Governor General. His views on public policy can only be the views of his Ministers. If he touches on the subject he must confine himself to what may be called Governor-Generalities.

John Buchan, Lord Tweedsmuir, served as Governor General from 1935 until his death in 1940. He was a canny Scot with a sense of occasion coupled with a sense of humour. The above remark comes from *Canadian Occasions: Addresses* (1940).

E.J. PRATT   1940

It took the sea a thousand years,
A thousand years to trace
The granite features of this cliff,
In crag and scarp and base.

It took the sea an hour one night,
An hour of storm to place
The sculpture of these granite seams
Upon a woman's face.

E.J. Pratt is the author of the short poem "Erosion" (1932). It appears in Pratt's *The Collected Poems* (2nd ed., 1958), edited by Northrop Frye.

EARLE BIRNEY   1940

I said that he fell straight to the ice where they found him.
And none but the sun and incurious clouds have lingered

Around the marks of that day on the ledge of the Finger,
That day, the last of my youth, on the last of our mountains.

These are the concluding lines of the powerful narrative poem "David" (1940), written by Earle Birney and found in his *Selected Poems* (1966). Controversy surrounded the appearance of the poem on high-school curricula and tests in the 1950s, since it touches on the subject of euthanasia, which is anathema to many religious and other special-interest groups.

N.W. ROWELL 1940

National unity must be based on provincial autonomy, and provincial autonomy cannot be assured unless a strong feeling of national unity exists throughout the country.

This paradoxical statement describes a dominion-provincial or federal-provincial relationship that is fraught with paradox. It comes from the Rowell-Sirois Report, *Report of the Royal Commission on Dominion-Provincial Relations* (1940), chaired by N.W. Rowell.

ADOLF HITLER 1940

In Canada, for example, there are 2.6 persons per square mile; in other countries perhaps 16, 18, 20, or 26 persons. Well, no matter how stupidly one managed one's affairs in such a country, a decent living would still be possible.

This observation on the relation between demographics and economics was made by the German dictator Adolf Hitler in a Berlin speech, Dec. 10, 1940. It was included in *Hitler's Words* (1944), edited by Gordon W. Prange.

SIR WINSTON CHURCHILL 1941

We have not journeyed all this way across the centuries, across the oceans, across the mountains, across the prairies, because we are made of sugar candy. . . . France would have held her place as a nation in the councils of the allies, and not at the conference table of the victors. But their generals misled them. When I warned them that Britain would fight on alone, whatever they did, their generals told their Prime Minister and his divided cabinet, "In three weeks England will have her neck wrung like a chicken." Some chicken! Some neck!

These are two excerpts from one of the most famous speeches associated with World War II. It was delivered in Ottawa by the British Prime Minister Sir Winston Churchill to a joint meeting of the Senate and the House of Commons, Dec. 30, 1941. Shortly afterwards, Churchill sat for Yousuf Karsh's celebrated "bulldog" photographic portrait.

YOUSUF KARSH 1941

I said, "Forgive me, sir," and plucked the cigar out of his mouth. By the time I got back to my camera, he looked so belligerent he could have devoured me. It was at that instant that I took the photograph. The silence was deafening.

The celebrated portrait photographer Yousuf Karsh of Ottawa is recalling how he took the inspired and inspiring "bulldog" photograph of British Prime Minister Sir Winston Churchill in the Speaker's Chambers, House of Commons, Dec. 30, 1941. The widely reproduced photographic portrait boosted morale by symbolizing resistance and no doubt helped substantially to win World War II. Karsh's account comes from *Karsh: A Fifty-Year Retrospective* (1983).

JOHN GILLESPIE MAGEE, JR. 1941

Oh, I have slipped the surly bonds of earth,
And danced the skies on laughter-silvered wings;
Sunward I've climbed and joined the tumbling mirth
Of sun-split clouds—and done a hundred things
You have not dreamed of—wheeled and soared and swung
High in the sunlit silence. Hov'ring there,
I've chased the shouting wind along and flung
My eager craft through footless halls of air.
Up, up the long delirious, burning blue
I've topped the wind-swept heights with easy grace,
Where never lark, or even eagle, flew;
And, while with silent, lifting mind I've trod
The high untrespassed sanctity of space,
Put out my hand and touched the face of God.

This sonnet, entitled "In High Flight," was chosen as the official poem of the Royal Air Force and of the Royal Canadian Air Force. It was written by John Gillespie Magee, Jr., a young American pilot who enlisted in Canada and flew with the RAF's Spitfire Squadron. He died in action on Dec. 11, 1941. The text of the poem, found among his personal effects, was reprinted by John Robert Colombo and Michael Richardson in *We Stand on Guard* (1985).

BRUCE HUTCHISON 1942

No one knows my country, neither the stranger nor its own sons. My country is hidden in the dark and teeming brain of youth upon the eve of its manhood. My country has not found itself nor felt its power nor learned its true place. It is all visions and doubts and hopes and dreams. It is strength and weakness, despair and joy, and the wild confusions and restless strivings of a boy who has passed his boyhood but is not yet a man.

Patriotic prose, the staple of other countries, has been a rarity in

Canada, so when newspaperman Bruce Hutchison wrote dithyrambic paragraphs that encompassed the whole of the land and all its peoples, he found readers anxious to discover the dynamism of their place in the sun. This passage of prose originally appeared in *The Unknown Country: Canada and Her People* (1942), and the book with its panoramas and vignettes of Canadian life sold a great many copies. It is currently out of print; apparently readers in the 1990s are no longer moved by romantic evocations of landscape and national character. Too much water has passed under the bridge for anyone to see Canada in the guise of a gangly adolescent. Perhaps the day of grand prose will return, or perhaps not.

W.L. MACKENZIE KING 1942

If, in reference to the very difficult question of service overseas, anyone can conceive of a policy which is better calculated to serve the national interest than the one the government has formulated, and which is clearly and concisely expressed in the words: "Not necessarily conscription, but conscription if necessary," I shall be the first to advocate its acceptance. . . . Those who oppose on other grounds do not differ fundamentally with the policy of the government with respect to service overseas: "Not necessarily conscription, but conscription if necesary."

W.L. Mackenzie King, ever the artful dodger, employed the seven words in quotation marks and repeated them like a mantra to cool the Conscription Crisis of World War II. His remarks come from his address on the National Resources Mobilization Act, House of Commons, July 7, 1942. His formulation is elastic to the point of being plastic. It is now believed that the phraseology originated in an unsigned editorial titled "Mr. King on Conscription" in *The Toronto Star*, June 11, 1942. The anonymous editorial writer argued as follows: "But the government says enough are coming forward; that enough may continue to come forward, and that conscription for overseas duty, which it is willing to impose if necessary, may never be necessary at all." According to writer David MacDonald, the wording of this passage was drawn to King's attention by his adviser J.S. (Jack) Pickersgill, and King eagerly adapted it to his own purposes.

J.H. ROBERTS 1942

Very heavy casualties in men and ships. Did everything possible to get men off but in order to get any home had to come to sad decision to abandon remainder. This was joint decision by Force Commanders. Obviously operation completely lacked surprise.

An Allied force of 4,963 Canadian soldiers of the 2nd Canadian Infantry Division and more than 1,000 British commandos launched a large-scale raid on the German-occupied stronghold at the northern France seaport of Dieppe, Aug. 19, 1942. In their first fighting the Canadians suffered 3,367 casualties, the Germans 333. The communication from Major-General J.H. Roberts was conveyed by pigeon to the 1st Canadian Corps Headquarters. It appeared in *Official History of the Canadian Army in the Second World War: Volume 1* (1955), by C.P. Stacey.

ARTHUR MEIGHEN 1942

Whether now judged right or wrong, whatever I have said, whatever I have done, is going to remain unrevised and unrepented. As it is, it will await whatever verdict may come.

Arthur Meighen, who served as Prime Minister in 1920-21 and for a few months in 1926, is identified with the uncompromising phrase "unrevised and unrepented." The passage comes from an address he delivered to the Conservative Party in Winnipeg, Dec. 9, 1942, which Meighen included in his suitably titled memoirs, *Unrevised and Unrepented* (1949).

JOSEPH GOEBBELS 1943

I also inspected a bombed-out hospital in Luetzow Street. Several corpses were just being carried out—a touching picture. One of the nurses killed was an air-raid warden. It drives one mad to think that any old Canadian boor, who probably can't even find Europe on the globe, flies to Europe from his super-rich country, which his people don't know how to exploit, and here bombards a continent with a crowded population. But let's hope we can soon deliver the proper reply.

This is one view of Allied intervention in Europe as expressed by Joseph Goebbels, Nazi leader and German Minister of Propaganda; diary entry, Feb.-March 1943, *The Goebbels Diaries* (1948), edited and translated by Louis P. Lochner.

A.M. KLEIN 1944

They are upon us, the prophets, minor and major!
Madame Yolanda rubs the foggy crystal.
She peers, she ponders, the future does engage her;
She sees the *Fuehrer* purged by Nazi pistol.

These are the opening lines of the poem "Psalm XXV," from *Poems* (1944), written by the Montreal poet A.M. Klein. The lines not only refer to prophecy, they even constitute a prophecy—two prophecies, in fact. They foretell the demise of Adolf Hitler, the Nazi *Fuehrer* and they foresee the manner of his death. Hitler shot himself with his own "Nazi pistol" on April 30, 1945. Klein probably wrote "Psalm XXV" in 1940; it was accepted for publication on Nov. 18, 1940 and first appeared in print in the magazine *Opinion*, Oct. 1941.

JACK MINER 1944

I know of no bird or animal that can equal the Canada Goose for getting well after being wounded. It is said that a cat has nine lives;

if that is true, the Canada Goose has at least eighteen, nine on each side of the border.

Jack Miner, the leading naturalist and conservationist of his day, was a self-taught ornithologist. In 1904, he opened a bird sanctuary at Kingsville, Ont., and he operated it until his death forty years later. Miner's observations on animal and human nature were so widely quoted for so many years that many of his statements (including the one above) have no known source.

PIERRE ELLIOTT TRUDEAU   1944

What sets a canoeing expedition apart is that it purifies you more rapidly and inescapably than any other. Travel a thousand miles by train and you are a brute; pedal five hundred on a bicycle and you remain basically a bourgeois; paddle a hundred in a canoe and you are already a child of nature.

This exceptional passage comes from an even more exceptional essay written by a most exceptional man, Pierre Elliott Trudeau. The future Prime Minister was only twenty-five when he penned the personal essay "Exhaustion and Fulfilment: The Ascetic in a Canoe" (1944), which was translated and included in *Wilderness Canada* (1970), edited by Borden Spears. Trudeau is known to be an expert canoeist.

HENRY A. LARSEN   1944

On September 27 we passed through the Bering Strait and docked in Vancouver on October 16, at 6:00 P.M. Behind us were 7,295 nautical miles, which we had covered in eighty-six days! There was nobody to meet us at the wharf. Canada was still at war and had no time for frivolous things.

Sergeant Henry A. Larsen, Captain of the RCMP vessel *St. Roch*, completed his return voyage through the fabled Northwest Passage in Oct. 1944. The eastern passage he had completed two years earlier, Sept. 1942. There was fanfare for neither event, as he noted in his autobiography, *The Big Ship* (1946), written with Frank R. Sheer and Edvard Omholt-Jensen.

W.L. MACKENZIE KING 1944

Over and over again, I have thought . . . that some day the world will know some of the things that I have prevented. . . . I must make increasingly clear to the world that prevention of wrong courses of evil and the like means more than all else that man can accomplish.

This admission was made by Prime Minister W.L. Mackenzie King in his diary on Dec. 8, 1944. It appears in *The Mackenzie King Record: Volume 2* (1968), edited by J.W. Pickersgill and D.F. Forster.

C.D. HOWE 1945

What's a million?

This catch-phrase is identified with C.D. Howe, who served as "Minister of Everything" in the Cabinets of Mackenzie King and St. Laurent. Howe never uttered these words. Howe may have been a pragmatist as well as a parliamentarian, but he was also a disciplinarian when it came to expenditures. He defended a review of budget estimates in the House of Commons on Nov. 19, 1945, with these words: "I daresay my honourable friend could cut a million dollars from this amount; but a million dollars from the war appropriation bill would not be a very important matter." The bill in question called for the expenditure of $1,365 million. The following day, John G. Diefenbaker, then a Conservative back-bencher, rose in the House of Commons and deliberately mis-quoted Howe. Diefenbaker claimed that Howe had said, "We may save a million dollars, but what of that?" Howe was outraged, but the pattern was set. Thereafter, the "Minister of Everything" was known as C.D. ("What's a million?") Howe.

F.R. SCOTT 1945

O Canada, O Canada, Oh can
A day go by without new authors springing
To plant the native maple, and to plan
More ways to set the selfsame welkin ringing?

F.R. Scott, poet and satirist, "The Canadian Authors Meet" (1945), *Selected Poems* (1966). The poem is a not-too-veiled satire on members of the Canadian Authors Association, which was founded in 1921 and is still going strong.

HUGH MACLENNAN 1945

Two solitudes.

The words "two solitudes" were introduced into intellectual discourse to refer to the mutual isolation of the French and English in Montreal, in Quebec, and in Canada, by the novelist and essayist Hugh MacLennan in his novel *Two Solitudes* (1945), which is set amid both communities in Montreal. MacLennan took the phrase from the German poet Rainer Maria Rilke, who introduced it into a letter written May 14, 1904, which appears in *Letters to a Young Poet* (1934), translated by M.D. Herter Norton. Rilke wrote about "the love that consists in this, that two solitudes protect and touch and greet each other." MacLennan discussed the phrase at least twice. In an essay in *Century 1867-1967* (1967), he wrote, "Our old division into two solitudes now seems to me to have been a blessing in disguise. It makes uniformity impossible in Canada. What lacked in the past was love and mutual respect.

What must come in the future—it is coming now, as a matter of fact—is affection and understanding." In an essay in *Maclean's,* Aug. 1971, he argued that Rilke's phrase is "surely the best practical definition of love ever uttered, whether applied to individuals or to two nations sharing a single state." It is difficult to imagine a time when the phrase will not be applicable to Canadian dualism.

A.R.M. LOWER 1946

In every generation Canadians have had to rework the miracle of their political existence. Canada has been created because there has existed within the hearts of its people a determination to build for themselves an enduring home. Canada is a supreme act of faith.

These lines come from A.R.M. Lower's popular yet scholarly history text, *Colony to Nation* (1946, 1964). A distinguished historian and a well-loved teacher at Queen's University, Kingston, Lower had a knack of finding the proper formulation for not only the facts but also the feelings of the subject at hand.

DREW PEARSON 1946

This is Drew Pearson with a flash from Washington. Canada's Prime Minister Mackenzie King has informed President Truman of a very serious situation affecting our relations with Russia. A Soviet agent surrendered some time ago to Canadian authorities and confessed to a gigantic Russian espionage network inside the United States.

Drew Pearson, the American broadcaster, broke the story of the defection of Igor Gouzenko on his radio program, Feb. 3, 1946. This occurred five months after the Soviet cipher clerk left the Russian Embassy in Ottawa with incriminating evidence of a Soviet spy network. Mackenzie King's government could not bring itself to release the information, according to June Callwood in *Emma* (1984).

HARRY S. TRUMAN 1947

Canada and the United States have reached the point where we no longer think of each other as "foreign" countries. We think of each other as friends, as peaceful and co-operative neighbours on a spacious and fruitful continent.

Harry S. Truman, U.S. President, addressing a joint meeting of the Senate and the House of Commons, June 11, 1947. Most Americans do indeed regard Canadians as neighbours rather than foreigners.

MORRIS C. SHUMIATCHER 1947

Every person and every class of persons shall enjoy the right to obtain and retain employment without discrimination with respect to the compensation, terms, conditions or privileges of employment because of the race, creed, religion, colour or ethnic or national origin of such person or class of persons.

This is one section of the Saskatchewan Bill of Rights Act, 1947, which became law in Saskatchewan on April 1, 1947. Other sections of the Act addressed the matter of discrimination in relation to land ownership, education, and religion. The Saskatchewan Bill of Rights preceded the United Nations' Universal Declaration of Human Rights by one full year; Diefenbaker's Canadian Bill of Rights by thirteen years; and the Canadian Charter of Rights and Freedoms by thirty-five years. Saskatchwan's Bill of Rights was the work of the Regina lawyer Morris C. Shumiatcher who, when counsel to T.C. Douglas, Premier of Saskatchewan, persuaded Attorney-General J.W. Corman to introduce the Bill in the Legislative Assembly, where it was debated briefly and passed unanimously. With some amendments over the years, it has remained a vital part of the annals and the law of Saskatchewan. Essential elements of the Bill have since been adopted by other provinces of Canada.

JOHN HUMPHREY 1948

It turns out the achievement of 1948 was much greater than anybody would have dared to imagine at the time.

The Canadian constitutional expert John Humphrey served as the United Nations' first Director of Human Rights and was the principal architect of the Universal Declaration of Human Rights, adopted by the U.N. on Dec. 10, 1948. He made the above remark at the U.N. headquarters in New York at a celebration to mark its fortieth anniversary, according to *The Toronto Star*, Dec. 9, 1988.

ARNOLD J. TOYNBEE 1948

Whatever the future of mankind in North America, I feel pretty confident that these French-speaking Canadians, at any rate, will be there at the end of the story.

Arnold J. Toynbee, the influential British historian, specialized in writing about great historical cycles. He made this prediction in *Civilization on Trial* (1948).

HAROLD ADAMS INNIS 1948

Canadian nationalism was systematically encouraged and exploited by American capital. Canada moved from colony to nation to colony.

The economist and historian Harold Adams Innis expressed this insight in the essay "Great Britain, the United States and Canada" (1948), included in *Essays in Canadian Economic History* (1956), edited by Mary Quayle Innis. Innis died in 1952; ten years later his description of the "neo-colonial" status of Canada had become something of a cliché.

DOUGLAS LEPAN 1948

You hesitate. The trees are entangled with menace.
The voyage is perilous into the dark interior.
But then your hands go to the thwarts. You smile. And so
I watch you vanish in a wood of heroes,
Wild Hamlet with the features of Horatio.

These are the last lines, and widely quoted ones at that, of the fine poem "Coureur de Bois" (1948), from *The Wounded Prince and Other Poems* (1948), written by the poet and essayist Douglas LePan. The lines may be otherwise interpreted, but they might suggest that behind the bland exterior characteristic of Canadians there lies an interior that is close to the world of nature and close to the heart of the native.

JAMES HOUSTON 1948

These Arctic carvings are not the cold sculptures of a frozen world. Instead, they reveal to us the passionate feelings of a vital people well aware of all the joys, terrors, tranquility, and wildness of life around them.

James Houston, artist and civil administrator for the Department of Northern Affairs from 1948 to 1962, encouraged the co-operative production of Eskimo soapstone sculpture and introduced printmaking to the Inuit on Baffin Island. Houston's remark was quoted by George Swinton in *Sculpture of the Inuit* (1971).

LISTER SINCLAIR 1948

"But we all hate Toronto."
"That's just it. We *all* hate Toronto! It's the only thing everybody's got in common."

Toronto appeared to be something of a spectre to the rest of the country in the late 1940s and 1950s. Lister Sinclair, the radio personality, caught this well in his CBC Radio play "We All Hate Toronto" (1946), which was included in *A Play on Words and Other Radio Plays* (1948). The tide of opinion began to abate in the 1960s, when Toronto became the New City, and ebbed when the recession of the late 1980s took hold.

LOUIS ST. LAURENT 1948

A small power is in a sense by its very smallness relieved from much of the responsibility which participation in decisions involves, and which the implementation of such decisions requires. At the other extreme the great powers can protect their positions with the veto. A "middle power" such as Canada, however, is in a different position. Its economic strength and political influence are of importance, and its prestige is high. The material and moral contribution which Canada can make to collective action, as the last two wars have shown, is significant.

This is an early use of the phrase "middle powers," which defined Canada's rank in world influence following World War II. Louis St. Laurent, then Secretary of State, employed the phrase on April 29, 1948, in a speech in the House of Commons concerning Canada's seat at the Security Council of the United Nations.

LOUIS ST. LAURENT 1948

Without sacrificing the universality of the United Nations, it is possible for the free nations of the world to form their own closer association for collective self-defence under article 51 of the charter of the United Nations . . . the formation of such a defensive group of free states would not be a counsel of despair but a message of hope.

On April 4, 1949, Canada and eleven other countries signed the treaty that established the North Atlantic Treaty Organization

149

(NATO) for collective security and mutual defence. As Secretary of State, Louis St. Laurent spoke on its behalf in the House of Commons, April 29, 1948.

LOUIS ST. LAURENT 1948

I didn't know at first that there were two languages in Canada. I just thought that there was one way to speak to my father and another to talk to my mother.

Louis St. Laurent, Prime Minister from 1948 to 1957, was a corporate lawyer who was dubbed "Uncle Louie" for his avuncular manner. He had a French father and an Engish mother and was fluently bilingual.

PAUL-EMILE BORDUAS 1948

Make way for magic! Make way for objective mystery! Make way for love! Make way for what is needed!

These are some lines from the artistic manifesto *Refus Global* (Global Refusal), which was released and distributed in Montreal on Aug. 9, 1948. The manifesto in favour of artistic and imaginative freedom was largely written by the painter Paul-Emile Borduas.

PERCY BENGOUGH 1949

Co-operation, Yes. Domination, No!

This celebrated statement of Canadian labour sovereignty is identified with Percy Bengough, who was President of the Trades and Labor Congress at the time when the American Federation of Labor was attempting to disenfranchise the TLC's Canadian members,

March 1949; quoted by Charles Lipton in *The Trade Union Movement in Canada* (1967).

LOUIS ST. LAURENT 1949

Socialists are Liberals in a hurry.

This aphorism was used in a speech by Prime Minister Louis St. Laurent, as reported in April 1949, according to Dale C. Thomson in *Louis St. Laurent* (1967). It was not entirely original, since the phrase "Liberals in a hurry" had been used in 1926 to refer to those Progressives and Liberal-Progressives in the House of Commons who joined the Liberal Party in 1926.

J.R. (JOEY) SMALLWOOD 1949

The only thing wrong with Confederation is that we didn't join in 1867.

J.R. (Joey) Smallwood became the first Premier of Newfoundland when the country that he loved so much—he called it "this poor bald rock"—joined Confederation on April 1, 1949. He was quoted by Richard Gwyn in *Smallwood: The Unlikely Revolutionary* (1968).

JOSEPH CHARBONNEAU 1949

We want social peace but we don't want the crushing of the working class. We are attached to man more than to capital. That's why the clergy has decided to intervene. It wants to have justice and charity respected and desires that there shall cease to be a situation where more attention is paid to money interests than to the human element.

Monseigneur Joseph Charbonnneau, Archbishop of Montreal, de-livered a controversial sermon at Notre-Dame Cathedral, Montreal,

Sunday, May 2, 1949. It supported the striking workers at Asbestos, Que. It was quoted by Charles Lipton in *The Trade Union Movement in Canada* (1967).

JAY SILVERHEELS 1949

Kemo Sabe

This catch-phrase is forever associated with Jay Silverheels. The Indian athlete and actor was born Harry Smith on the Six Nations Reserve. In Hollywood he changed his name to Jay Silverheels and played the Lone Ranger's "faithful Indian companion Tonto" in countless radio, movie, and television productions between 1949 and 1958. It seemed he was always saying, "Yes, Kemo Sabe." Dick Brown, in *The Canadian*, Aug. 9, 1975, quoted Silverheels as explaining, "Kemo Sabe. Good friend. . . . Actually, I never did find out what it really means." It may be pidgin Spanish for "don't understand," though David Rothel in *Who Was that Masked Man?* (1976) maintained the words mean "trusty scout" and were derived from the name of a boy's camp at Mullet Lake, Michigan. A younger generation prized Tonto's contribution to popular culture but complained that his roles were as stereotypical as those of Aunt Jemimah and Stefin Fetchit. The following joke made the rounds in the 1960s: "They're surrounding us," said the Lone Ranger, pointing to a band of hostile Indians. "What do you mean *us?*" replied Tonto.

JOHN DRAINIE 1949

The same as before—just the same—the long, magnificent delirious swoop of dizziness . . . the Great Circle . . . the swift pathway to Arcturus. All as before but now infinitely more rapid. Never have I had such speed. Beyond the Moon and past the North Star in a twinkling, swooping in a long bright curve round the Pleiades. . . . Hello, there, old Betelgeuse,

I'm off to the little blue star that points the way to the unknown. Forward into the untrodden.

These lines come from the radio play "Mr. Arcularis" and they were read with extraordinary feeling by the veteran actor John Drainie. "Mr. Arcularis," based on the short story by Conrad Aiken, was adapted for radio by Gerald Noxon. Produced for CBC Radio's "Stage" series by Andrew Allan, it was first broadcast on Nov. 18, 1949. It is the story of an elderly man whose path to death takes him across the heavens. The production is considered a jewel in the crown of CBC Radio drama.

J.S. WOODSWORTH 1950

I am no longer interested in the Heaven above. I believe it is the duty of the CCF to make a Kingdom of Heaven on earth.

This was the credo adopted in his mature years by J.S. Woodsworth, leader of the Co-operative Commonwealth Federation. The sentences come from an address delivered in April 1950, as quoted by Ivan Avakumovic in *Socialism in Canada* (1978).

ANDREI GROMYKO & A.G.L. MCNAUGHTON 1950s

GROMYKO: What Canadian apples do you recommend?
McNAUGHTON: McIntosh Reds and Northern Spies.

It is said that this exchange took place at the United Nations in New York between Soviet Ambassador Andrei Gromyko and the Canadian Ambassador A.G.L. McNaughton at the height of the Cold War in the 1950s.

FOLK SONG 1950s

I'se the b'y that builds the boat,
And I'se the b'y that sails her!

I'se the b'y that catches the fish
And takes 'em home to Lizer.

This is the first verse of "I'se the B'y," a very popular Newfoundland song, one that is well-known across Canada. In the 1950s, it was sung and recorded by the Leslie Bell Singers.

C.D. HOWE 1951

Who would stop us? Don't take yourself too seriously. If we wanted to get away with it who would stop us?

At one time "Who would stop us?" was a catch-phrase that epitomized the arrogant use of political power in the House of Commons by the Liberal Party. The words come from a debate in the House of Commons, May 21, 1951, between the powerful cabinet minister C.D. Howe and the Opposition critic Howard Green. The Conservative Party eventually stopped Howe and the Liberals in their tracks.

CHARLOTTE WHITTON 1951

Whatever women do they must do twice as well as men to be thought half so good . . . luckily, it's not difficult.

Charlotte Whitton was the first woman to serve as the mayor of a Canadian city. The outspoken Whitton was Mayor of Ottawa in 1951-56 and 1960-64. Salty remarks peppered her speech; not for nothing did *Reader's Digest* call her "hell on wheels."

VINCENT MASSEY 1951

Canadian achievement in every field depends mainly on the quality of the Canadian mind and spirit. This quality is determined by what Canadians think, and think about; by the books they read, the pictures

154

they see and the programmes they hear. These things, whether we call them arts and letters or use other words to describe them, we believe to lie at the roots of our life as a nation.

The Massey Report was titled *Report of the Royal Commission on National Development in the Arts, Letters and Sciences, 1949-51* (1951). The Commission was headed by Vincent Massey, later Governor General. Its Report led to the formation of the Canada Council in 1957.

B.K. SANDWELL 1952

Let the Old World, where rank's yet vital,
Part those who have and have not title.
Toronto has no social classes—
Only the Masseys and the masses.

B.K. Sandwell was the editor of *Saturday Night* when he was moved to compose this ditty, which he titled "On the Appointment of Governor-General Vincent Massey, 1952." It was generally felt that members of the wealthy Massey family, especially Vincent and his actor brother Raymond, "put on airs." The ditty appeared in *The Blasted Pine* (1957), edited by F.R. Scott and A.J.M. Smith.

BRUCE HUTCHISON 1952

The mystery of William Lyon Mackenzie King is not the mystery of a man. It is the mystery of a people. We do not understand King because we do not understand ourselves.

Bruce Hutchison, newspaperman, came to this conclusion after writing *The Incredible Canadian* (1952), his biographical study of Prime Minister Mackenzie King. Earlier, in 1948, historian F.H. Underhill had maintained of King: "He has been the representative

Canadian, the typical Canadian, the essential Canadian, the ideal Canadian, the Canadian as he exists in the mind of God." In later years the historian C.P. Stacey was able to show from King's diaries that the "ideal Canadian" was a man for the ages . . . especially the New Age, because of his spiritualistic practices.

C.L. BURTON 1952

Life, if you have a bent for it, is a beautiful thing. It consists, I do believe, of having a sense of urgency.

C.L. Burton was Chairman of The Robert Simpson Co. Ltd. He expressed his views in his memoir titled, fittingly, *A Sense of Urgency* (1952).

CONN SMYTHE 1952

If you can't lick 'em in the alley, you can't beat 'em on the ice.

This is one of the most widely quoted maxims of professional hockey. It has been used to justify both manly qualities and hockey violence. It was first recorded in an interview with hockey personality Conn Smythe conducted by Trent Frayne in 1952. Smythe backtracked somewhat for Bob Pennington of *The Toronto Star*, Oct. 1, 1973: "I did not mean that you scare the other guy but that you show him there is no fear in you."

E.W.R. STEACIE 1952

An efficient organization is one in which the accounting department knows the exact cost of every useless administrative procedure which they themselves have initiated.

The distinguished chemist E.W.R. Steacie was appointed President of the National Research Council in 1952. He exerted an immense influence on national science policy. J.D. Babbitt, editor of Steacie's *Science in Canada* (1965), quoted this observation and dated it 1952.

W.A.C. BENNETT 1952

I'm plugged into God.

This is the most characteristic remark attributed to the controversial and quotable W.A.C. Bennett, who served as Premier of British Columbia from 1952 to 1972. Bennett never uttered these words, although millions of people believe that he did. According to Roger Keene, writing in *Conversations with W.A.C. Bennett* (1980), the Premier, wanting to demonstrate the nature of power to a reporter, plugged in an electric lightbulb and explained, "You see, when I plug it in, the light will come on again. That law has always been there. It's not new." The demonstration led an editorial writer at *The Toronto Star* to compose the following headline: "Bennett Plugged into God." Thereafter, the "I'm plugged into God" label stuck to him.

IRVING LAYTON 1953

Death is a name for beauty not in use.

This lovely line was written by the poet Irving Layton and comes from the poem "Composition in Late Spring" (1953), which appears in *The Collected Poems of Irving Layton* (1971).

JOHN G. DIEFENBAKER 1953

As Prince Albert goes, so goes the nation.

This statement is something of a political truism. Prince Albert has become the bellwether in Canadian politics, playing the same role that the Illinois town of Peoria plays in American politics. The aphorism is attributed to John G. Diefenbaker, who represented the

Prince Albert constituency in the House of Commons from 1953 to 1979. Prince Albert has been represented in the House of Commons by three Prime Ministers: Wilfrid Laurier, Mackenzie King, John Diefenbaker.

WILLIAM SHAKESPEARE 1953

Now is the winter of our discontent
Made glorious summer by this sun of York.

These were the first words to be recited from the open stage of the Stratford Shakespearian Festival on the evening of July 13, 1953, with the premiere of William Shakespeare's *The Tragedy of King Richard III* (c. 1594). The lines were recited by Alec Guinness in the title role under the direction of Tyrone Guthrie. A Shakespearian festival in Ontario's Stratford was the brain-child of journalist Tom Patterson, and to everyone's surprise, it came to pass. Drama critic Herbert Whittaker declared, "July 13, 1953, was the most exciting night in the history of Canadian theatre." How does the New World fare in Shakespeare's dramatic works? There is a reference to it in *The Comedy of Errors* (c. 1591): "Where America, the Indies?" The North Pole is the subject of a pun in *Love's Labour's Lost* (c. 1594): "By the north pole, I do challenge thee. I will not fight with a pole, like a northern man: I'll slash; I'll do it by the sword." An allusion to the Northwest Passage occurs in *Hamlet* (c. 1601): "I am mad north-north-west; when the wind is southerly, I know a hawk from a handsaw."

DWIGHT D. EISENHOWER 1953

Defensively, as well as geographically, we are joined beyond any possibility of separation.

Dwight D. Eisenhower, U.S. President, addressing a joint sitting of the Senate and the House of Commons, Nov. 14, 1953.

ALLAN LAMPORT 1954

If somebody's gonna stab me in the back, I wanna be there.

This celebrated remark originated with Allan Lamport, Mayor of Toronto, 1952-54. For his malapropisms, Lamport has been called "Metro's Goldwyn Mayor," as noted by John Robert Colombo in *Quotations from Chairman Lamport* (1990). Here are some other "lampys": "Why, I even went so far as to be fair!" "I'm lost, but I'm making record time," "Toronto is a city of the future and always will be."

F.R. SCOTT 1954

The advantages of living with two cultures
Strike one at every turn,
Especially when one finds a notice in an office building:
"This elevator will not run on Ascension Day";
Or reads in the *Montreal Star:*
"Tomorrow being the Feast of the Immaculate Conception,
There will be no collection of garbage in the city";
Or sees on the restaurant menu the bilingual dish:

DEEP APPLE PIE

TARTE AUX POMMES PROFONDES

Satire is sometimes the only way to deal with deep divisions and simplistic attempts to bridge them. Satire was the special talent of F.R. Scott, poet and expert on constitutional law. This classic poem, titled "Bonne Entente" (1954), appears in Scott's *Selected Poems* (1966).

REUBEN SHIP 1954

The Investigator took a deep breath before speaking. "In all humility I dedicate myself to the task of bringing to light the facts of their monstrous conspiracy that threatens our way of life Up Here. I shall pursue this objective, relentlessly, disregarding all attempts at intimidation by persons in high places who may be implicated by these facts; and I shall not cease until I have fixed the blame for a thousand years of treason!"

One of the highlights of CBC Radio's famed "Stage" series was its production of *The Investigator*, a satire on the anti-Communist "political witchhunt" initiated by U.S. Senator Joseph McCarthy. Based on an original script written by Reuben Ship, directed by Andrew Allan, it was broadcast May 30, 1954. It starred actor John Drainie as the unnamed demagogue. The production elicited U.S. congressional disapproval followed by Canadian parliamentary "questions." A bootleg album was sold in the United States; for a British publisher, Ship novelized the script as *The Investigator: A Narrative in Dialogue* (1956).

MARILYN BELL 1954

I did it for Canada!

Marilyn Bell, a sixteen-year-old marathon swimmer, became the first person to swim Lake Ontario, Sept. 9, 1954. It took her 20 hours and 59 minutes to cover 51 kilometres of choppy water. Bell's explanation was echoed by marathon swimmer Cindy Nicholas when she swam across the English Channel, Aug. 7, 1975. Nicholas boasted, "I really did it for Canada."

J. SCOTT FEGGANS 1955

It's mainly because of the meat.

For at least two decades the slogan of Dominion Stores was kept before the eyes and ears of the buying public. An advertising campaign that focused on the supermarket's values in meat was devised in 1955 by J. Scott Feggans, the chain's head of advertising, who maintained that the words came to him one night and that the following morning he wrote them down on the back of the proverbial envelope, according to an article in *The Toronto Star*, Aug. 9, 1975. Robert Henry Hahn composed the catchy tune for the jingle's use on radio and television.

C.P. STACEY 1955

Canada is an unmilitary community. Warlike her people have often been forced to be; military they have never been.

These are the opening sentences of the *Official History of the Canadian Army in the Second World War, Volume 1* (1955), written by the military historian C.P. Stacey.

GEORGE DREW 1956

Now that the trained seals are silent. . . .

George Drew, Leader of the Opposition, referred to those Government Members of Parliament who submitted to party discipline as "trained seals." This was during the Pipeline Debate in the House of Commons, May 15, 1956. "Trained seals" are presumably the opposite of "loose fish," Sir John A. Macdonald's phrase for undisciplined members of one's own party. Both Prime Minister Trudeau and Premier Lévesque referred to members of the press as "trained seals" in 1977. Two years later, René Lévesque described those francophones who lived outside the Province of Quebec as "dead ducks." Novelist Yves Beauchemin, in his presentation to the Bélanger-Campeau Commission on the Future of Quebec in Nov. 1990, added a new ethnic slur: "French Canadians who live outside Quebec are still-warm corpses."

HANS SELYE 1956

> Stress is the state manifested by a specific syndrome which consists of all
> the nonspecifically induced changes within a biologic system.

This definition of stress was developed by the endocrinologist Hans
Selye, who founded the Institute of Experimental Medicine and
Surgery at the University of Montreal in 1945 and continued as its
director until his retirement in 1976. The definition above comes from
his book *The Stress of Life* (1956). A simpler definition also appears
in the book: "Stress is essentially the rate of all the wear and tear
caused by life."

HUMPHRY OSMOND 1956

> To make this mundane world sublime,
> Take half a gram of phanerothyme.
> To sink in Hell or soar angelic,
> You'll need a pinch of psychedelic.

This ditty was composed by Dr. Humphry Osmond, who coined
the word *psychedelic* to refer to "mind-expanding" drugs in 1956.
At the time he was Director of Psychiatric Research, Department
of Public Health, Saskatoon, Sask. Osmond introduced LSD to
Aldous Huxley, but the California-based novelist took a dislike
to the word *psychedelic,* preferring his own word *phanerothyme,*
which means "to reveal the soul." Details appear in Huxley's
Moksha: Writings on Psychedelics and the Visionary Experience
(1977), edited by Michael Horowitz and Cynthia Palmer. LSD
guru Timothy Leary liked to quote Marshall McLuhan's ditty:
"Lysergic acid hits the spot. / Forty billion neurons, that's a lot."
Psychedelic is the most widely known adjective of Canadian
origin.

WOODY GUTHRIE & MARTIN BOCHNER 1956

This land is your land, this land is my land,
From Bona Vista to Vancouver Island,
From the Arctic Islands to the Great Lakes waters;
This land was made for you and me.

"This Land Is Your Land" is one of the most widely sung of modern folk songs. It was written in 1956 by the American singer and songwriter Woody Guthrie; shortly afterwards, with the composer's blessing, Martin Bochner adapted the lyrics for the Toronto-based folk group The Travellers. The original refrain runs: "From California to the New York Island, / From the redwood forest to the Gulf-stream waters." There are now versions suitable for singing in many countries of the world.

F.R. SCOTT 1957

He skilfully avoided what was wrong
Without saying what was right,
And never let his on the one hand
Know what his on the other hand was doing.

In these well-chosen words, F.R. Scott offered a psychological and political profile of Prime Minister W.L. Mackenzie King. He did so in the satiric poem "W.L.M.K." (1957), which appears in Scott's *Selected Poems* (1966). In 1974, fellow poet Dennis Lee rhymed: "William Lyon Mackenzie King / Sat in the middle & played with string / And he loved his mother like *any*thing— / William Lyon Mackenzie King."

ROBERTSON DAVIES 1957

There is more to marriage than four bare legs under a blanket.

This happy line comes from *Love and Libel* (1957), Robertson Davies's stage adaptation of his novel *Leaven of Malice* (1954).

ROY THOMSON 1957

A TV licence is a licence to print money.

This statement is known around the world, or wherever there is television, and its currency gave Roy Thomson, Lord Thomson of Fleet, some pleasure and much notoriety. He made the observation as a boast to fellow businessmen after his company, Scottish Television Limited, based in Edinburgh, Scotland, was awarded the coveted licence to operate a national television service, June 19, 1957. Thomson remarked in his memoirs, *After I Was Sixty* (1975), "Perhaps this remark was injudicious but it was certainly right." When he visited China, he met Chou En-lai who inquired, "Is it not true, then, that you had a licence to print money?"

JOHN G. DIEFENBAKER 1957

My fellow Canadians....

With these words John G. Diefenbaker, who served as Prime Minister of Canada from 1957 to 1963, began many of his speeches to the people of Canada.

GEORGE R. PEARKES 1957

I now have the pleasure of unveiling the Avro Arrow—Canada's first supersonic aircraft—a symbol of a new era for Canada in the air.

So spoke George R. Pearkes, Minister of National Defence, addressing twelve thousand spectators at the "official roll-out" of the Avro Arrow, Malton, Ont., Oct. 4, 1957, as quoted by Richard Organ *et al.* in *Avro Arrow* (1980). The event was marred by an eerie coincidence. The advanced jet fighter plane designed and built by the A.V. Roe Company was unveiled the very day the Soviet Union launched its Sputnik satellite!

LESTER B. PEARSON 1957

> The grim fact, however, is that we prepare for war like precocious giants and for peace like retarded pygmies.

Lester B. Pearson, former President of the United Nations General Assembly and future Prime Minister of Canada, was awarded the Nobel Prize for Peace in Oslo, Norway, Dec. 11, 1957. The text of the address he delivered on that occasion appeared in *The Four Faces of Peace and the International Outlook* (1964), edited by Sherleigh G. Pierson.

JOHN G. DIEFENBAKER 1958

> One Canada, one Canada where Canadians will have preserved to them the control of their own economic and political destiny. Sir John A. Macdonald gave his life to this party. He opened the west. He saw Canada from east to west. I see a new Canada—a Canada of the North!

Prime Minister John G. Diefenbaker, elected in 1957, called an election for the following year and delivered rousing campaign speeches on two subjects, "One Canada" and the "Northern Vision." This passage comes from his address in Winnipeg, Man., Feb. 12, 1958.

JOHN G. DIEFENBAKER 1958

> I am the first prime minister of this country of neither altogether English nor French origin. So I determined to bring about a Canadian citizenship that knew no hyphenated consideration.

Prime Minister John G. Diefenbaker boasted of his German ancestry and gave special recognition to the national contributions of people of other than British and French extraction. The "hyphenated consideration" comes from an interview with him conducted by Jeannine Locke in *Maclean's*, March 29, 1958.

JOHNNY WAYNE & FRANK SHUSTER 1958

> If I told him once, I told him a thousand times, I said, "Julie, don't go!"

The comedy team of Johnny Wayne and Frank Shuster began in radio and switched to television. The team achieved its widest audience by appearing a record fifty-eight times on "The Ed Sullivan Show." They performed their fondly remembered "Julius Caesar skit" on Sullivan's popular weekly show on May 4, 1958. The line above was spoken by Sylvia Lennick.

BOARD OF BROADCAST GOVERNORS 1958

> Canadian content.

The concept of "Canadian content" goes back to the Broadcasting Act of 1958, which established the Board of Broadcast Governors; the chairman was broadcaster Andrew Stewart. The act required the BBG to ensure that all radio and television be "basically Canadian in content and character." The BBG ruled that all TV stations be required to telecast a minimum of "45% Canadian content" as of April 1, 1961, and that by April Fool's Day of the following year there was to be "55% Canadian content." The public broadcasters (CBC Radio and TV) met the "Canadian content" regulations, but the private broadcasters, regarding them as "guidelines," paid them lip service—and continue to do so to the present day.

SELWYN DEWDNEY 1958

> I stared. A huge animal with crested back and horned head. There was no mistaking him. And there, a man on a horse—and there four suns—and

there, canoes. I felt the shivers coursing my back from nape to tail—the Schoolcraft site! Inscription Rock! My fourteen months' search was over.

The revival of interest in the continuing or enduring tradition of native art may be dated from the summer of 1958, when art instructor Selwyn Dewdney located the fabled Agawa Site of "rock art" in northwestern Ontario. It had been described a century earlier by Indian agent H.R. Schoolcraft. Two years later, in 1960, in Beardmore, Ont., Dewdney gave painting supplies to a fledgling native artist—Norval Morrisseau. Dewdney's description of the Agawa Site, now a major tourist attraction, appeared in *Indian Rock Paintings of the Great Lakes* (1967).

EWAN MACCOLL & PEGGY SEEGER 1958

In the town of Springhill, Nova Scotia,
Down in the dark of the Cumberland Mine,
There's blood on the coal and the miners lie,
In roads that never saw sun nor sky,
Roads that never saw sun nor sky.

The Springhill Mine in Nova Scotia, the deepest mine in North America, collapsed on Oct. 23, 1958, crushing seventy-four miners. So moved were the Anglo-American folksingers Ewan MacColl and Peggy Seeger that they composed their ballad "The Springhill Mining Disaster" with its deeply moving lines.

PIERRE ELLIOTT TRUDEAU 1958

French Canadians are perhaps the only people in the world who "enjoy" democracy without having had to fight for it.

This observation was made by Pierre Elliott Trudeau, professor, intellectual, and future Prime Minister, in his essay "Some Obstacles to Democracy in Quebec" (1958), in *Federalism and the French Canadians* (1968).

GEORGE P. GRANT 1959

We listen to others to discover what we ourselves believe.

The first moral philosopher to gain a wide following in Canada was George P. Grant. Years before the publication of his major essay *Lament for a Nation* (1965), he hosted and conducted a series of interviews with prominent world thinkers for CBC-TV, beginning with these words, as quoted in *CBC Times*, Feb. 18, 1959.

H. LANDON LADD 1959

We are only loggers.

This was the slogan of District 2 (Newfoundland) of the International Wood Workers of America, adopted by the local's president H. Landon Ladd in 1959. It was coined, according to Richard Gwyn in *Smallwood: The Unlikely Revolutionary* (1968), "after a retired logger heard him speak, and then told him: 'What you say is right, and what you are trying to do is right. But you'll never get it. We are only loggers.'"

CHRISTOPHER DAFOE 1959

For it's forty below in the winter,
    And it's twenty below in the fall.
It just rises to zero in summer,
    And we don't have a springtime at all.

These lines come from the refrain of a song known as "Forty Below." The four-verse song plus refrain is a parody of the folk song "Red River Valley." The lyrics of the parody, long believed to be traditional, were written by the journalist Christopher Dafoe and published in his column "Coffee Break by Wink," in *The Winnipeg Free Press*, May 39, 1959. The experience of writing the lyrics is recalled by Dafoe in his article "Part of the Oral Tradition," *The Beaver*, Feb.-March 1993. He registered surprise upon later learning they were being ascribed to "Anon." He concluded modestly, "It should be reward enough to know that after a lifetime of earnest effort at the typewriter the result of an idle half-hour is likely to outlive me. It is an honour to be a colleague, however humble, of the authors of *Western Wind* and *The Blue Tail Fly*." In the same vein, singer and songwriter Marie-Lynn Hammond wrote "Canadian Love" (1980), which begins, "Oh Canadian love, Canadian love / it's either 40 below or it's 90 above."

INSCRIPTION 1959

This stone bears witness to the common purpose of two nations, whose frontiers are the frontiers of friendship, whose ways are the ways of freedom, and whose works are the works of peace.

This inscription appears in bronze embedded in black granite on the International Friendship Memorial erected to mark the opening of the St. Lawrence Seaway and Power Project, dedicated by Queen Elizabeth II, Prime Minister John G. Diefenbaker, and U.S. President Dwight D. Eisenhower, outside Prescott, Ont., June 26, 1959.

MARSHALL MCLUHAN 1959

The medium is the message.

This is the most widely quoted aphorism of Canadian origin of all time. Coined by communications consultant Marshall McLuhan, it is known from Toronto to Timbuktu. McLuhan first uttered the now-famous formulation on the evening of July 30, 1959, at a reception in the Vancouver home of educator Alan Thomas, following a symposium at the University of British Columbia on the subject of music and the mass media. McLuhan first included the aphorism in his book *Understanding Media* (1964) and thereafter punned (or "funned") with it: "The medium is the mess-age," "The medium is the massage," etc. What McLuhan meant was that the content of any form of communication is influenced by the form taken by the communication. According to anthropologist Edmund Carpenter, writing in *Canadian Notes & Queries*, Spring 1992, the talismanic sentence came from a lecture delivered by Ashley Montague titled "The Method is the Message." Carpenter, a close associate of McLuhan, added, "Marshall improved the wording and extended the concept." Philip Marchand, writing in *Marshall McLuhan: The Medium and the Messenger* (1989), stated that the now-famous formulation was first publicly uttered at the annual convention of the National Association of Educational Broadcasters, Omaha, Nebraska, 1958; but all the evidence (statements by educator Alan Thomas, broadcaster Eugene Hallman, and McLuhan hiself) points to Vancouver in 1959.

EDMUND CARPENTER 1959

No word meaning "art" occurs in Aivilik, nor does "artist": there are only people. Nor is any distinction made between utilitarian and decorative objects. The Aivilik say simply, "A man should do all things properly."

Edmund Carpenter was among the first anthropologists to make creative use of the insights of the Inuit. This insight about the Inuktitut language spoken by the Aivilik comes from his book *Eskimo* (1959). Carpenter's colleague Marshall McLuhan made use of the insight in *From Cliché to Archetype* (1970): "The Balinese say, 'We have no art, we do everything as well as possible.'"

ANDRÉ LAURENDEAU 1959

Am I cherishing an illusion? It seems to me we used to speak better, not so slurred, not so coarse, not so screechy, not so *joual*. But who will settle that? When the universities get their millions, they will be able to commission linguists to conduct an inquiry into the state of our language. Maybe then we shall learn how many good intentions can bring about such pitiful results.

From time to time intellectuals in Quebec, like their counterparts in France, express deep concern about the state of spoken or written French. The distinguished editor André Laurendeau, in "The Language We Speak," *Le Devoir*, Oct. 21, 1959, voiced his concerns about the language heard in the streets of the Province of Quebec. *Joual* is the word he used to refer to what he heard, a slangy way of pronouncing *cheval*, the French word for "horse." *Joual* was taken up by a group of poets and novelists. Like the language of the "beat generation," *joual* recalls an earlier era and seems to have vanished from the scene.

MORDECAI RICHLER 1959

A man without land is nobody. Remember that, Duddel.

This is the grandfather's advice to the young Duddel or Duddy. The acquisition of land, and hence stature and status, is the theme of Mordecai Richler's novel *The Apprenticeship of Duddy Kravitz* (1959) and the movie based on it, directed by Ted Kotcheff in 1974.

ANONYMOUS 1960s

So farewell to Alberta, farewell to the west,
It's backwards I'll go to the girl I love best.
I'll go back to the east and get me a wife
And never eat cornbread the rest of my life.

This is the last verse of a traditional folk song, "The Alberta Homesteader." Edith Fowke obtained it from traditional singer Ivan

Brandick in the early 1960s. The full text appears in *Canada's Story in Song* (1965), edited by Edith Fowke and Alan Mills.

E. HEATHER SCOTT 1960s

As Canadian as possible—under the circumstances.

Details are surprisingly scarce, but in a CBC Radio contest held in the early 1960s, listeners were asked to complete the following statement: "As Canadian as possible. . . ." Listener E. Heather Scott completed it in this fashion and won the contest, according to Peter Gzowski writing in *This Country in the Morning* (1974).

HUGH MACLENNAN 1960

Boy Meets Girl in Winnipeg and Who Cares?

This is the title of a magazine article written by essayist and novelist Hugh MacLennan about the fact that Canadian editors, publishers, and readers prefer their romance and drama to be set in foreign locales rather than in presumably non-romantic and non-dramatic places like Winnipeg. MacLennan's article is reprinted in *Scotchman's Return and Other Essays* (1960).

BRENDAN BEHAN 1960

Montreal is the only place where a good French accent isn't a social asset.

This judgement may have been valid when it was made in 1960 by the visiting Irish playwright Brendan Behan, as quoted in *The Wit of Brendan Behan* (1968). In the 1990s it is certainly untrue, though amusing.

ROBERTSON DAVIES   1960

Where are the clerisy? They are people who like to read books . . . the
clerisy are those who read for pleasure, but not for idleness; who read for
pastime but not to kill time; who love books, but do not live by books.

Robertson Davies helped revive the use of the word "clerisy" for a
certain kind of readership. He argued on behalf of the needs of the
"clerisy" in his collection of essays *A Voice from the Attic* (1960).

TOMMY THOMPSON   1960

Please Walk on the Grass.

The first sign with this message was erected in Edwards Gardens in
Toronto in 1960; it attracted national and international attention for
its "hands-on" approach. The brain-child of Tommy Thompson,
Metropolitan Toronto's Parks Commissioner, it was adopted as the
motto of the Parks Department.

HOWE MARTYN   1961

The multinational firm.

The concept of business "multinationality," which evolved into the
staple of the economic life of the Western world in the last decades of
the twentieth century, was independently conceived and given wide
currency in 1961 by Howe Martyn, Professor of Political Economy,
the American University, Washington, D.C. In a letter written in
1973, Martyn, a Canadian citizen, noted: "I coined the term for a
course, finding subsequently, however, a similar earlier use. I prefer
my original term 'multinational *firm*' because it avoids the suggestion
of an American monopoly of this development conveyed by
'corporation' which is the American term for what others call limited
company or *société anonyme*." From the first, Canadian nationalists

were wary of the so-called multinational firm. As Mel Watkins wrote in *Gordon to Watkins to You* (1970), "The multinational corporation is like the man who came to dinner. You welcome him as a guest and then find that he's making the rules and giving the orders for the household."

HUGH MACLENNAN 1961

In the early October of that year, in the cathedral hush of a Quebec Indian summer with the lake drawing into its mirror the fire of the maples, it came to me that to be able to love the mystery surrounding us is the final and only sanction of human existence.

These are the thoughts of the narrator of the powerful novel *The Watch that Ends the Night* (1961), written by Hugh MacLennan.

JOHN F. KENNEDY 1961

We share common values from the past, a common defence line at present, and common aspirations for the future, and indeed the future of all mankind. Geography has made us neighbours. History has made us friends. Economics has made us partners. And necessity has made us allies. Those whom nature hath so joined together, let no man put asunder. What unites us is far greater than what divides us.

John F. Kennedy, U.S. President, addressed a joint sitting of the Senate and the House of Commons, May 17, 1961.

W.L. MORTON 1961

Not life, liberty, and the pursuit of happiness, but peace, order, and good government are what the national government of Canada guarantees. Under these, it is assumed, life, liberty, and happiness may be achieved, but by each according to his taste. For the society of allegiance admits of a diversity the society of compact does not, and one of the blessings of

Canadian life is that there is no Canadian way of life, much less two, but a unity under the Crown admitting of a thousand diversities.

This influential passage, with its repeatedly reproduced insight, draws attention to the differences between the United States and Canada through sections of the Declaration of Independence, 1776, and the British North America Act, 1867. The notion of paralleling the two passages may have originated with the historian W.L. Morton, who so expressed it in his book *The Canadian Identity* (1961).

EARLE BIRNEY 1962

We French, we English, never lost our civil war,
endure it still, a bloodless civil bore;
no wounded lying about, no Whitman wanted.
It's only by our lack of ghosts we're haunted.

There is an audaciousness to these lines that is exciting. They come from the poem "Can.Lit." (1962), composed by Earle Birney. The text of the poem appears in Birney's *Selected Poems 1940-1966* (1966).

MARSHALL MCLUHAN 1962

The new electronic independence recreates the world in the image of a global village.

This is the first known appearance in print of the words "a global village." The sentence appears in the seminal book *The Gutenberg Galaxy* (1962), written by communications theorist Marshall McLuhan. What McLuhan had in mind is that electronic communication, which is instantaneous and may be reactive or interactive, has the effect of shrinking an immense world into a tiny village and turning strangers into neighbours. According to Philip Marchand in *Marshall McLuhan: The Medium and the Messenger* (1989), the germ of the idea grew from the following sentence from

America and Cosmic Man (1948) by Wyndham Lewis, an Ontario resident in the 1940s: "The earth has become one big village, with telephones laid on from one end to the other, and air transport, both speedy and safe." Edmund Carpenter, writing in *Canadian Notes & Queries,* Spring 1992, argued, "A more accurate phrase, as Marshall later realized, was *global theatre.* But this proved unappealing to journalists who considered themselves neutral reporters, not theatrical producers." The notion of the "global village" is one that a Canadian thinker has contributed to international intellectual discourse.

MARSHALL MCLUHAN 1962

The media.

Credit for the first use of the words *the media* to embrace all forms of communication must go to communications theorist Marshall McLuhan, according to cultural commentator Thomas Wolfe, interviewed on CBC-TV's *Marshall McLuhan: The Man with the Message,* Oct. 18, 1984. McLuhan used it in *Counterblast* (1954), where he wrote, "The media are not toys; they should not be in the hands of Mother Goose and Peter Pan executives. They can be entrusted only to new artists, because they are art forms." McLuhan was alone in using *the media* in the mid-1950s; but by the mid-1960s a chorus of cultural commentators throughout North America and the United Kingdom chanted the words in this sense, sometimes as a noun in the singular, sometimes in the plural. The subject of the *mass media* was much discussed in the United States in the 1950s. As H.L. Mencken noted, the words *mass media* were used as early as 1923 in the United States. Wolfe asked the following question about McLuhan and his media theories in the article "The New Life Out There" (1965), *McLuhan: Hot & Cool* (1967), edited by Gerald Emmanuel Stearn: "Suppose he is what he sounds like, the most important thinker since Newton, Darwin, Freud, Einstein, and Pavlov—what if he is right?"

McLuhan, when he learned of the rhetorical question, was not amused. His reply was characteristic: "I'd rather be wrong."

VAL SEARS 1962

Come, gentlemen, we have a government to overthrow.

Newspaperman Val Sears has written thousands of news stories and articles and millions of words, but what the public remembers is this single remark. He made it upon boarding a press plane in Ottawa prior to the general election of June 18, 1962. The remark was tinged with sarcasm, as if to draw attention to the fact that Prime Minister John G. Diefenbaker was constantly complaining about the Liberal bias of the press and the Socialist bias of the CBC.

RENÉ LÉVESQUE 1962

Maîtres chez nous.

The political and economic slogan "Maîtres chez nous" (Masters in our own house) is associated with the provincial Liberal Party and Quebec Premier Jean Lesage, who inaugurated the so-called Quiet Revolution. In Oct. 1962, René Lévesque, then a Liberal cabinet minister, led the move to nationalize Hydro-Québec. He credited the use of the slogan to "a small group of us" who realized that "the moment those three words rang out, the search was over." His account appears in "To Be Masters in Our Own House" (1968), in *Canada: A Guide to the Peaceable Kingdom* (1970), edited by William Kilbourn. Maurice Duplessis had used the slogan in 1943; it was the maxim of the civil servant R.E. Bouchette, who promoted Quebec's economic interests as early as 1901. In 1968, Prime Minister Trudeau, no separatist, added: "Masters in our own house we must be, but our house is the whole of Canada." The description "Quiet

Revolution" has been credited to Brian Upton, a reporter with *The Toronto Telegram*, about 1962.

IAN TYSON 1963

Four strong winds that blow lonely,
Seven seas that run high,
All those things that don't change come what may,
But our good times are all gone.
And I'm bound for movin' on,
I'll look for you if I'm ever back this way.

These are lines from the country song "Four Strong Winds" (1963), composed by Ian Tyson and closely identified with the singer Sylvia Fricker.

OSCAR BRAND 1963

From the Vancouver Island to the Alberta highland,
Cross the prairie, the Lakes, to Ontario's towers.
From the sound of Mount Royal's chimes, out to the Maritimes,
Something to sing about, this land of ours.

Folksinger and songwriter Oscar Brand composed and performed "Something to Sing About" (also called "This Land of Ours") in 1963, and the rousing song has been popular with folk groups ever since.

RALPH MELNYK 1963

English was good enough for Jesus Christ.

When the Royal Commission on Bilingualism and Biculturalism was established in 1963, its commissioners criss-crossed the country listening to citizens' briefs and griefs about language and culture. Ed Ogle, head of *Time*'s Canadian bureau, went off the beaten track to interview ordinary Canadians, one of whom gave him an answer that has never been bettered. Ralph Melnyk, a Saskatchewan farmer, expressed the standard discontent with the "Bi & Bi" commission, which he said was finding reasons to "stuff French down his throat." When Ogle pressed him about the use of French in the workplace, Melnyk explained that English was good enough for him because it was good enough for Jesus Christ. The remark has since become a commonplace, but it originated with Ogle in 1963.

MORDECAI RICHLER 1963

"I'm world-famous," Dr. Parks said, "all over Canada."

Mordecai Richler popularized the notion of relative fame in his satiric novel *The Incomparable Atuk* (1963). Everyone is familiar with Andy Warhol's prediction: "In the future everyone will be famous for fifteen minutes." Not everyone knows the Canadian variant: "In the future everyone will be famous for fifteen minutes, thirty in Newfoundland."

NORTHROP FRYE 1963

Literature is a human apocalypse, man's revelation to man, and criticism is not a body of adjudications, but the awareness of that revelation, the last judgment of mankind.

Northrop Frye, literary philosopher, "The Keys of Dreamland," *The Educated Imagination* (1963).

VINCENT MASSEY 1963

Nothing touched me quite so much as this comment in a Canadian newspaper: "He made the Crown Canadian." It was too generous a tribute; but that was what I had tried to do.

Vincent Massey served as Governor General from 1952 to 1959, the first native-born Canadian to be appointed to that office. The observation above appears in his memoirs, *What's Past Is Prologue* (1963). As research has failed to locate the "Canadian newspaper" in question, the "too generous a tribute" is assumed to be hyperbole, what Lord Tweedsmuir, one of Massey's predecessors in the office, called a "Governor-Generality."

GLENN GOULD 1964

The concert is dead.

This declaration is associated with Glenn Gould, pianist and musical theorist. Although the sentiment is undeniably his, nowhere does he seem to have said or written the words. Gould performed his last concert at the Wilshire Abell Theatre, Los Angeles, California, April 10, 1964. Thereafter the performing artist was the recording artist. Richard Kostelanetz, in *Master Minds* (1969), quoted Gould as saying, "The habit of concert-going and concert-giving, both as a social institution and as chief symbol of musical mercantilism, will be . . . dormant in the twenty-first century."

ABRAHAM ROTSTEIN 1964

Much will have to change in Canada if the country is to stay the same.

This pronouncement, which would be characterized as Zen-like but for the fact that it turned out to be prophetic, was made by political economist Abraham Rotstein in 1964, as mentioned in his book *The Precarious Homestead* (1973).

F.H. UNDERHILL 1964

A nation is a body of people who have done great things together in the past and who hope to do great things together in the future.

Historian F.H. Underhill characterized a nation in these words in his collection of radio talks, *The Image of Confederation* (1964). The notion has also been attributed to the nineteenth-century French philosopher Ernest Renan. In 1963, Quebec sociologist Jean-Charles Bonenfant approached the idea obliquely: "Most nations have been formed, not by people who desired intensely to live together, but rather by people who could not live apart."

F.R. SCOTT 1964

The world is my country
The human race is my race
The spirit of man is my God
The future of man is my heaven.

This poem was the maxim of F.R. Scott, the distinguished poet, essayist, lawyer, and teacher. Called "Creed" (1964), it appears in his collection *Selected Poems* (1966). The four lines neatly and expressively summarize an involvement with humankind that remains characteristic of the man who died in 1985.

F.R. SCOTT 1964

I used to say to my classes in constitutional law, "We have a *rendez-vous* with the BNA Act. It's going to come some day!"

F.R. Scott was a specialist in constitutional law as well as a poet. With colleague King Gordon, he watched the *rendez-vous* take place on television—Queen Elizabeth II signing the Constitution Act, 1982, on Parliament Hill, Ottawa, April 17, 1982.

LORD BEAVERBROOK 1964

Here I must say, in my eighty-sixth year, I do not feel greatly different from when I was eighty-five. This is my final word. It is time for me to become an apprentice once more. I have not settled in which direction. But somewhere, sometime soon.

There was an impressive banquet held in London, England, May 25, 1964, to honour Max Aitken, Lord Beaverbrook, on his eighty-fifth birthday. Tendered by Lord Thomson of Fleet, it was the last public appearance of Beaverbrook, the Canadian-born British "press lord." (He died two weeks later.) "The Beaver" put the occasion to magnificent use, recalling his past and his chequered contribution to it, and alluding to the impending future. By all reports, an impressive silence followed the emotional speech.

LESTER B. PEARSON   1964

This is the flag of the future, but it does not dishonour the past.

These words come from the speech delivered by Prime Minister Lester B. Pearson in the House of Commons on Dec. 15, 1964, when Canada acquired its own distinctive flag, the Maple Leaf flag, to replace the Union Jack of Great Britain. Three hundred and eight speeches were delivered in the House before it voted acceptance. Opposition leader John G. Diefenbaker spoke against adoption, one reason being the resemblance between the Maple Leaf flag and the flag of Peru. Indeed, from a distance the two flags look somewhat alike. Both are red and white, both have three panels, both have devices in the centre panel, a maple leaf in the case of Canada, a crest with bearings in the case of Peru.

TAKEO NAKANO   1964

As final resting place,
Canada is chosen.
On citizenship paper,
Signing
Hand trembles.

Takeo Ujo Nakano, the Japanese-born Canadian poet, composed this short poem—the traditional five-line tanka—and accepted the invitation to read it before Emperor Hirohito and Empress Nagako of Japan in 1964. The story is told in *Within the Barbed Wire Fence: A Japanese Man's Account of His Internment in Canada* (1980), written with Leatrice Nakano.

VILHJALMUR STEFANSSON 1964

A land may be said to be discovered the first time a European, preferably an Englishman, sets foot on it.

Vilhjalmur Stefansson was regarded as controversial and outspoken for uttering sentiments like the one above. It comes from the Arctic explorer's autobiography, *Discovery* (1964). In the intervening years, the traditions and sentiments of the native peoples and ethnic minorities have been asserted, so that today the remark may sound obvious rather than outspoken.

LUCIEN RIVARD 1965

I'm going out to flood the rink.

With this explanation to the prison guards, convicted drug peddler Lucien Rivard gained access to the prison yard and leapt over the wall of Bordeaux Jail, Montreal, 6:30 P.M., March 2, 1965. Opposition leader John G. Diefenbaker delighted in describing Rivard's feat. "It was a balmy night, with above-zero weather," Diefenbaker would begin, as noted by Richard Gwyn in *The Shape of Scandal* (1965).

EDMUND WILSON 1965

The reviewer, at the end of this article, after trying to give an account of these books, is now wondering whether the primary reason for the current underestimation of Morley Callaghan may not be simply a general incapacity—apparently shared by his compatriots—for believing that a writer whose work may be mentioned without absurdity in association with Chekhov's and Turgenev's can possibly be functioning in Toronto.

The American literary critic Edmund Wilson made these observations in his study of the fiction of Morley Callaghan in his book of criticism *O Canada* (1965). In much the same way, the English man-of-letters Anthony Burgess paid a compliment to another Toronto novelist when he wrote in 1986: "With Robertson Davies the Canadian novel may at least claim to be taken very seriously indeed."

JEAN-PAUL DESBIENS 1965

Education is impossible without love, without loving a few of the great men of the past.

This is one of the many insightful aphorisms of Jean-Paul Desbiens, known as Frère Untel (or Brother Anonymous), the author of *For Pity's Sake* (1965), translated by Frédéric Côté.

GILLES VIGNEAULT 1965

Mons pays ce n'est pas un pays c'est l'hiver
Mon jardin ce n'est pas un jardin c'est la plaine
Mon chemin ce n'est pas un chemin c'est la neige
Mon pays ce n'est pas un pays c'est l'hiver

Gilles Vigneault wrote a short poem called "Mon Pays" (My Country), which he published in his collection *Avec les Vieux Mots* (1965). When he became a *chansonnier*, he set the evocative lines to music and began to sing them in an impassioned manner. "Mon Pays" was accepted as the unofficial anthem of Quebec. The first verse appears here. Here is the English translation: "My country is not a country it's the winter / My garden is not a garden it's the plain / My road is not a road it's the snow / My country is not a country it's the winter."

NORTHROP FRYE 1965

A garrison is a closely knit and beleaguered society, and its moral and social values are unquestionable. In a perilous enterprise one does not discuss causes or motives: one is either a fighter or a deserter. . . . The real terror comes when the individual feels himself becoming an individual, pulling away from the group, losing the sense of driving power that the group gives him, aware of a conflict within himself far subtler than the struggle of morality against evil. . . . But at present I am concerned rather with a more creative side of the garrison mentality, one that has had positive effects on our intellectual life.

The literary philosopher Northrop Frye was a social critic as well as a literary critic. In the Preface to *The Bush Garden: Essays on the Canadian Imagination* (1971) he wrote that Canada is "practically the only country left in the world which is a pure colony, colonial in psychology as well as in mercantile economics." One of his most striking observations about Canadian society in the late eighteenth, nineteenth, and early twentieth centuries is that it once resembled and still perhaps continues to resemble a military garrison characterized by "the garrison mentality." Frye expressed this insight or opinion in the superb essay "Conclusion to a *Literary History of Canada*" (1965), which he reprinted in his collection *The Bush Garden.* Elsewhere he noted with a sense of dismay or disappointment how inarticulate was the society of Upper Canada and southern Ontario.

NORTHROP FRYE 1971

Literature is conscious mythology: as society develops, its mythical stories become structural principles of story-telling, its mythical concepts, sun-gods and the like, become habits of metaphoric thought. In a fully mature literary tradition the writer enters into a structure of traditional stories and images.

The first four words of this passage epitomize the thought of the literary philosopher Northrop Frye. The passage comes from Frye's "Conclusion to a *Literary History of Canada*" (1965), reprinted in *The Bush Garden* (1971).

GEORGE P. GRANT 1965

The impossibility of conservatism in our era is the impossibility of Canada. As Canadians we attempted a ridiculous task in trying to build a conservative nation in the age of progress, on a continent we share with the most dynamic nation on earth.

These two sentences express the central theme of *Lament for a Nation* (1965). The philosophical work, a moral meditation on nationhood, was written by philosopher George P. Grant. It considered the nature of conservatism and the notion of progress in the post-war period in North America.

JOHN ROBERT COLOMBO 1965

Canada could have enjoyed:
English government,
French culture,
And American know-how.

Instead it ended up with:
English know-how,
French government,
And American culture.

This *bon-mot* was conceived by the editor and poet John Robert Colombo. It appeared as a free-verse poem titled "O Canada" (1965) in *The New Romans* (1986), an anthology edited by Al Purdy. The sentiment may be less true in the future than it has been in the past; but again, it may be even more true.

NORTHROP FRYE 1965

But Canada has, for all practical purposes, no Atlantic seaboard. The traveller from Europe edges into it like a tiny Jonah entering an inconceivably large whale, slipping past the Straits of Belle Isle into the Gulf of St. Lawrence, where five Canadian provinces surround him, for the most part invisible. Then he goes up the St. Lawrence and the inhabited country comes into view, mainly a French-speaking country, with its own cultural traditions. To enter the United States is a matter of crossing an ocean; to enter Canada is a matter of being silently swallowed by an alien continent.

Northrop Frye, literary philosopher, "Conclusion to a *Literary History of Canada*" (1965), *The Bush Garden: Essays on the Canadian Imagination* (1971).

ROBERT M. FOWLER 1965

The only thing that really matters in broadcasting is program content; all the rest is housekeeping.

The 1960s were characterized by the striking of a succession of quasi-government committees of inquiry into all aspects of private and public broadcasting in Canada, but particularly into the affairs of the CBC. Robert M. Fowler, a business executive, chaired not one but two such committees. The memorable statement above comes from *The Royal Commission Report of the Committee on Broadcasting* (1965), called the Fowler Report, prepared by Fowler with the assistance of Marc Lalonde and G.C.E. Steele. Except for the occasional aphorism, little if any good flowed from these reports.

187

PADDY SHERMAN 1966

Here we lead a privileged life; we are able to golf, ski, sail, climb mountains, garden, ten months every year. Philosophical discussion is not popular in B.C.

When Paddy Sherman made this observation about the British Columbia of his day, he was editor of *The Vancouver Province*. Sherman's observation—or opinion—received wide coverage in Solange Chaput-Rolland's book, *My Country, Canada or Quebec?* (1966).

ROBERT REGULY 1966

Star Man Finds Gerda Munsinger.

This was the headline on "the scoop of the Sixties." It appeared on the front page of *The Toronto Star,* March 11, 1966. Investigative reporter Robert Reguly, travelling to Munich, West Germany, succeeded in locating Gerda Munsinger, the former Miss Garmisch-Partenkirchen, a woman of East German background, who seems to have been intimate with at least one federal cabinet minister during her brief stay in Montreal and Ottawa in the 1960s. The Munsinger Affair was Canada's first—and so far sole—"sex and security" scandal, involving as it did Conservative Cabinet Minister Pierre Sévigny. A commission of inquiry (which failed to interview Mrs. Munsinger) concluded that although sex may have been involved, security was not an issue. Wags attributed to Mrs. Munsinger the quip: "I want my bedtime Tory."

GAD HOROWITZ 1966

Red Tory.

The term "Red Tory" was popularized in Canada by the political scientist Gad Horowitz in the article "Conservatism, Liberalism and Socialism: An Interpretation," *Canadian Journal of Economics and Political Science,*

May 1966. The term defines "a conscious ideological Conservative with some 'odd' socialist notions (W.L. Morton) or a conscious ideological socialist with some 'odd' tory notions (Eugene Forsey)." Its opposite is presumably a "blue Grit," a non-progressive Liberal.

PAUL JOSEPH CHARTIER   1966

Mr. Speaker, Gentlemen, I might as well give you a blast to wake you up. For one whole year, I have thought of nothing but how to exterminate as many of you as possible. . . . The only bills you pass are the ones that line your pockets, while the rest of the country has to eat spaghetti and meat balls.

Paul Joseph Chartier is remembered as the Mad Bomber of Parliament Hill. An unemployed truck driver from Alberta, he carried a homemade bomb into the Centre Block on Parliament Hill with the intention of pitching it into the Commons chamber from the visitor's gallery. He was killed when it exploded prematurely in the men's room, May 18, 1966. No one else was hurt. Fragments of a speech he had hoped to deliver survived and were quoted by Harry Bruce in *The Canadian*, Sept. 10 and 17, 1966.

ROBERT H. WINTERS   1966

You have perhaps heard the story of the four students—British, French, American, Canadian—who were asked to write an essay on elephants. The British student entitled his essay "Elephants and the Empire." The French student called his "Love and the Elephant." The title of the American student's essay was "Bigger and Better Elephants," and the Canadian student called his "Elephants: A Federal or a Provincial Responsibility?"

It is not certain that Robert H. Winters, former Minister of Trade in Liberal administrations, originated this joke. But he Canadianized it and used it to good effect in his speeches in 1966.

LEONARD COHEN 1966

God is alive. Magic is afoot. God is alive. Magic is afoot. God is afoot. Magic is alive. Alive is afoot. Magic never died.

This mantra-like passage attesting to the power of magic and miracle appeared in the novel *Beautiful Losers* (1966), written by poet and songwriter Leonard Cohen.

LEONARD COHEN 1967

And you want to travel with her,
And you want to travel blind;
And you know that you can trust her,
For she's touched your perfect body with her mind.

This is the refrain of the hauntingly memorable lyrics of "Suzanne" (1967), which the poet and singer Leonard Cohen composed and performed to much acclaim at the Newport and Mariposa folk festivals in the summer of 1967.

KENNETH CARTER 1967

A buck is a buck.

This was the maxim of Kenneth Carter, Chairman of the Carter Commission on Tax Reform. As Carter concluded in its report, released on Feb. 24, 1967, the tax system should exist to raise revenue, not to right social wrongs, and all earnings should be taxed as such.

ANTOINE DE SAINT-EXUPÉRY 1967

Terre des Hommes / Man and His World.

World expositions have themes, and the theme chosen for Expo 67 was "Terre des Hommes / Man and His World." It is not widely known that the theme of the Montreal fair was taken from the writing of the French aviator, artist, and author Antoine de Saint-Exupéry, best remembered as the creator of *The Little Prince* (1943). Expo's theme comes directly from Saint-Exupéry's book *Terre des Hommes* (1939), which is known in English as *Wind, Sand and Stars* (1939). Saint-Exupéry's humanistic philosophy is predicated on people "looking together in the same direction." The novelist Gabrielle Roy drew the attention of the fair's organizers to the phrase *Terre des Hommes*.

RICHARD MORRIS & DORIS CLAMAN   1967

Give us a place to stand
And a place to grow
And call this land
Ontario.

This is the chorus of the theme song "Ontar-i-ar-i-ar-io," which was loudly sung throughout the documentary film *A Place to Stand*, directed by Christopher Chapman for the Ontario Pavilion at Expo 67 in Montreal. The catchy words were written by songwriter Richard Morris; the lively tune, by Dolores Claman.

A.J.M. SMITH   1967

McLuhan put a telescope to his ear;
What a lovely smell, he said, we have here.

This satirical couplet was written by the poet and critic A.J.M. Smith. Called "The Taste of Space," it appears in Smith's *Poems* (1967). When McLuhan first heard it, his response was "Synaesthesia!"

MARSHALL MCLUHAN 1967

Canada is the only country in the world that knows how to live without an identity.

This is one of Marshall McLuhan's famous "probes." With verbal economy, it turns the absence of something into the presence of something else, in this instance the lack of national identity into the ability to function without superfluous intellectual baggage. It comes from the broadcast "Canada: A Borderline Case" on CBC Radio, May 29, 1967.

CHIEF DAN GEORGE 1967

O God! Like the Thunderbird of old I shall rise again out of the sea; I shall grab the instruments of the white man's success—his education, his skills, and with these new tools I shall build my race into the proudest segment of your society. Before I follow the great Chiefs who have gone before us, O Canada, I shall see these things come to pass.

Chief Dan George delivered a powerful poetic address titled "A Lament for Confederation" at Empire Stadium, Vancouver, July 1, 1967. The elected chief of the Salish, a man of considerable dignity, Dan George played Indian chiefs in a slew of movies and television programs. Playing the part of Old Lodge Poles, he addresses the following words to his son (played by Dustin Hoffman) in the Hollywood film *Little Big Man* (1974): "My heart soars like a hawk."

BLAIR FRASER 1967

We all, I'm sure, have many hopes for Canada on this Centennial day—that she may grow, thrive, prosper in all things. To these I would add one hope more: that Canada will not so greatly grow, and not so grossly thrive, as to destroy this heritage of solitude which makes us what we are and which our children will know perhaps better than we how to value.

The year 1967 marked the Centennial of Confederation and a coming of age for Canada. There was a national spirit in the land, the arts flourished, and Quebec was able to make a special and individual contribution through hosting the world's fair, Expo 67. The journalist Blair Fraser summarized much of this spirit in the Centennial Sermon he delivered at the Church of the Messiah, Montreal, July 2, 1967. It was included in *"Blair Fraser Reports"* (1969), edited by John Fraser and Graham Fraser. The Centennial year marked a high point; low points followed, notably the October Crisis of 1970.

CHARLES DE GAULLE 1967

Vive le Québec! Vive le Québec libre! Vive le Canada français! Vive la France!

French President Charles de Gaulle made an official visit to Canada to attend Expo 67 and addressed a crowd from the balcony of Montreal's City Hall, July 24, 1967. In his speech he deliberately incurred the wrath of federalists and curried favour with the separatists by employing their slogan "Québec libre." Montreal Mayor Jean Drapeau and Prime Minister Lester B. Pearson disavowed de Gaulle's *démarche*. De Gaulle cancelled his visit to Ottawa and promptly returned to Paris. To this day, commentators and historians debate whether the intervention or indiscretion was planned or impromptu. The most stylish response to the French President was made by Pauline Vanier, widow of the Governor General; she had the following terse comminiqué conveyed to de Gaulle: "1940."

GORDON LIGHTFOOT 1967

There was a time in this fair land when the railroad did not run,
When the wild majestic mountains stood alone against the sun,

Long before the white man and long before the wheel
When the green dark forest was too silent to be real.

These are the opening lines of composer and singer Gordon Lightfoot's moving ballad "Canadian Railroad Trilogy," first written and performed in 1967.

EMIL L. FACKENHEIM 1967

Jews are forbidden to give Hitler a posthumous victory.

This is one of the most widely quoted injunctions of the era. It is recognized wherever there are Jewish people. It was originated by Emil L. Fackenheim, rabbi and philosopher at the University of Toronto, who explained, "In 1967 I formulated the only statement I ever made that became famous: that there now exists a six hundredth and four-teenth commandment—Jews are forbidden to give Hitler a posthumous victory. . . . If we live as if nothing had happened we imply that we are willing to expose our children or their offspring to a second Holocaust—and that would be another way of giving Hitler a posthumous victory." The explanation comes from Fackenheim's article "To Mend the World," *Viewpoints: The Canadian Monthly*, Oct.-Nov. 1985. The Torah, the Hebrew Bible, has a total of 613 commandments; Fackenheim—or the Holocaust—added one new one.

ROBERT THOMPSON 1967

The Americans are our best friends, whether we like it or not.

This malapropism is identified with Robert Thompson, who served as national leader of the Social Credit Party from 1961 to 1967. Peter C. Newman recalled the oft-quoted remark in *Home Country* (1973), along with two other "Thompsonisms": "Social Credit is above politics" and "Parliament is being turned into a political arena."

PIERRE ELLIOTT TRUDEAU 1967

There's no place for the state in the bedrooms of the nation.

Pierre Elliott Trudeau was Minister of Justice and not yet Prime Minister when he tossed off this now-celebrated *bon mot* during the course of an Ottawa interview, Dec. 22, 1967. This is what he actually said, in reference to changes in the Criminal Code: "The state has no place in the nation's bedrooms." Like many well-known aphorisms, it is seldom quoted in its original form (it is generally cited in the longer form given above) and it is not the work of a single person. Trudeau's aphorism is an adapation of lines that originally appeared in an editorial published in *The Globe and Mail* on Dec. 12, 1967: "Obviously, the state's responsibility should be to legislate rules for a well-ordered society. It has no right or duty to creep into the bedrooms of the nation." Journalist Martin O'Malley wrote the unsigned editorial, so he contributed to the formulation of one of the most celebrated of modern Canadian aphorisms, one that brought the name "Trudeau" to the lips of the electorate.

BARBARA WARD 1968

A Canada prepared to pioneer with lucidity and daring the role of the first "international nation" in history would not only have an immense impact on its fellow states. It might also transform its own political life. It could, conceivably, turn the present rather bored citizen acquiescence in modern politics into something more exciting and active, into participation, into enjoyment, into purpose, even into fun.

The notion that Canada would become the first "international nation," whatever that means, is associated with the British social activist Barbara Ward. She expressed the idea in her essay "The First International Nation" (1968), reprinted by William Kilbourn in *Canada: A Guide to the Peaceable Kingdom* (1970).

Emil L. Fackenheim   1968

> Had every Christian in Hitler's Europe followed the example of the king
> of Denmark and decided to put on the yellow star, there would be today
> neither despair in the church nor talk of the death of God.

Emil L. Fackenheim, rabbi and philosopher, expressed a fundamental
truth when he made this observation not about the Jewish problem, but
about the Christian problem in *Quest for Past and Future* (1968).

Pierre Elliott Trudeau   1968

> La raison avant la passion.

This French adage is said to be the personal maxim of Pierre Elliott
Trudeau, who was sworn in as Prime Minister on April 20, 1968. He
served in that office (except for the period between June 1, 1979, and
March 3, 1980) until his resignation, June 30, 1984. The phrase is
translated "Reason over passion"; the artist Joyce Wieland worked
the words into an elaborate quilt.

T.C. Douglas   1968

> A recession is when your neighbour has to tighten his belt. A depression
> is when you have to tighten your own belt. And a panic is when you have
> no belt to tighten and your pants fall down.

T.C. (Tommy) Douglas, the leader of the New Democratic Party,
had a popular touch. He made this remark in 1968.

Marshall McLuhan   1968

> Life. Consider the alternative.

This is one of communications theorist Marshall McLuhan's famous "probes." It appeared in *War and Peace in the Global Village* (1968), written with Quentin Fiore.

MARSHALL MCLUHAN 1968

Canada is the only country in the world that has never had a national identity. In an age when all homogenous nations are losing their identity images through rapid technological change, Canada alone can "keep it cool." We have never been committed to a single course or goal. This is now our greatest asset.

Communications theorist Marshall McLuhan expressed this conception of Canada in a letter written to Prime Minister Pierre Elliott Trudeau dated Dec. 2, 1968, which is included in *Letters of Marshall McLuhan* (1987), edited by Matie Molinaro, Corinne McLuhan, and William Toye. Fans of Sherlock Holmes often write to their favourite fictional detective at 221b Baker Street in London, England. Apparently, one Canadian fan once wrote as follows: "We've been searching for Canadian identity for several years now and we would greatly appreciate your assistance in finding it."

CLAUDE T. BISSELL 1969

It's ironical that the first people to demand free speech are the first people to deny it to others.

Claude T. Bissell, President of the University of Toronto, made this point about the clamour of unruly student action. They were protesting the appearance on the campus of Clark Kerr, former President of Berkeley, a favourite target of student protesters. They interrupted his address at the Royal Ontario Museum, Feb. 5, 1969. Bissell described the incident in his memoirs, *Halfway up Parnassus* (1974).

Irving Layton 1969

Only the tiniest fraction of mankind want freedom. All the rest want someone to tell them they are free.

This is an aphorism from Irving Layton's book *The Whole Bloody Bird* (1969).

Irving Layton 1969

In Pierre Elliott Trudeau, Canada has at last produced a political leader worthy of assassination.

The poet Irving Layton included this aphorism in his book *The Whole Bloody Bird* (1969). At the time Trudeau had been Prime Minister for just over a year, and there was a sense that publishing such a statement or even quoting it was "tempting the gods." Trudeau was the target of no assassination attempt, though on at least one occasion he was showered with rotten eggs. Canadian leaders who have been killed or harmed for political reasons include Father of Confederation Thomas D'Arcy McGee, Doubkhobor leader Peter V. Verigen, Communist leader Tim Buck, and Quebec Minister Pierre Laporte. The British consular official James Cross was kidnapped by the FLQ in October 1970, one year after Layton made his observation about Trudeau.

Pierre Elliott Trudeau 1969

Living next to you is in some ways like sleeping with an elephant. No matter how friendly and even-tempered the beast, one is affected by every twitch and grunt.

Prime Minister Trudeau's image of Canada lying in bed next to the American "elephant" is as fresh today as it was the day he introduced it during the course of a speech to members of the National Press Club, Washington, D.C., March 25, 1969. Lawrence Martin, in *The Presidents and the Prime Ministers* (1982), attributed the authorship of the speech to Trudeau's adviser, Ivan Head.

JOHN LENNON & YOKO ONO 1969

> All we are saying is give peace a chance.
> All we are saying is give peace a chance.

These two lines come from "Give Peace a Chance," the anti-war anthem written and recorded by Beatle John Lennon and his artist wife Yoko Ono during their "bed-in for peace" conducted in Room 1742, Queen Elizabeth Hotel, Montreal, May 30, 1969. Lennon and Ono were campaigning for world peace. They admired Canada and its Prime Minister. "Everything points to Canada as being one of the key countries in the new race for survival," Lennon told the press on Parliament Hill, Ottawa, Dec. 1969. "If all politicians were like Mr. Trudeau, there would be world peace. You people in Canada don't realize how lucky you are to have a man like Mr. Trudeau." Ono added: "We're just enthralled meeting Mr. Trudeau, he is Beautiful People."

GREG CLARK 1969

> I tell you what you do, boy. Or girl. Go and look at the western sky where the new moon, the silver shaving of the moon, hangs. Look at it over your *left* shoulder, and wish. Wish that your first love shall be your last love. And if your wish is granted, you will have put on the whole armour of life.

This piece of advice—or wisdom—was proffered by veteran newspaperman and crackerbarrel philosopher Greg Clark in his book *May Your First Love Be Your Last* (1969).

PETER MATTHEWS 1969

Only in Canada. . . . Pity.

This line comes from a classic—and immensely popular—advertising campaign in television commercials for Red Rose Tea, the idea being that discriminating Britishers are unable to purchase Red Rose Tea because it is available "only in Canada" and more's the pity. The concept was created for Brooke Bond Inc. by Peter Matthews under the direction of Jack Cronin, creative director of J. Walter Thompson in Montreal. The campaign, launched in 1969, is still running.

LAURENCE J. PETER 1969

In a hierarchy, every employee tends to rise to his level of incompetence.

This is the world-famous Peter Principle, as propounded by Dr. Laurence J. Peter, psychologist and educator, one-time Vancouver resident. It appeared in print for the first time, along with a number of other "laws of human behaviour," in *The Peter Principle* (1969), coauthored by West Coast writer Raymond Hull.

ROBERT BOURASSA 1970

Will it sell in St. Agapit?

This was said to be the political maxim of Robert Bourassa, who served as Premier of Quebec from 1970 to 1976 and from 1985 to 1994. St. Agapitville is a village on the South Shore east of Laurier Station. It serves as something of a social and political bellwether for Quebeckers, being to that province what Prince Albert is to the rest of Canada and Peoria is to the United States.

BILL DARNELL 1970

Make it a *green* peace.

The Greenpeace Foundation was so named by Bill Darnell, an original member in Vancouver in 1970 of the Don't Make a Wave Committee, which preceded the formation of Greenpeace. "The word *Greenpeace* had a ring to it—it conjured images of Eden; it said ecology and antiwar in two syllables; it fit easily into even a one-column headline," noted co-founder Robert Hunter in *Warriors of the Rainbow* (1979). Hunter deserves credit for selecting the name *Rainbow Warrior* for Greenpeace's series of protest vessels. On July 10, 1985, French government operatives blew up Greenpeace's flagship *Rainbow Warrior*—which was being used to draw world attention to French nuclear tests in Polynesia—in Auckland Harbour, New Zealand. Thereupon, Greenpeace proclaimed: "You Can't Sink a Rainbow."

CHIEF DAN GEORGE 1970

O Great spirit, whose voice I hear in the winds, and whose breath gives life to the world, hear me. I come to you as one of your many children. I am small and weak. I need your strength and your wisdom. May I walk in beauty. Make my eyes ever behold the red and purple sunset. Make my hands respect the things that you have made and my ears sharp to hear your voice. Make me wise so that I may know the things you have taught your children, the lessons you have hidden in every leaf and rock. Make me strong, not to be superior to my brothers, but to be able to fight my greatest enemy, myself. Make me ever ready to come to you with straight eyes, so that when life fades as the fading sunset, my spirit may come to you without shame.

This prayer was composed by the native leader Chief Dan George. The elected chief of the Salish and sometime actor spoke with considerable eloquence and elegance. He recited his prayer at the close of the program devoted to him and his ideals on CBC-TV's "Telescope," Sept. 7, 1970.

FLQ MANIFESTO 1970

> The people in the *Front de Libération du Québec* are neither Messiahs nor modern-day Robin Hoods. They are a group of Quebec workers who have decided to do everything they can to assure that the people of Quebec take their destiny into their own hands, once and for all.

These are the opening words of the FLQ Manifesto, written by the Quebec terrorists who on Oct. 5, 1970, kidnapped British consular official James Cross from his residence in Westmount, Montreal, and sparked the October Crisis. Three days later, as the FLQ demanded, the full text of the manifesto was read in French and English on network television. The text appears in Marcel Rioux's *Quebec in Question* (1971), translated by James Boake. The terrorists felt themselves to be unduly "terrorized by the Roman Capitalist Church" and "terrorized by the payments owing to Household Finance." A second kidnapping—that of Pierre Laporte—led the Trudeau administration to consider that there was a state of "apprehended insurrection" and to invoke the War Measures Act, Oct. 16, 1970.

PIERRE ELLIOTT TRUDEAU 1970

> TRUDEAU: Yes, well there are a lot of bleeding hearts around who just don't like to see people with helmets and guns. All I can say is, go on and bleed, but it is more important to keep law and order in the society than to be worried about weak-kneed people who don't like the looks of—
>
> RALFE: At any cost? How far would you go with that? How far would you extend that?
>
> TRUDEAU: Well, just watch me. . . . Yes, I think the society must take every means at its disposal to defend itself against the emergence of a

parallel power which defies the elected power in this country and I think that goes at any distance.

On Oct. 13, 1970, just over a week after the onset of the October Crisis, Prime Minister Pierre Elliott Trudeau was interviewed by CBC-TV reporter Tim Ralfe on Parliament Hill about the measures the government would take to deal with the emergency. The exchange was telecast that evening, and the text was reproduced by *The Toronto Star* the following day. The War Measures Act was invoked on Oct. 16, 1970.

ROBERT FULFORD 1970

My generation of Canadians grew up believing that, if we were very good or very smart, or both, we would someday *graduate* from Canada.

Writer and editor Robert Fulford made this admission about intellectual life in English Canada in the 1950s, in "Notebook," *Saturday Night*, Oct. 1970.

DONALD G. CREIGHTON 1970

Confederation had been a political union of several provinces, not a cultural compact between two ethnic communities, English and French.

The eminent historian Donald G. Creighton distinguished between two conceptions of Canada, political union vs. cultural pact, arguing that the Fathers of Confederation took the Conservative view, envisioning a union, not the Liberal view, opting for a pact. Creighton offered evidence for his conviction in *Canada's First Century* (1970).

WILDER PENFIELD 1970

In all our studies of the brain, no mechanism has been discovered that can force the mind to think, or the individual to believe, anything. The mind continues free. This is a statement I have long considered. I have made every effort to disprove it, without success. The mind, I must conclude, is something more than a mechanism. It is, in a certain sense, above and beyond the brain, although it seems to depend upon brain action for its very existence. Yet it is free.

Wilder Penfield, one of the world's most eminent neurosurgeons, was also an essayist and philosopher. He made this observation in _Second Thoughts: Science, the Arts, and the Spirit_ (1970).

DICK BEDDOES 1970

The sportswriting confraternity is burdened with hacks who make tin-can gods out of cast-iron jerks.

Dick Beddoes, sportswriter, had a way with words. He made this widely quoted remark in his appearance before the Special Senate Committee on the Mass Media (the Davey Commission) in 1970.

DAVEY COMMISSION 1970

The most insidious effect of journalist monopolies, however, is the atmosphere they breed. Every reporter soon learns that there are only a few newspapers where excellence is encouraged. If they are lucky or clever or restless, they will gravitate to those newspapers. If not, they will stay where they are, growing cynical about their work, learning to live with a kind of sour professional despair. Often you can see it in their faces. Most Canadian city-rooms are boneyards of broken dreams.

The words "corporate concentration" were widely used in the business world in the 1960s to refer to the concentration of the ownership of once-independent companies by a decreasing number of giant firms, usually national or multinational corporations. In government circles there was some worry that increased ownership of the organs of mass communication—the periodical press and radio and televi-

sion broadcasting in particular—would result in monopolies. Indeed, as lawyer-poet F.R. Scott once noted, "Newspapers are born free and everywhere are in chains." (He might well have applied the observation to television stations, networks, and cable companies.) Senator Keith Davey, a former broadcaster, was appointed chairman of the Special Senate Committee on Mass Media to study the situation. The Davey Commission surveyed it with respect to both "media concentration" and "excellence." *Report of the Special Senate Committee on Mass Media: The Uncertain Mirror* (1970) was written with some style and offered many insights. It was largely the work of magazine editor and journalist Alexander (Sandy) Ross. Like many other special committees and royal reports, its findings made the headlines but remade no rules or regulations. "Corporate concentration" in the guise of "globalization" continues unaffected. The Report is mainly remembered for Ross's observation about "boneyards" and "broken dreams."

PIERRE ELLIOTT TRUDEAU 1971

Fuddle-duddle.

This amusing Canadianism was created out of the blue by Prime Minister Pierre Elliott Trudeau. Accused of uttering "a four-letter word" in the House of Commons, Feb. 16, 1971, and of directing it at two Conservative members, Trudeau denied the charge as "an absolute untruth." Later, outside the House, asked by CTV's parliamentary reporter Max Keeping if he had told the Tory M.P.'s to "fuck off," Trudeau replied, "No, it was fuddle-duddle." That led M.T. McCutcheon, M.P., to quip, "Mr. Trudeau wants to be obscene but not heard." The cheeky euphemism appealed to the younger generation and the words even appeared on T-shirts.

CAMPBELL HUGHES 1971

A Canadian is someone who drinks Brazilian coffee from an English teacup, and munches a French pastry, while sitting on his Danish furniture, having just come home from an Italian movie in his German car. He picks up his Japanese pen and writes to his member of Parliament to complain about the American takeover of the Canadian publishing business.

This definition of a Canadian remains as true today as when it first appeared in print (with some substitutions: a Japanese car rather than a German one, for instance). The editors of *Time*, March 1, 1971, attributed it to Campbell Hughes, Canadian head of an American-owned publishing conglomerate. Hughes was a serious-minded person; when asked about the witticism, he maintained that he was merely repeating "someone else's" definition of the Canadian way of life.

T.C. DOUGLAS 1971

Canadians do not want to escape from the tyranny of big business only to fall into the clutches of big government.

T.C. (Tommy) Douglas, leader of the New Democratic Party, farewell address, leadership convention, Ottawa, April 21, 1971.

MORDECAI RICHLER 1971

The Canadian kid who wants to grow up to be Prime Minister isn't thinking big, he is setting a limit to his ambitions rather early.

This remark was made by novelist and essayist Mordecai Richler and was quoted in *Time*, May 31, 1971.

PIERRE VALLIÈRES 1971

The Canadian Confederation was nothing more than a vast financial transaction carried out by the bourgeoisie at the expense of the workers of the country, and more especially the workers of Quebec.

With the publication of his tract *White Niggers of America* (1971), translated by Joan Pinkham, Pierre Vallières became the first well-known Quebecker to bring to the separatist cause the insights of Marxism and the anti-racist and anti-colonialist rhetoric of French thinker Franz Fanon. Vallières wrote this semi-biographical, semi-political work while serving time in the New York prison known as The Tombs for his involvement in a plot to blow up the Statue of Liberty to bring attention to the cause of Quebec separatism.

PIERRE ELLIOTT TRUDEAU 1971

I wish to emphasize the view of the government that a policy of multiculturalism within a bilingual framework is basically the conscious support of individual freedom of choice. We are free to be ourselves. But this cannot be left to chance. It must be fostered and pursued actively.

With these words, Prime Minister Pierre Elliott Trudeau committed the Government of Canada to implement across the country the main recommendations of the Royal Commission on Bilingualism and Biculturalism, House of Commons, Ottawa, Oct. 8, 1971.

GEZA MATRAI 1971

Freedom for Hungary! Freedom for all!

This was the cry of the Hungarian-born Canadian protester Geza Matrai as he was physically restrained from further assaulting Alexei Kosygin. At the time, the Soviet Premier was strolling across Parliament Hill with Prime Minister Pierre Elliott Trudeau, Oct. 19, 1971.

IRVING LAYTON 1971

By the way
she moved
away
I could see

her devotion
to literature
was not
perfect.

"Misunderstanding" is the title of this amusing little verse, which may
be found in *The Collected Poems of Irving Layton* (1971).

LOUIS DUDEK   1971

Reading a dead poet
Who complained in his time
Against bad laws, bad manners,
And bad weather in bad rhyme,

I thought how glad he'd be
To be living in our time
To damn worse laws, worse manners,
And worse weather, in worse rhyme.

"The Progress of Satire" is the title of this satiric verse, which was
written by the poet Louis Dudek and included in his *Collected Poetry*
(1971).

RICHARD M. NIXON   1972

MR. NIXON: Canada is the largest trading partner of the United States.
HON. MEMBERS: Hear, hear!
MR. NIXON: It is very important that that be noted in Japan, too.
HON. MEMBERS: Hear, hear!

U.S. President Richard M. Nixon made this point in an address
delivered before a joint sitting of the Senate and the House of
Commons, April 14, 1972. Nixon was correcting the error he made
when, at a press conference in the White House, Washington, D.C.,

Sept. 16, 1971, he had identified Japan as the U.S.'s largest trading partner.

ROBERT BOURASSA 1972

We will do our best to spread the wealth of Ontario across our country.

Was Quebec Premier Robert Bourassa speaking for effect when he made this statement to journalist Richard Cleroux, who quoted it in *The Globe and Mail*, May 1, 1972? By "our country" he meant Quebec. The words "profitable federalism" are associated with Bourassa's first administration (1970-76), according to Quebec political adviser Léon Dion in *Quebec: The Unfinished Revolution* (1976), translated by Thérèse Romer.

DAVID LEWIS 1972

Corporate welfare bums.

This phrase has passed into the Canadian political lexicon. It was coined by David Lewis, leader of the New Democratic Party, and introduced in a speech in New Glasgow, N.S., Aug. 3, 1972, according to Walter Stewart in *Divide and Con* (1973). Lewis branded as "corporate welfare bums" those corporations, large and small, which avoided paying their fair share of business taxes as well as those businesses which pressed all levels of government for additional grants, concessions, subsidies, deferrals, remissions, depreciations, and incentives. According to former NDP researcher Boris Celovsky, what sparked research into this matter was business writer Alexander Ross's column in *The Toronto Star*, April 17, 1972, which named some of the corporations in question. Twenty years later Revenue Canada was still eliminating loopholes in the Income Tax Act that were allowing, for instance, "several hundred Canadian corporations to avoid taxes on billions of dollars in foreign investments," according to *Bottom Line*, June 1993.

DONALD G. CREIGHTON 1972

> History is the record of an encounter between character and circumstance . . . the encounter between character and circumstance is essentially a story.

Few historians would attempt so fundamental a definition of the nature of history as did Donald G. Creighton in *Towards the Discovery of Canada* (1972).

RAYMOND SOUSTER 1972

> ". . . But only God can make a tree."
> (He'll never try it in Sudbury.)

The poet Raymond Souster wrote "Very Short Poem" in the 1960s. It appears in his *Selected Poems* (1972). Perhaps the satiric verse had its effect in Sudbury; since the 1960s, "greening" has taken precedence in the northern Ontario mining community.

ROBERTSON DAVIES 1972

> Canada is not really a place where you are encouraged to have large spiritual adventures.

Robertson Davies, man-of-letters, quoted by Peter C. Newman, "The Master's Voice," *Maclean's*, Sept. 1972.

MARGARET ATWOOD 1972

> This above all, to refuse to be a victim. Unless I can do that I am nothing.

These are the thoughts of the narrator of the novel *Surfacing* (1972), written by Margaret Atwood.

PAUL HENDERSON 1972

When I scored that final goal, I finally realized what democracy was all about.

Hockey fans in Canada and the former Soviet Union will never forget the evening of Sept. 28, 1972, when Team Canada battled the Soviet team in Moscow's Luzhniki Stadium. With thirty-four seconds left in the game, left-winger Paul Henderson scored the winning goal. Dick Beddoes covered the momentous event, describing it moment by moment in *Hockey Night in Minsk* (1972). Beddoes attributed the above words to Henderson after he scored the all-important goal. Throughout all eight games in the Canada-Soviet series, Canadian fans chanted, "Da, da, Canada! / Nyet, nyet, Soviet!"

JEAN DRAPEAU 1973

The Montreal Olympics can no more have a deficit than a man can have a baby.

This diverting remark was made by Jean Drapeau, Mayor of Montreal, announcing the "self-financing" Olympic budget of $310 million at a press conference in Montreal, Jan. 29, 1973. Thereafter, Aislin published his celebrated cartoon in *The Montreal Gazette* which showed the pregnant Mayor on the phone yelling, "'Ello, Morgentaler?" (Aislin is the pen-name of cartoonist Terry Mosher; Dr. Henry Morgentaler is known for his advocacy of abortion on demand.) As poet and aphorist Louis Dudek noted in 1991, "Montreal is still paying forty million a year for two weeks of the Olympics."

KEITH SPICER 1973

Westmount Rhodesians.

Keith Spicer, Commissioner of Official Languages, compared—or seemed to compare—the English who live in the affluent Montreal district of Westmount with those privileged white citizens of Rhodesia who opposed black rule in their part of Africa. Spicer was addressing a conference at Johns Hopkins University, Washington campus, April 1973. The comparison caused much comment—and much criticism—at the time.

GORDON SINCLAIR 1973

This Canadian thinks it is time to speak up for the Americans as the most generous and possibly the least appreciated people in all the earth. . . . I can name to you 5,000 times when Americans raced to the help of other people in trouble. Can you name me one time when someone else raced to the Americans in trouble?

Newspaperman and broadcaster Gordon Sinclair made a splash when he devoted one of his daily "Let's Be Personal" radio broadcasts to praising Americans and honouring the American spirit. "Americans" was first heard on CFRB Radio in Toronto, June 5, 1973. The station was deluged with requests for scripts and tapes. Sinclair rerecorded the script ("The Battle Hymn of the Republic" playing in the background), and sales of the recording generated millions of dollars for the American Red Cross, as noted by Scott Young in *Gordon Sinclair: A Life . . . and Then Some* (1987).

GABRIELLE ROY 1973

Every writer must eventually write his Ninth Symphony or give in to despair.

The novelist and memoirist Gabrielle Roy expressed this view of the psychology of the writer in a letter dated Aug. 1, 1973, quoted by Joan Hind-Smith in *Three Voices* (1975).

MORLEY CALLAGHAN 1973

> The thing is that you must not have a kind of nationalism which is an
> insistence on the protection of the third-rate, do you see? All you should
> say is, I know it's excellent, and the world will discover it *is* excellent.
> They'll discover it's Canadian, because they'll ask where it came from.

**Morley Callaghan held out for excellence in his fiction. He was
interviewed by Donald Cameron in *Conversations with Canadian
Novelists* (1973).**

KEITH MCKERRACHER 1973

> These men are about evenly matched. That's because the average
> thirty-year-old Canadian is in about the same shape as the average
> sixty-year-old Swede. Run. Walk. Cycle. Let's get Canada moving again.
> This message is from the Canadian movement for personal fitness,
> PARTICIPaction.

**This now-famous fitness commercial appeared on national television a
total of six times in the fall of 1973. It was conceived by Keith
McKerracher, President of the Institute of Canadian Advertising, and
was sponsored by the Fitness and Amateur Sports' National Advisory
Council. No advertising agency was involved, no research was conducted, but it struck a responsive chord in the psyches of Canadians.**

MICHEL BRUNET 1973

> The thing which amazes me is that I know perfectly well, as a historian,
> that there is corruption in any government—there's always corruption.
> It's bad when it's more than fifteen percent.

**This oh-so-human observation was made by Quebec historian
Michel Brunet during an interview conducted by Ramsay Cook,
included in *The Craft of History* (1973), edited by Eleanor Cook.**

PETER C. NEWMAN 1973

And what I've learned is not to believe in magical leaders any more; that character and compassion are more important than ideology; and that even if it's absurd to think you can change things, it's even more absurd to think that it's foolish and unimportant to try.

Peter C. Newman has written informed biographies of Diefenbaker and other national figures, and in the mid-1990s is writing a biography of former Prime Minister Brian Mulroney. Newman gave expression to his political, social, and personal philosophies in *Home Country: People, Places, and Power Politics* (1973).

ROD SYKES 1973

That "Eastern Bastard" Is My Brother!

The oil crisis of 1973 left Albertans furious with the Trudeau administration's National Energy Policy. In November, bumper-stickers on automobiles in Alberta sported the message "Let the Eastern Bastards Freeze in the Dark." Rod Sykes, Mayor of Calgary, was appalled and responded with his own bumper-sticker, which read "That 'Eastern Bastard' Is My Brother!" The incident was noted by James H. Gray in *The Toronto Star,* Dec. 15, 1973.

PIERRE BERTON 1973

A Canadian is somebody who knows how to make love in a canoe.

This amusing definition of a Canadian links him—or her—with the wilderness. Pierre Berton, author and media personality, made the widely quoted remark during an interview conducted by Dick Brown in *The Canadian*, Dec. 22, 1973.

AL PURDY 1974

Hockey is the Canadian specific.

It took a poet, Al Purdy, to express the Canadian fascination with hockey so aptly and succinctly. Purdy's remark was quoted by Dick Beddoes and John Roberts in their account of the second Canada-Soviet games, *Summit 74* (1974).

ANONYMOUS 1974

The world will end at midnight tonight; 11:30 in Newfoundland.

Regular listeners to CBC Radio are reminded every time they hear a program announcement of the fact that Newfoundland time is thirty minutes ahead of mainland time, regardless of time zone. The catch-phrase is often attributed to Tom Cahill, CBC producer in St. John's, Nfld. It was discussed in *Peter Gzowski's Book About This Country in the Morning* (1974). *A propos* time, the National Research Council Time Signal, heard over CBC Radio each day at 1:00 P.M., may be the longest-running if shortest radio program (it lasts as little as fifteen seconds). It runs: "The beginning of the long dash, followed by ten seconds of silence, indicates exactly one o'clock. . . . "

DENNIS LEE 1974

Mackenzie was a crazy man,
He wore his wig askew.
He donned three bulky overcoats
In case the bullets flew.
Mackenzie talked of fighting
While the fight went down the drain.
But who will speak for Canada?
Mackenzie, come again!

William Lyon Mackenzie, one of the leaders of the Rebellion of 1837, stood for "popular rights" and republicanism. This verse comes from the comic-yet-serious poem "1838" in *Nicholas Knock and Other People* (1974), by the poet Dennis Lee.

HERSCHEL HARDIN 1974

Canada, in its essentials, is a public enterprise country, always has been, and probably always will be. Americans have, or at least had, a genius for private enterprise; Canadians have a genius for public enterprise. As long as we describe Canada in terms of the American model, we will continue to see ourselves as second-rate Americans, because we *are* second-rate Americans, not being Americans at all.

Many passages have been written in praise of private enterprise, but very few have been written extolling public enterprise, especially when it is the "mixed economy" variety. Here is one that praises the economy that melds private initiative and public interest. It comes from *A Nation Unaware* (1974), written by Herschel Hardin, playwright and nationalist.

HUGH MACLENNAN 1974

Ours is not the only nation which has out-travelled its own soul and now is forced to search frantically for a new identity. No wonder, for so many, the past Canadian experience has become not so much a forgotten thing as an unknown thing.

Hugh MacLennan, novelist and essayist, made this observation in his lyrical volume *Rivers of Canada* (1974). The observation was true when he made it; it is even truer twenty years later. The past receives short shrift from the present. The achievements of the past are barely appreciated if recognized at all. In the same vein, historian Michael

Bliss noted in 1975, "Canadians are a people who remember their present and think it's their history."

JORGE LUIS BORGES 1974

Canada is so far away it hardly exists.

Was the Argentine writer Jorge Luis Borges fooling when he made this statement? He was being interviewed by poet and broadcaster Robert Zend in his apartment in Buenos Aires, Oct. 4, 1974. Zend asked him, "What do you think of when you think of Canada?" Borges made the above reply.

PIERRE JUNEAU 1974

For God's sake. Either we have a country or we don't. Let's decide!

Pierre Juneau, Chairman of the Canadian Radio-Television and Tele-communications Commission, tried to balance the demands of private broadcasters and the needs of public broadcasting. The above remark was attributed to him during one of his appearances before the Senate Committee on Communications in Oct. 1974, during which he defended the mandate of the Canadian Broadcasting Corporation.

GORDON (GORDIE) HOWE 1975

All pro athletes are bilingual. They speak English and profanity.

Bilingualism was much in the news in the decade that followed the passage of the Official Languages Act of 1969. Bilingualism in the sports world was no problem, according to hockey star Gordie Howe, as quoted by George Gamester in *The Toronto Star*, May 27, 1975.

BETTE STEPHENSON 1975

Men are very fragile creatures. Their psyches are so closely tied to their epididymis.

When this remark appeared in print, there was a rush to dictionaries to learn the meaning of the word "epididymis." The remark was made by Bette Stephenson, former President of the Canadian Medical Association and future Ontario Minister of Health, during an interview by Christina McCall Newman in *The Globe and Mail*, July 12, 1975. Stephenson added, "The epididymis is the little tube that carries the sperm from the testicle to the *vas deferens.*"

DENE DECLARATION 1975

We the Dene of the Northwest Territories insist on the right to be regarded by ourselves and the world as a nation.

Opening statement of the Dene Declaration, passed at the Second Joint General Assembly of the Indian Brotherhood of the Northwest Territories, Fort Simpson, N.W.T., July 19, 1975. The text appears in Mel Watkins's *Dene Nation* (1977).

JOHN G. DIEFENBAKER 1975

While there's snow on the roof, it doesn't mean the fire has gone out in the furnace.

John G. Diefenbaker, who was in his sixties when he became Prime Minister of Canada (1957-63), was active in politics well into his eighties. He made the above remark at his eightieth birthday party, Ottawa, Sept. 17, 1975. Prime Minister Trudeau attended the celebration and greeted Diefenbaker "at eighty, at the midpoint in his political career. . . ."

LAURA SABIA 1975

I'm a Roman Catholic and I take a dim view of 2,500 celibates shuffling back and forth to Rome to discuss birth control and not one woman to raise a voice.

Laura Sabia, chairperson of the Ontario Advisory Council on the Status of Women, made this widely quoted personal statement in 1975.

JAN MORRIS 1976

The genius of Canada remains essentially a deflationary genius.

The truth of this observation resonates in Canadian hearts and minds. The observation was made by the Anglo-Welsh travel writer Jan Morris in "On the Confederation Special," *Travels* (1976). Over the years, Morris has described and redescribed the Canadian national style, finding something appealing in either the pattern or the cut of the cloth. "After a few days in Ottawa I began to think that perhaps some recondite accommodation kept this city itself in a balance—that some unwritten compact between the prosaic and the fantastic sustained its bland composure," she wrote of Ottawa in "Government Town," *Saturday Night*, Jan. 1987. "It is part of the civic genius—part of the Canadian genius, too—to reduce the heroic to the banal," she noted in "Suddenly Saskatoon," *Saturday Night*, July-Aug. 1990. "Cheer up! You have drawn a second prize, I would say, in the Lottario of Life," she advised Torontonians in "Flat City," *Saturday Night*, June 1984. In the Introduction to *City to City* (1990), she wrote of the country: "I think it deserves better of itself—more recognition of its own virtues, more readiness to blow its own trumpet, a little less becoming diffidence, a bit more vulgar swagger. Sometimes Canada's modesty touches me, but sometimes it makes me feel like giving it a kick in the seat of its ample pants, to get its adrenalin going." Morris, a world traveller and perceptive essayist, concluded: "While it may not be the most thrilling of countries, [Canada] has a genuine claim to be considered the best."

JOE CLARK 1976

Joe Who?

This was the main headline on the front-page news story in *The Toronto Star*, Feb. 23, 1976, devoted to the election of dark-horse candidate Joe Clark to the leadership of the federal Conservative Party. The catch-phrase caught on, becoming the nickname of the future Prime Minister. When Clark showed a determination to make changes, he was rechristened (briefly) "Joe Do."

LÉON DION 1976

A nation may be considered as a community of communities. The nation is an organic entity of goals and resources.

This view of nationhood was advanced by the sociologist and Quebec government adviser Léon Dion in *Quebec: The Unfinished Revolution* (1976), translated by Thérèse Romer. Prime Minister Joe Clark was comfortable with the notion that Canada was a "community of communities" for it met the needs of Conservatives and seemed to solve some of the problems that exist for separatists. Pierre Elliott Trudeau ridiculed the idea as "ten premiers and the Prime Minister as a kind of head waiter to take their orders" and also as "a loose confederation of shopping centres."

STOMPIN' TOM CONNORS 1976

The girls are out to Bingo and the boys are gettin' stink-o;
We think no more of Inco on a Sudbury Saturday night.

Stompin' Tom Connors rose to fame composing, performing, and recording songs like "Sudbury Saturday Night" (1976), which was included by Bob Davis in *Singin' about Us* (1976).

CHARLES BRONFMAN 1976

> I have a fantasy about holding the next Seagram's annual meeting and telling the shareholder it's the last one to be held in Montreal. If, God forbid, the PQ is elected, I will make that statement.

Charles Bronfman, Canadian corporate head of the giant Seagram's distillery empire, made this threat during the course of an address delivered at the Allied Jewish Community Services Building, Montreal, Nov. 14, 1976. The next day saw the election of the Parti Québécois; yet Seagram's remains a Montreal-based company, as noted by Peter C. Newman in *Bronfman Dynasty: The Rothschilds of the New World* (1978).

PIERRE ELLIOTT TRUDEAU 1976

> Our forefathers willed this country into being. Times, circumstances and pure will cemented us together in a unique national enterprise, and that enterprise, by flying in the face of all expectations, of all experiences, of all conventional wisdom, that enterprise provides the world with a lesson in fraternity. This extraordinary undertaking is so advanced in the way of social justice and of prosperity, that to abandon it now would be to sin against the spirit, to sin against humanity.

Prime Minister Pierre Elliott Trudeau waxed eloquent about the history and nature of Canada and about what values and ideals the country could represent to the rest of the world. He spoke on the eve of the Parti Québécois's electoral victory, Nov. 15, 1976, and the text of his address appeared in *The Globe and Mail* the next day.

RENÉ LÉVESQUE 1976

> I never thought I could be as proud to be a Quebecker as I am tonight. . . . We're not a minor people. We're maybe something like a great people.

René Lévesque, separatist leader and Quebec Premier-designate, made these remarks following the victory of his Parti Québécois in Montreal, Nov. 15, 1976. The next day the cartoonist Aislin drew for *The Montreal Gazette* the image of a surprised Lévesque saying, "O.K., everybody, take a Valium!" The "proud-to-be-a-Quebecker" reference was recalled by Prime Minister Trudeau following the outcome of the Quebec referendum on sovereignty-association, May 20, 1980.

J.C.M. OGELSBY 1976

Canada and Mexico, as the saying goes, have one common problem between them. This problem, of course, is their relationship with the United States.

This saying was first recorded by historian J.C.M. Ogelsby in *Gringos from the Far North: Essays in the History of Canadian-Latin American Relations, 1866-1968* (1976). No doubt the North American Free Trade Agreement will bring this saying into relief.

THOMAS R. BERGER 1977

The risk is in Canada. The urgency is in the United States.

Appointed to inquire into the need, both national and continental, for the proposed Mackenzie Valley Pipeline, Thomas R. Berger came to the above conclusion, expressed in *Northern Frontier, Northern Homeland: The Report of the Mackenzie Valley Pipeline Inquiry* (1977). He recommended a ten-year moratorium on the construction of any such line. His report was received with relief and even enthusiasm by the northern people.

CAMILLE LAURIN 1977

There will be no longer any question of a bilingual Quebec.

This statement was made by Camille Laurin, Quebec Cabinet Minister, tabling Bill 1 in Quebec's House of Assembly, April 1, 1977. Bill 1, like its successor Bill 101, provided for a unilingual province, contrary to the provisions of the BNA Act, 1867. On another occasion Laurin expressed the aim of the Parti Québécois: "We want to make Quebec as French as Ontario is English."

MEL HURTIG 1977

I am absolutely convinced that if there was a stronger national spirit across Canada there would be less need for Quebec nationalism, and there would be fewer Western separatists. I am equally convinced that no such national pride and spirit will ever be generated in a country that is increasingly becoming the world's foremost example of a branch-plant colony.

This statement, which appeared in the Presentation to the Task Force on Canadian Unity, Edmonton, Nov. 18, 1977, was prepared by publisher and future political-party leader Mel Hurtig. Applicable in the 1970s, the words remain applicable in the 1990s.

NORTHROP FRYE 1977

Where is here?

This conundrum-like question was posed by literary philosopher Northrop Frye in "Haunted by Lack of Ghosts," *The Canadian Imagination* (1977), edited by David Staines. Frye contrasted "Where is here?" with unanswerable questions about the ever-elusive Canadian identity.

NAT TAYLOR 1978

Cineplex.

The word *cineplex* was coined in 1978 by Nat Taylor, Toronto film exhibitor, former head of Famous Players, and partner in the

Cineplex Corp. The term combines two words, *cinema* and *complex*, and refers to the installation of multiple movie screens in one movie theatre, generally located in a shopping centre or mall. The world's first cineplex opened in Toronto's Eaton Centre in 1979 with eighteen movie screens under one roof, and more have since been added there.

HEADLINE 1978

One Million Unemployed.

This banner headline appeared on *The Toronto Star*, March 14, 1978. The lead story was filed from the nation's capital by correspondent Terrance Wills. It began: "Ottawa—For the first time in Canada's history, more than a million people are officially out of work."

YVON DESCHAMPS 1978

All we want is an independent Quebec within a strong and united Canada.

There is a lot of wisdom in this wisecrack. It is associated with one of the comic routines of Quebec comedian Yvon Deschamps, and it was quoted by Peter C. Newman in *Maclean's,* Nov. 13, 1978. In French it goes like this: "Un Québec independant dans un Canada uni!"

ROBERT MCCLURE 1979

No. 1. Adventure equals Risk with Purpose.
No. 2. Satisfaction gained from a job is in inverse proportion to the money earned.
No. 3. Satisfaction equals service over income.

These are the maxims of Robert McClure, who led a varied and active life as physician, educator, long-time missionary in China and elsewhere, and served as the independent-minded Moderator of the United

Church of Canada (1968-71). McClure's maxims appeared in this form in Munroe Scott's biography, *McClure: Years of Challenge* (1979).

FLORA MACDONALD 1979

It involves the lives of American human beings who are hostages in Iran. It involves, as well, the lives of Canadians who are in Iran—and that is something we must not forget.

Flora MacDonald, Minister of External Affairs, came close to revealing, under close questioning in the House of Commons, Nov. 27, 1979, that six Americans were "house guests" of Canadian Embassy officials in the Iranian capital of Tehran. But she succeeded in keeping the information secret, as Jean Pelletier and Claude Adams noted in *The Canadian Caper* (1981). Ambassador Kenneth Taylor is credited with coining the word "exfiltrate" to refer to the way he engineered the Americans' escape to the West on Jan. 28, 1980.

ANTONINE MAILLET 1979

We don't have much to say. Just that we're alive.

When author and historian Antonine Maillet was awarded France's Prix Goncourt for her novel *Pélagie—La Charrette* (1979), world attention was focused on the Acadian people of New Brunswick. Maillet made this characteristically modest remark about her remarkable people on CBC-TV, Dec. 5, 1979.

ANATOL RAPOPORT 1979

Cooperate on move one; thereafter, do whatever the other player did the previous move.

These innocent-seeming imperatives are the two commands that govern the operation of the computer program known as TIT FOR

TAT. It was devised and designed by Anatol Rapoport, psychologist and philosopher at the University of Toronto, who is specially concerned with the nature of international cooperation and the systemic causes of warfare. His TIT FOR TAT program outperformed all other such programs in the scenario known as the Prisoners' Dilemma at an international computer tournament held at Indiana University in 1979, and it continues to excel. It initiates reciprocal cooperation through characteristic features: niceness (it never defects first), provocability (it is tough and responds in kind), forgiveness (it rewards good behaviour by cooperating the next time), clarity (its strategy is straightforward and apparent to all). The moral to be derived from TIT FOR TAT seems to be (in the words of mathematician Douglas R. Hofstadter) that "mutual cooperation can emerge in a world of egoists without central control, by starting with a cluster of individuals who rely on reciprocity."

JEAN CHRÉTIEN 1980

The Rockies are my Rockies. They were discovered by the voyageurs Radisson, des Groseilliers and La Vérendrye. I want them for my children and grandchildren.

A strong note of pan-Canadianism was sounded by Jean Chrétien in the speeches he delivered as a cabinet minister in the Trudeau administrations between 1968 and 1984. Robert Sheppard quoted one of Chrétien's "my Rockies" speeches in *The Globe and Mail*, April 29, 1980.

STAN ROGERS 1980

Ah, for just one time, I would take the Northwest Passage
To find the hand of Franklin reaching for the Beaufort Sea
Tracing one warm line through a land so wild and savage
And make a Northwest Passage to the sea.

Stan Rogers died in a fire on board Air Canada Flight 797 in June 1983. Only thirty-three, he had many more songs to write and sing. He composed and performed with such passion and gusto that someone called him "the Mount St. Helens of folk." His one hundred or so songs decry the loss of the land and the sea and the traditional way of life. With the chorus of his song "Northwest Passage," included in his album *Northwest Passage* (1980), he struck a vital chord. His masterly song recalls the endurance of Sir Alexander Mackenzie, David Thompson, and other explorers in search of "the sea-route to the Orient for which so many died." So the singer resolves "to seek a Northwest Passage at the call of many men / To find there but the road back home again." As Chris Gudgeon noted in *An Unfinished Conversation: The Life and Music of Stan Rogers* (1993), "The linear quality of communications is a very Canadian concept. We see it in our routes of transportation: rivers, railways, roads and even airway, all of which are oriented along an east-west line."

NATIONAL ANTHEM 1980

O Canada! Our home and native land!
True patriot love in all thy sons command!
With glowing hearts we see thee rise,
The True North strong and free!
From far and wide, O Canada,
We stand on guard for thee.
God keep our land glorious and free!
O Canada, we stand on guard for thee.
O Canada, we stand on guard for thee.

    *

O Canada! Terre de nos aïeux,
Ton front est ceint de fleurons glorieux!
Car ton bras sait porter l'épée,
Il sait porter la croix!

Ton histoire est une epopée,
Des plus brillants exploits.
Et ta valeur, de foi trempée,
Protégera nos foyers et nos droits.
Protégera nos foyers et nos droits.

Here are the words of the official English and French texts of "O Canada" as they appear in the National Anthem Act, 1980, where they are identified as the "National Anthem—Hymne national." Calixa Lavallée composed the stirring tune for Sir Adolph-Basile Routhier's words in 1880; R. Stanley Weir wrote the verses for the English version in 1908. Of related interest is the Royal Salute, which is a short composition that cunningly combines bars of music from both "O Canada" and "God Save the Queen"; it is played but not sung on semi-official occasions.

RENÉ LÉVESQUE 1980

If I understand you properly, you are saying, "Until next time."

René Lévesque, Quebec Premier and Parti Québécois leader, expressed dismay with the results of the Quebec referendum on sovereignty-association in his speech at the Paul Sauvé Arena, Montreal, May 20, 1980. In hockey parlance, it was federalists 60, separatists 40. The referendum was dubbed "the René-rendum" and "the referen*dumb*." Crestfallen, Lévesque employed the French "goodbye"—*à la prochaine fois.*

PIERRE ELLIOTT TRUDEAU 1980

I never thought I could be as proud to be a Quebecker and a Canadian as I am tonight.

Prime Minister Pierre Elliott Trudeau addressed the nation on television following the pro-federalist outcome of the Quebec referendum on sovereignty-association, Ottawa, May 20, 1980. He echoed the words that René Lévesque had spoken following the victory of the Parti Québécois in the provincial election of Nov. 15, 1976.

TERRY FOX 1980

> Somewhere the hurting must stop. . . . I'm not a dreamer . . . but I believe in miracles. I have to.

Terry Fox, a young amputee who lived in New Westminster, B.C., sent a letter to the head office of the Canadian Cancer Society on Oct. 15, 1979, in which he requested the society's aid in sponsoring his "run across Canada to raise money for the fight against cancer." The society agreed, and Fox's Marathon of Hope raised millions for cancer research. The one-legged runner jogged from St. John's, Nfld., to Thunder Bay, Ont., two-thirds of the way across Canada. He died of cancer on June 28, 1981.

W.P. KINSELLA 1980

> There was silence in the room. Then a voice, stunning as thunder, clear and common as a train whistle—the voice of a ball-park announcer: "If you build it, he will come."

These dramatic lines come from the short story "Shoeless Joe Jackson Comes to Iowa" (1980) by fiction writer W.P. Kinsella, who expanded the story into the novel *Shoeless Joe* (1982), which was filmed as *Field of Dreams* (1989) by writer-director Phil Alden Robinson. The disembodied voice urges an Iowa farmer to clear a baseball diamond in his wheat field and await the arrival of deceased baseball player Shoeless Joe Jackson, who was wrongly disgraced in the 1919 White Sox scandal. The line "If you build it, he will come" has gained wide currency, as has the movie's title "field of dreams." The image of the baseball diamond has been re-imagined to apply to the ice rink by columnist Joey Slinger writing in *The Toronto Star*,

May 10, 1993: "The field of our dreams is flooded and frozen and has a net at either end."

WILLIAM GIBSON 1980

Cyberpunk.

The term *cyberpunk* refers to a school of postmodernist science fiction that developed in North America during the 1980s. As critic Peter Nicholls noted, the word itself dates from the story "Cyberpunk" (1983) by U.S. writer Bruce Bethke; but the term, which combines the words *cybernetics* and *punk* as in *punk rock*, is identified with the Vancouver-based writer William Gibson. In the title story of the collection *Burning Chrome* (1980), and especially in the novel *Neuromancer* (1984), Gibson presents a futuristic world of "consensual hallucination" characterized by urban decay, media overload, and drugs, and co-extensive with "virtuality" or virtual reality (computer simulation and stimulation of sensory experience). In 1982, two cyberpunk movies were released: *Blade Runner* and *Videodrome* (directed by David Cronenberg).

RONALD REAGAN 1981

We are happy to be your neighbour. We want to remain your friend. We are determined to be your partner and we are intent on working closely with you in a spirit of co-operation. We are much more than acquaintances.

U.S. President Ronald Reagan addressed a joint sitting of the Senate and the House of Commons, March 11, 1981.

LARKIN KERWIN 1981

Canadarm marks a new approach to space: We humans come here no longer as wary explorers, but to stay and build. This progression to the commercialization of space demands new ways of doing things. . . . Canada can be proud of its world leadership in this branch of robotics. We have a Canadian first, which is an achievement quite as beautiful as any other work of art.

Larkin Kerwin, President of the National Research Council, expressed national pride in the success of the Remote Manipulator System (Canadarm) designed and built by the NRC and Spar Aerospace for NASA's Space Shuttle. Canadarm first flew on the second Shuttle flight, Nov. 12, 1981. Later that very day Kerwin addressed his remarks to the Empire Club of Canada, Toronto.

CANADIAN CHARTER OF RIGHTS AND FREEDOMS 1982

Everyone has the following fundamental freedoms: (a) freedom of conscience and religion; (b) freedom of thought, belief, opinion and expression, including freedom of the press and other media of communication; (c) freedom of peaceful assembly; and (d) freedom of association.

This is a key clause from the Canadian Charter of Rights and Freedoms, part of the Constitution Act, 1982, proclaimed by Queen Elizabeth II, Parliament Hill, Ottawa, April 17, 1982.

EUGENE FORSEY 1982

Dominion as the title of a country is a distinctively Canadian word. It is the only distinctive word we have contributed to political terminology. Other countries throughout the Commonwealth borrowed it from us.

Historian Eugene Forsey felt that the name Dominion Day was preferable to that of Canada Day, in a letter to the editor of *The Globe and Mail*, July 16, 1982.

HENRY MORGENTALER 1982

Every child a wanted child, every mother a willing mother.

This credo appears in the book *Abortion and Contraception* (1982), written by the proponent of abortion on demand, Dr. Henry Morgentaler.

JACK LENZ AND TONY KOSINEC 1983

You've got a diamond,
You've got nine men,
You've got a hat and a bat
And that's not all.
You've got the bleachers,
Got 'em from spring 'til fall,
You got a dog and a drink
And the umpire's call,
Waddaya want?
Let's play ball!

Chorus: *Okay* (Okay),
Blue Jays (Blue Jays),
Let's (Let's) *Play* (Play) BALL!

These are the catchy words of the "Blue Jays Song," the theme song composed for the Blue Jays Baseball Club of Toronto by songwriters Jack Lenz and Tony Kosinec. First performed at the seventh inning stretch in 1983 at CNE Stadium, its use has continued to this day at the SkyDome. The Blue Jays won World Series pennants in 1992 and 1993.

GAETAN DUGAS 1984

I've got gay cancer. I'm going to die and so are you.

Gaetan Dugas was an Air Canada flight attendant and early AIDS carrier who boasted of infecting at least 2,500 men across North

America during the last decade of his life. He died of complications from the Acquired Immune Deficiency Syndrome in Quebec City in 1984, according to Randy Shilts in *And the Band Played On: Politics, People and the AIDS Epidemic* (1987).

PIERRE ELLIOTT TRUDEAU 1984

I went home, discussed it with the boys, put them to bed. I walked until midnight in the storm, then I went home and took a sauna for an hour and a half. It was all clear. I listened to my heart and saw if there were any signs of my destiny in the sky, and there were none—there were just snowflakes.

Prime Minister Pierre Elliott Trudeau announced his decision to retire from public office at a press conference in Ottawa, Feb. 29, 1984. The tongue-in-cheek account of how he "went for a walk in the snow" is recalled at four-year intervals, as the event occurred on Leap Year Day. Before Leap Year 1984, associations with Feb. 29 were Sadie Hawkins' Day, invented by cartoonist Al Capp, and the birthday of hockey player Henri (Pocket) Richard. There is even a clerihew about it: "Poor Kim Campbell— / Deprived of an amble / In the snow / By an early overthrow." Warren Clements published it in *The Globe and Mail*, Dec. 4, 1993. It was written by reader Merle Young, Willowdale, Ont.

BRIAN MULRONEY 1984

In Quebec—and it is very obvious—there are wounds to be healed, worries to be calmed, enthusiasms to be rekindled, and bonds of trust to be established. The men and women of the province have undergone a collective trauma.

Brian Mulroney was speaking as Conservative leader at his nomination meeting in his own riding in the city of Sept-Iles, Que., April 6, 1984, when he first moved to "bring Quebec into the Constitution . . .

with honour and enthusiasm." Mulroney wrote the speech with the assistance of his long-time friend Lucien Bouchard. The speech succeeded in planting the seeds of Quebec's dissatisfaction, supposedly stemming from Prime Minister Trudeau's 1982 patriation of the Constitution that occurred without the participation of the Province of Quebec. Trudeau would later dismiss the idea of Quebec's discontent as "humiliation at every streetcorner."

JOHN TURNER & BRIAN MULRONEY 1984

TURNER: Well, I have told you and told the Canadian people, Mr. Mulroney, that I had no option.

MULRONEY: You had an option, sir. You could have said, "I am not going to do it. This is wrong for Canada. And I am not going to ask Canadians to pay the price." You had an option, sir, to say no, and you chose to say yes, yes to the old attitudes and the old stories of the Liberal party.

TURNER: I had no option, I. . . .

This confrontation between Prime Minister John Turner and Conservative leader Brian Mulroney took place during the national leaders' debate, national television, July 25, 1984. The issue was whether John Turner, as the incoming Prime Minister, had the right or responsibility to refuse to countenance the eleventh-hour patronage appointments approved by retiring Prime Minister Trudeau. Also at stake was the nature of leadership.

RENÉ LÉVESQUE 1984

Obviously, there is an element of risk. But it is a beautiful risk, and we don't have the luxury of not taking it.

Quebec Premier René Lévesque referred to separatism in the guise of sovereignty-association as "*un beau risque*" (a beautiful risk) in an address, Quebec City, Sept. 22, 1984. The words are not without a certain raffish charm. Robert Bourassa, when he resumed the premiership in 1985, turned them 180 degrees by referring to "the fine risk of federalism."

MARC GARNEAU 1984

My country is very fantastic. We are lucky to be Canadian, to have such a big and wonderful country.

The astronaut Marc Garneau was the first Canadian in space. He described his feelings as he whirled 350 kilometres above his native Quebec, spending eight "days" in space aboard the Space Shuttle, launched Oct. 5, 1984.

BRIAN MULRONEY 1984

As for us, we have only been in power for two months, but I can tell you this: Give us twenty years, and it is coming, and you will not recognize this country. Moreover, the whole area of federal-provincial relations will also be completely changed.

These words proved to be prophetic in ways unanticipated by Brian Mulroney. They come from his first address as Prime Minister in the House of Commons, Nov. 7, 1984.

BRIAN MULRONEY 1984

The concept of universality is a sacred trust, not to be tampered with.

The words "sacred trust" are associated in a negative fashion with Prime Minister Brian Mulroney and his two Conservative administrations. Between 1984 and 1993, Mulroney governments did what they could to chip away at the country's social programs, not just their universality. The statement above is adapted from a remark quoted in *The Globe and Mail*, Dec. 29, 1984. "Sacred Trust" is associated with Mulroney in the same way "Joe Who?" clings to Joe Clark and "Shrug" to Pierre Elliott Trudeau.

BRYAN ADAMS 1985

We can bridge the distance
Only we can make the difference
Don't you know that Tears Are Not Enough
If we can pull together
We can change the world for ever
Heaven knows that Tears Are Not Enough.

Singer-songwriter Bryan Adams composed the words and music of the pop song "Tears Are Not Enough" with Jim Vallance. In Feb. 1985, it was recorded by more than fifty popular Canadian artists and groups to benefit Ethiopian Famine Relief.

DAVID CRONENBERG 1985

More blood! More blood!

This is said to be the favourite on-set declaration of horror-film director David Cronenberg, according to Neil Gaiman and Kim Newman in *Ghastly beyond Belief* (1985). He once wrote, "Canadians are very reluctant to confront the creature from the Black Lagoon— which is our collective unconscious, really. But that creature wants to come out."

ANASTASIA M. SHKILNYK 1985

Love has to become a stronger power than the poisons of self-interest and powerlessness or else we will all perish.

Sociologist Anastasia M. Shkilnyk came to this conclusion after studying the erosion of life and culture caused by mercury pollution

236

of the water source, from 1963 on, at the Grassy Narrows Reserve, Ont. It comes from her harrowing study *A Poison Stronger than Love: The Destruction of an Ojibwa Community* (1985).

MICHAEL WILSON 1985

> No matter how we define the term, Canada has an acute shortage of rich people.

Michael Wilson, Minister of Finance, gave this as one reason why taxing the wealthy would not ensure the continuation of social services. He was speaking about the newly tabled federal budget at the annual meeting of the Canadian Economics Association, Montreal, May 30, 1985.

JACQUES PLANTE 1985

> How would you like a job where, every time you make a mistake, a big red light goes on and 18,000 people boo?

Jacques Plante, one of hockey's great goalkeepers, donned a protective face mask 1959, the first professional goalie to do so. The above remark was attributed to the hockey star the year before his death in Switzerland on Feb. 26, 1986.

WAYNE GRETZKY 1985

> I skate to where the puck is going to be, not where it's been.

With this statement, hockey superstar Wayne Gretzky expressed an intriguing insight into how one may be trained to anticipate future conditions and change. It appeared in *Let's Do It! A Vision of Canadian Broadcasting Proposed by the CBC to the Federal Task Force on Broadcasting Policy*, released Dec. 1985.

TOURISM CANADA 1986

Canada. The World Next Door

This is the theme of the major advertising campaign created for Tourism Canada for use in the United States; the concept was devised by Arnold Wicht (art director) and John McIntyre (writer) of Camp Associates Advertising (now Axmith McIntyre Wicht) and launched on March 5, 1986.

CLAUDE CHARRON 1986

They were the two poles of Quebec politics. Lévesque is what we are; Trudeau is what we would like to be.

The spectacle of the Québécois voting simultaneously for the separatist René Lévesque provincially and the federalist Pierre Elliott Trudeau federally is matched by the insight of Claude Charron, former Quebec Cabinet Minister, quoted by Donald Brittain in the NFB/CBC-TV production "The Champions," Sept. 14-16, 1986.

KIM CAMPBELL 1986

Charisma without substance is a dangerous thing.

Dangerous thing indeed! This aphorism came to haunt its creator, Kim Campbell. It was first heard on Oct. 22, 1986, when she unsuccessfully contested the leadership of the Social Credit Party of British Columbia, which was won by William Vander Zalm. She recalled her own aphorism when she declared her candidacy for the leadership of the Conservative Party in Vancouver, March 25, 1993, adding, "My great fear was that I might become known as the candidate of substance without charisma." Thereafter, she began to mint catchy phrases that showed her in a bad light. As Minister of National Defence, she equated "enemies of the Progressive Conservative Party" with "the enemies of Canadians" (echoing the suggestion made the previous year by Prime Minister Mulroney, who identified enemies of the Charlottetown Accord with "enemies of Canada"). She called people with political "apathy" "such condescending SOBs." As Prime Minister, she eschewed debating "the modernization of social programs in forty-seven days" left to the campaign. Conceding defeat for herself and her party on election night, Oct. 25, 1993, she joked: "Gee, I'm glad I didn't sell my car." (For the record, she owned a 1980 Honda Civic.) To the degree that her short but striking political career illustrates anything at all, it is that making memorable remarks may be the undoing of a public figure. Mackenzie King avoided such remarks like the plague. As Ontario Premier William Davis observed, "Bland works."

JOHN C. POLANYI 1986

I know of no other place where princes assemble to pay their respects to molecules. When, as we often must do, we fear science, we really fear ourselves. Human dignity is better served by embracing knowledge.

John C. Polanyi, Professor of Chemistry, University of Toronto, accepted the Nobel Prize for Chemistry (for work on chemiluminescence, which has applications to laser technology) in Stockholm, Sweden, Dec. 10, 1986.

MEECH LAKE ACCORD 1987

Quebec constitutes, within Canada, a distinct society.

This was a key provision of the Meech Lake Constitutional Accord, adopted for future provincial ratification at an all-ministers' conference, Ottawa, June 3, 1987. The Accord, by granting constitutional recognition of the distinctive character of the Province of Quebec, sought to provide for "two distinct societies (*deux nations*)" in Canada. The Accord failed to meet ratification in Manitoba and Newfoundland.

As Manitoba Premier Gary Filmon explained, "We have an aboriginal past and a multicultural future . . . not just the French-English duality that is seen as the fundamental characteristic." Newfoundland Premier Clyde Wells stated, "I am not rejecting Quebec. I am rejecting a Canada with a Class A province, a Class B province and eight Class C provinces."

PETER USTINOV 1987

Toronto is a kind of New York operated by the Swiss.

Peter Ustinov, theatre personality and frequent visitor to Toronto, made this appreciative comment, which was quoted by John Bentley Mays in *The Globe and Mail*, Aug. 1, 1987. When reminded of the insight at a reception on June 20, 1992, Ustinov replied, "I've been here so many times, I've learned it's really run by the Canadians."

PRESTON MANNING 1987

The West Wants In.

This is an early slogan of the Reform Party of Canada. The party was founded at a convention in Winnipeg in Oct. 1987, and western reformer Preston Manning was elected its founding leader. At the party's convention in April 1991, Manning announced that the western protest party would henceforth be a national party. It won 52 seats (principally in the West) in the federal election of 1993.

RONALD REAGAN 1988

There are indeed no limits to what people can accomplish when they are free to follow their dreams. We're making that dream a reality. It is the American dream.

U.S. President Ronald Reagan made this point in his speech at the signing of the Free Trade Agreement, White House, Washington, D.C., Jan. 2, 1988. The agreement became effective Jan. 1, 1989; it was branded by critics as "the Free Trade Disagreement" and "the Free Raid Agreement." Retired judge Marjorie Montgomery Bowker, after studying the text of the agreement, opined that "the free-trade agreement has no clothes." She concluded, "I began and ended my study as a supporter of free trade. I ended as an opponent of this particular Free Trade Agreement." The entertainer Don Harron added the following suggestion: "If we go ahead with Free Trade with the United States, and it really works, we should try it with the provinces of this country." Another comedian, Dave Broadfoot, posed the following question: "Will it make us more competitive, or will it continue to let us act like Canadians?"

NORTHROP FRYE 1988

> The knowledge that you can have is inexhaustible, and what is inexhaustible is benevolent. The knowledge that you cannot have is of the riddles of birth and death, of our future destiny and the purposes of God. Here there is no knowledge, but illusions that restrict freedom and limit hope. Accept the mystery behind knowledge: It is not darkness but shadow.

Northrop Frye, the literary philosopher, was also an ordained minister of the United Church of Canada. These profound words come from his address at the annual baccalaureate service, Metropolitan United Church, Toronto, April 10, 1988, as quoted by Alexandra Johnston in *Vic Report*, Spring 1991.

CONRAD BLACK 1988

> Journalists as a group, unlike all other powerful groups, require some protection from themselves, and from their own excesses.

Conrad Black, capitalist, publisher of newspapers with a global daily circulation in excess of 4.5 million copies, expressed this opinion of journalists at the annual dinner, Canadian Press, April 20, 1988, as reported in *The Globe and Mail* the following day.

JEFF MACINNIS 1988

The Passage is beaten.

This was the boast of Arctic explorer Jeff MacInnis at Pond Inlet, Baffin Island, N.W.T., Aug. 17, 1988. MacInnis (the son of undersea explorer Dr. Joseph MacInnis) became the first person to navigate the Northwest Passage solely by breeze and brawn. He covered a distance of 4,000 kilometres in a catamaran over three summers.

DIANE DUPUY 1988

Always, always I.Q.s. Always how intelligent people are. They forget the soul. To us there's no I.Q. Everything is done by soul.

Diane Dupuy is the founder of Famous People Players, the puppet-and-light show that employs developmentally handicapped young people. She always stresses the ability of people to learn and was quoted by Catherine Dunphy in *The Toronto Star*, Oct. 27, 1988.

BRIAN MULRONEY 1988

Nearly half a century ago, in the crisis of wartime, the Government of Canada wrongfully incarcerated, seized the property, and disenfranchised thousands of citizens of Japanese ancestry. We cannot change the past. But we must, as a nation, have the courage to face up to these historical facts.

Prime Minister Brian Mulroney offered the apologies of the government and people of Canada to Japanese Canadians for the injustices visited upon them during World War II. The apology, accompanied by a comprehensive redress, was delivered in the House of Commons, Sept. 22, 1988. The Prime Minister addressed a similar apology to "our fellow Canadians of Italian origin during World War II" in Concord, Ont., Nov. 4, 1990.

A. ALAN BOROVOY 1988

> I would renounce, therefore, the attempt to create heaven on earth, and focus instead on reducing the hell.

This is the maxim of A. Alan Borovoy, General Counsel, Canadian Civil Liberties Association, who established the present organization in Toronto in 1964. The maxim appears in *When Freedoms Collide: A Case for Our Civil Liberties* (1988).

BEN JOHNSON 1988

> I have never, ever knowingly taken illegal drugs, and I would never embarrass my family, my friends, my country, and the kids who love me.

Ben Johnson, the champion sprinter who was billed as "the fastest man in the world," made this statement after he was stripped of his Olympic gold medal, speaking at a press conference in Toronto, Oct. 4, 1988. Johnson subsequently admitted to the use of banned anabolic steroids. The International Amateur Athletics Federation banned him from competition for life on March 5, 1993, after it was learned that again he had been caught making use of illegal, muscle-building steroids. Two days later, Johnson admitted to a Toronto news conference, "I had hoped not to end my career in this way." The ambivalent response of Canadians to the Johnson affair found classic expression in the editorial cartoon drawn by Frank Edwards in *The Kingston Whig-Standard*, Sept. 18, 1988. Edwards drew three identical drawings of the sprinter and captioned them "Canadian Wins Gold Medal," "Jamaican-Canadian Accused of Steroid Use," and "Jamaican Stripped of Gold Medal."

STEPHEN JAY GOULD   1989

The animals of the Burgess Shale are the world's most important fossils, in part because they have revised our view of life, but also because they are objects of such exquisite beauty. . . . The animals of the Burgess Shale are holy objects—in the unconventional sense that word conveys in some cultures. . . . They are grubby little creatures of a sea floor 530 million years old, but we greet them with awe because they are the Old Ones, and they are trying to tell us something.

Paleontologists and biologists have long recognized the unique importance of the marine-animal fossils found in the Burgess Shale, Yoho National Park, British Columbia. The fossil-bearing area, accidentally discovered in 1909, is now a World Heritage Site. The amazing variety of life forms found here, including at least one that prefigures invertebrate zoology, inspired Stephen Jay Gould's masterful meditation titled *Wonderful Life: The Burgess Shale and the Nature of History* (1989).

GORDON (GORDIE) HOWE   1989

I feel I've gained more than I lost. I lost a record, but I gained a lot of friends.

Thus did hockey great Gordie Howe gracefully acknowledge the record-breaking achievement of Wayne Gretzky, hockey's superstar. In Edmonton on Oct. 15, 1989, playing for the Los Angeles Kings against his old team the Edmonton Oilers, Gretzky exceeded by one goal Howe's long-standing record of 1,850 career points. Howe was quoted by Al Strachan in *The Globe and Mail* the following day. By the end of the 1993 season, Gretzky established 2,328 points. Gordie predicted, "Wayne will get at least 3,000 points before he's finished."

MARC LÉPINE 1989

Women to one side. You're all a bunch of feminists! . . . Women to one side. You are all feminists, I hate feminists.

This was the cry of sometime student and mass murderer Marc Lépine, who shot and killed fourteen women students of engineering and wounded twelve others before taking his own life at the Ecole Polytechnique, Université de Montréal, 4:30 P.M., Dec. 6, 1989.

LUCIEN BOUCHARD 1990

RÉMILLARD: Canada can survive very well without Newfoundland.

BOUCHARD: We can imagine a situation where English Canada will have to choose between Quebec or Newfoundland.

This exchange took place between Gil Rémillard, Quebec's Minister of Intergovernmental Affairs, and Lucien Bouchard, federal Environment Minister, news conference, Quebec City, April 6, 1990. Thereafter, Bouchard was saddled with the sentiment if not the statement "English Canada will have to choose between Quebec and Newfoundland." Prime Minister Brian Mulroney was conciliatory: "Canada needs all of its component parts, including Newfoundland and Labrador."

LUCIEN BOUCHARD 1990

If you think this is a bluff, then I called my bluff. I quit the Cabinet.

Lucien Bouchard resigned from the Cabinet and from the Conservative Party over Prime Minister Brian Mulroney's willingness to make the twenty-three changes to the Meech Lake Constitutional Accord recommended by the Charest Commission. Bouchard announced his resignation at a press conference, Ottawa, May 22, 1990, in the process lapsing into somewhat unidiomatic English. Bouchard—who had been co-writer of the speech delivered by Mulroney at Sept-Iles, April 6, 1984, about Quebec's "humiliation"— went on to found the separatist Bloc Québécois in July 1990 and to head a party of 54 members in the House of Commons following the election of Oct. 25, 1993.

BRIAN MULRONEY 1990

> Right here, I told them when it would be. I told them a month ago when we were going to meet. It's like an election campaign; you count backward. I said, "That's the day we're going to roll the dice."

Prime Minister Brian Mulroney, during the course of an interview at 24 Sussex Drive in Ottawa, June 11, 1990, boasted to reporters how one month earlier he and his advisers had gathered to determine the federal strategy to deal with the Meech Lake Constitutional Accord and to set a First Ministers' meeting the first week of June. Mulroney assumed, mistakenly, that the outcome was "in the bag." The pressure tactic backfired, in part because of the boast made above, as noted by Susan Delacourt and Graham Fraser in *The Globe and Mail,* June 12, 1990. Newfoundland Premier Clyde Wells, for one, was offended. The dice image stuck to Mulroney and the Meech Lake Accord like glue: "It gives the impression that we're being manipulated. I saw that 'roll of the dice' and I'm still having trouble squaring that with his comments to me," said Wells. Jean Chrétien, the newly elected Liberal leader, told the Liberal Leadership Convention, Calgary Saddledome, June 22, 1990, "Canada has been ill-served by Brian Mulroney, who played poker with our country. Every time Mulroney rolls the dice, Canada pays the price. We must not allow the bungling of one Prime Minister to deprive us of the kind of Canada we love." In late June 1990, Manitoba Premier Gary Filmon, when he learned that the federal government planned to ask the Supreme

Court to rule on a deadline extension, told reporters, "This appears to be another roll of the dice by the federal government."

ELIJAH HARPER 1990

No, Mr. Speaker.

These three words have had a greater impact on the state of the nation than any words written or uttered since the passage of the Constitution Act in 1982. They changed the face of the country in the 1990s. They were spoken by Elijah Harper, Ojibwa-Cree Member, in Manitoba's Legislative Assembly. They withheld the unanimity required for the Legislature to table and then ratify the Meech Lake Constitutional Accord by its deadline. Harper said "No, Mr. Speaker" a total of nine times between June 12 and June 22, 1990.

BRIAN MULRONEY 1990

In politics, madame, you need two things: friends, but above all an enemy.

Prime Minister Brian Mulroney made this observation following the by-election victory of Liberal leader Jean Chrétien, Dec. 10, 1990, Beauséjour, N.S. It was quoted two days later by Graham Fraser in *The Globe and Mail*.

LÉON DION 1990

English Canada will not make concessions—and we are not even sure of that—unless it has a knife to its throat.

Léon Dion, constitutional expert and adviser to the Bourassa administration, testifying before the Bélanger-Campeau Commission on the future of Quebec, Dec. 12, 1990. He suggested that the "knife" should be Quebec's threat to English Canada to hold a referendum on independence.

EUGENE FORSEY 1990

No one can deny that Quebec is, culturally and sociologically, a distinct society. So is Newfoundland.

Eugene Forsey, authority on the constitution and critic of the Meech Lake Constitutional Accord, *A Life on the Fringe* (1990).

LENORE KEESHIG-TOBIAS 1991

The people who have control of your stories, control of your voice, also have control of your destiny, your culture.

Lenore Keeshig-Tobias, Ojibwa storyteller and writer, expressed the view of many native elders that their traditions remain theirs to tell, and theirs alone, despite the meaning of the Copyright Act. She was interviewed by Hartmut Lutz in *Contemporary Challenges: Conversations with Canadian Native Authors* (1991).

MAUDE BARLOW 1991

If you want to know who is going to change this country, go home and look in the mirror.

Maude Barlow, Chairperson, Council of Canadians, address, League of Canadian Poets, Toronto, May 25, 1991.

CYNTHIA KERR 1991

Who's going to break the silence?
Who's going to fight the fight?

Stand up and be counted
And give us back the night.

Cynthia Kerr, composer, refrain of "Give Us Back the Night," quoted by Kerr in "Have Your Say," *The Toronto Star*, 8 Sept. 1991. This song, associated with the Montreal Massacre, was recorded in Jan. 1991. One of the voices of the chorus was that of Nina De Villiers, a high-school student from Hamilton, Ont., who one evening in Aug. 1991 was raped and murdered.

DOUGLAS COUPLAND 1991

Generation X.

The generation of North Americans born in the mid-1960s who are in no hurry "to find themselves" because they give equal value to life experience and education was given its title Generation X by the Vancouver-based fiction writer Douglas Coupland in his satiric novel. It is not certain whether he originated the phrase; he certainly adopted it and is identified with it following the publication of his work of fiction *Generation X: Tales for an Accelerated Culture* (1991). *Shampoo Planet* (1992), his second work, surveyed the adolescent world of "global teens" who are most at home in shopping malls. Apparently, the descriptions "Generation X" and "Xers" have some history of being used in Britain to refer to their post-Baby Boom Punkers. "One generation is IBM. The next is Macintosh. They can communicate, but they're different." Coupland made this observation on CBC-TV's "Prime Time News," Nov. 4, 1992.

PIERRE ELLIOTT TRUDEAU 1992

You think you'll have peace if you vote Yes. You'll have peace if you vote No. Because No means we've had enough of the Constitution, we don't want to hear any more about it. . . . The blackmail will continue if you vote Yes. . . . They made a mess that deserves a big No.

It is commonly said that "the élites" endorsed the Charlottetown Constitutional Accord. One member of "the élite" who decried it was former Prime Minister Pierre Elliott Trudeau, who in one widely publicized speech delivered off-camera in a Chinese restaurant, Maison du Egg Roll in Montreal, Oct. 1, 1992, administered the crippling blow to the ill-conceived Accord.

BRIAN MULRONEY 1992

Canadians today face the choice we have faced repeatedly throughout our history: in 1774, 1791, in 1840, in 1867 and 1980. That choice is simple: Quebec will either be a distinct society within Canada or it will develop as a distinct society outside Canada. The French language and culture, in such a minority position in North America, must continue to find in Canada the freedom and oxygen that will enable them to flourish and endure.

The notion of Quebec as a "distinct society," soon to be associated with the Charlottetown Constitutional Accord, appealed to Prime Minister Brian Mulroney. He gave it expression in an address to a group of businessmen in Montreal, Oct. 23, 1992, as quoted by Graham Fraser in *The Globe and Mail*, Oct. 26, 1992.

CHARLOTTETOWN ACCORD 1992

Quebec constitutes within Canada a distinct society, which includes a French-speaking majority, a unique culture and a civil law tradition. . . .

This clause was the most contentious of many clauses in the Charlottetown Constitutional Accord. Another point of contention was the provision that "the Senate should initially total 62 Senators and should be composed of six Senators from each province and one Senator from each territory." Also divisive was "a guarantee that

Quebec would be assigned no fewer than 25 per cent of the seats in the House of Commons. . . ." The text of the Charlottetown Accord of the First Ministers and Native and Territorial Leaders for Constitutional Reform, Aug. 28, 1992, was reproduced in *The Globe and Mail*, Sept. 1, 1992. The referendum itself was held on Oct. 26, 1992.

JOE CLARK 1992

When the United Nations . . . looks at all other countries and says this is the best place in the world to live, we should take this seriously. And we should recognize that, once, Beirut was one of the best places in the world to live, and it gave in to anger—that so many of the things that we see on the news today used to be whole communities until they gave in to anger. This could happen here. If we lose this, we lose the country.

Joe Clark, Minister of Constitutional Affairs, speaking on CBC-TV's "Midday," quoted by Edison Stewart in *The Toronto Star*, Sept. 17, 1992. This is the origin of Clark's notorious "second Beirut" remark, the dire warning being that if Canadians rejected the Charlottetown Constitutional Accord, the country would descend into the chaos characterized by Beirut, the capital of strife-torn Lebanon. Michael Bliss and other commentators took exception to Clark's "scare tactics." The electorate decisively rejected the Accord in the referendum held on Oct. 26, 1992.

SUE RODRIGUEZ 1992

I want to ask you gentlemen, if I cannot give consent to my own death, then whose body is this? Who owns my life?

Sue Rodriguez, victim of ALS (amyotrophic lateral sclerosis, Lou Gehrig's disease, a progressive and terminal illness), made a video-taped presentation to a House of Commons justice subcommittee in Nov. 1992 in which she urged amendments to the section of the Criminal Code that makes it a crime for one person to assist another's suicide; quoted by Deborah Wilson in *The Globe and Mail*, Dec. 5, 1992. Subsequently the Supreme Court of Canada denied Rodriguez's request for a physician-assisted death.

LEONARD COHEN 1992

> Give me back the Berlin Wall
> Give me Stalin and St. Paul
> I've seen the future, brother:
> it is murder.

These powerful and possibly prophetic lines come from the song "The Future," composed and performed by Leonard Cohen on his CD album *The Future* (1992).

BRIAN MULRONEY 1993

> You can be, these days, a popular prime minister or you can be an effective one. You can't be both.

When he made this observation, Prime Minister Brian Mulroney was referring to his own unpopularity and to that of British Prime Minister John Major. He was speaking at a press conference at 10 Downing Street, London, England, May 11, 1993, quoted by Paul Koring in *The Globe and Mail* the following day.

LEWIS W. MACKENZIE 1993

> If you are a commander of a U.N. mission, don't get in trouble after 5:00 P.M. or on the weekend. There is no one in the U.N. to answer the phone!

Lewis W. MacKenzie, Major-General, retired, U.N. Chief of Staff for peacekeeping in Sarajevo, Yugoslavia, Aug. 1992. In his memoirs

Peacekeeper: The Road to Sarajevo (1993), MacKenzie explained: "Yes, I said that. My friends and former bosses in the U.N. were hurt and replied that, indeed, they had talked to me many times after 5:00 P.M. They were absolutely right, but they missed my point: They talked to me from home, a reception or, in some cases, from bed, but that isn't the same as being able to report to a command headquarters on a twenty-four-hour basis." In his letter on his retirement, *The Globe and Mail*, Jan. 21, 1993, he noted: "Countries that have soldiers in charge seem, more often than not, to be the ones where democracy is but a flickering candle sitting in an open window with a forecast of rain."

MORDECAI RICHLER 1993

Another defining phrase is *distinct society*. French-speaking Quebecers—arguably hypersensitive, clearly insecure, but not necessarily separatist—have pleaded for this interpretation of themselves to be stitched into our constitution, but each time it has stuck in the craw of the rest of Canada. My solution was for the rest of Canada (dubbed R.O.C. in our vernacular) to declare themselves an "indistinct society," confirming what the rest of the world thinks of us in any event, but it didn't fly.

Mordecai Richler, author and critic of Quebec's language policy, "Gros Mac Attack," *The New York Times Magazine*, June 18, 1993. Richler, a resident of Quebec's Eastern Townships, expatiated on these notions in his book *Oh Canada! Oh Quebec!: Requiem for a Divided Country* (1992).

MICHAEL SMITH 1993

There's a little bit of a tendency to feel that we cannot do first rate things in Canada because we're too small. This award says the science done here is as good as the science done anywhere, and you can do science in B.C. as well as anywhere in the world.

Michael Smith, biochemist at the University of British Columbia, co-winner of the 1993 Nobel Prize for Chemistry, was interviewed by Robert Matas in *The Globe and Mail*, Oct. 14, 1993.

FRANK OGDEN 1993

My suggestion was to consider selling the Yukon to a country like Taiwan, which with $88 billion in foreign reserves is the cash-richest country on the planet. Maybe, for $200-250 billion, they might be interested. Say $50 billion down and $10 billion a year for 15-20 years. If present residents of the Yukon were offered $100,000 to move, they might consider this form of "early retirement." Native people should get $100,000 each and have the choice of staying or moving. Quite possibly their new owners might treat them better than the previous ones.

*

Another "elite" is developing. The "have" and the "have nots" of the Industrial Age have been replaced by the "know" and the "know nots" of the Communications Age. The gap between the masses of techno-peasants and the new elite will grow ever wider as the new age progresses. Because the more we know makes it even easier to know more. Those that are behind at the start of the race may never catch up.

Outlandish? Obvious? Provocative? Prophetic? Imaginative? Insightful? Reasonable? Unreasonable? These are merely two of the multitude of suggestions that were made in seminars and addresses in Canada and around the world by the Vancouver-based futurist Frank Ogden in 1993. If one thread runs through all of Ogden's probes, it is the need for change: "As this bulldozer of change rolls over our planet, we all have to learn that if we don't become part of the bulldozer, we'll become part of the road." / "Although I am a futurist today, if I don't change tomorrow I will be a historian." / "The cardinal sin of the 1990s is to be boring." / "Personally, I believe you could put a kid through high school in four months." / "If schools were factories, we would have closed them ten years ago because they're not producing a saleable product. Kids can't get jobs because they don't know what's happening." / "In the era of AIDS, CyberSex may be the ultimate in safe sex." / "By the start of the third millennium, Spanish, not French, will be the second language in Canada." / "Holidays are the greatest learning experience unknown to man." / "Techno-peasant." / "On a cold, wet Canadian winter night, there's nothing like crawling into bed with your laptop and curling up with a good disc."

JUDITH MERRIL 1995

Human cultures and consciousness on Earth evolved in many languages from widely scattered and vastly varied enclaves: some broiling hot, some bitter cold, desert-dry or drenched with rain, on mountaintops, at the seaside. But the earliest legends of each and every unique culture show that we were all, from the beginning, gazing in awe at the night skies, imagining ourselves somehow descended from those wondrous lights, looking to them for blessings, fearing their displeasure, hoping somehow, some day, to ascend once more to the brightness of the stars.

In the late fall of 1994, according to schedule, the Mars Observer spacecraft will leave the bounds of Earth; in the early spring of the following year, if all goes according to plan, its Lander will alight on the planet Mars and report on its surface and atmosphere. Affixed to the Lander will be a CD-ROM called *Visions of Mars*, which will offer audio and video messages, a gallery of artwork, and an anthology of works of science fiction about Mars and Martians written over the centuries by imaginative authors in eight languages. *Visions of Mars* is edited by artist and writer Jon Lomberg for The Planetary Society; Time Warner Interactive Group is releasing a replica of the CD-ROM on Earth. In the words of Carl Sagan, President of The Planetary Society, "This collection is intended as a gift from our era to the future generations of human beings who will one day explore and perhaps settle the planet Mars." The special video messages on the CD-ROM were prepared by scientist and author Arthur C. Clarke, astrophysicist Vyacheslav Linkin, astronomer and author Carl Sagan, and science-fiction author Judith Merril. What appears here is a passage of Toronto-based Merril's moving testament from *Visions of Mars*. It is the last of the "all-time great Canadian quotations." So far.

INDEX OF CONTRIBUTORS

The index consists of names of contributors followed by summaries of quotations with relevant page numbers. Also included are names and quotations found in commentaries. Statutes, folk songs, mottos, slogans, etc., appear under Anonymous.